How to
Think Straight
About Psychology

HOW TO THINK STRAIGHT ABOUT PSYCHOLOGY

Fourth Edition

Keith E. Stanovich

Ontario Institute for Studies in Education

HarperCollins*College*Publishers

To my parents, Betty and Mike Stanovich

Acquisitions Editor/Editor in Chief: Jill Lectka/Priscilla McGeehon
Design Manager/Text and Cover Designer: John D. Sparks
Electronic Production Manager: Alexandra Odulak
Manufacturing Manager: Hilda Koparanian
Electronic Page Makeup: Bookworks
Printer and Binder: R.R. Donnelley & Sons Company
Cover Printer: New England Book Components

How to Think Straight About Psychology, Fourth Edition
Copyright © 1996 by Keith E. Stanovich

HarperCollins ® and ® are registered trademarks of HarperCollins Publishers Inc.

Library of Congress Cataloging-in-Publication Data
Stanovich, Keith E., 1950-
   How to think straight about psychology/Keith E. Stanovich.— 4th ed.
     p. cm.
   Includes bibliographical references and index.
   ISBN 0-673-99439-2 (alk. paper)
   1. Psychology—Research—Methodology. 2 Mass media—Psychological aspects. 3. Mass media—Objectivity. I Title.
BF76.5.S68 1996
150'.72—dc20   95-12238
                                             CIP

95 96 97 98 9 8 7 6 5 4 3 2 1

Contents

Chapter 4

Chapter 5

Chapter 6

Chapter 11

Notes on the Fourth Edition

The fourth edition of *How to Think Straight About Psychology* has fewer structural revisions than the third edition because of the major chapter reorganization that occurred in the previous edition. The content and order of the chapters remain the same in the fourth edition. However, I have continued to update and revise the examples that are used. I have replaced some dated examples with more contemporary studies and/or issues. I have made a major effort to keep contemporary the citations that are relevant to the various concepts and experimental effects that are mentioned. As a result a total of 157 *new* citations appear in this edition, so that the reader continues to have up-to-date references on all of the examples and concepts.

Based on comments spontaneously sent to me by readers and on several comprehensive reviews commissioned by HarperCollins, I have moved certain sections. For example, the discussion of the Clever Hans case has been moved from Chapter 4 to Chapter 6, and the section on the anecdote war has been moved from Chapter 10 to Chapter 4. A discussion of the important issue of clinical versus actuarial prediction has been added to the chapter on probabilistic reasoning (Chapter 10). At the request of readers, I have bolstered the "Our Own Worst Enemies" section of Chapter 11. The goal of the book remains what it always was: to present a short introduction to critical thinking skills within the context of the subject matter of psychology.

Many of the individuals I have acknowledged in earlier editions continue to contribute ideas for the book. However, I must single out Richard West of James Madison University, who has been a most valuable continuing contributor to the book's evolution. This time around, I received some extremely thorough reviews from HarperCollins readers: Angela M. Birkhead-Flight, University of Cincinnati; Ronald Gandelman, Rutgers University; Joseph E. Morrow, California State University at Sacramento; John F. Pfister, Dartmouth College; Toni G. Wegner, University of Virginia; Murray S. Work, California State University at Sacramento. Many of their suggestions were incorporated into this edition. Additional helpful comments were received from Ludy Benjamin, Texas A&M University; Stephen Louisell, Kalamazoo Community College; Douglas Mook, University of Virginia; Marjorie Semonick, University of Minnesota; David Share, University of Haifa; Linda Siegel, Ontario Institute for Studies in Education; Frank Smoll, University of Washington; Mike Stadler, University of Missouri; and Marty Wall, University of Toronto. My new acquisitions editor at HarperCollins, Jill Lectka, has provided guidance, enthusiasm, and support for the book.

As before, readers are encouraged to send me comments by corresponding with me at the following address: Keith E. Stanovich, Department of Applied Psychology, Ontario Institute for Studies in Education, 252 Bloor St. W., Toronto, Ontario, Canada M5S 1V6. E-mail: KStanovich@oise.on.ca

Keith E. Stanovich

Preface

There exists a body of knowledge that is unknown to most people. This information concerns human behavior and consciousness in their various forms. It can be used to explain, predict, and control human actions. Those who have access to this knowledge use it to gain an understanding of other human beings. They have a more complete and accurate conception of what determines the behavior and thoughts of other individuals than do those who do not have this knowledge.

Surprisingly enough, this unknown body of knowledge is the discipline of psychology.

What can I possibly mean when I say that the discipline of psychology is unknown? Surely, you may be thinking, this statement was not meant to be taken literally. Bookstores contain large sections full of titles dealing with psychology. Television and radio talk shows regularly feature psychological topics. Newspapers and magazines run psychology columns. Nevertheless, despite this attention, there is an important sense in which the field of psychology is unknown.

Despite much seeming media attention, the discipline of psychology remains for the most part veiled from the public. The transfer of "psychological" knowledge that is taking place via the media is largely an illusion. Few people are aware that the majority of the books they see in the "psychology" sections of many book stores are written by individuals with absolutely no standing in the psychological community. Few are aware that many of the people to whom the media apply the label "psychologist" would not be considered so by the American Psychological Association or the American Psychological Society. Few are aware that many of the most visible psychological "experts" have contributed no information to the fund of knowledge in the discipline of psychology.

The flurry of media attention paid to "psychological" topics has done more than simply present inaccurate information. It has also obscured the very real and growing knowledge base in the field of psychology. The general public is unsure about what is and is not psychology and is unable to independently evaluate claims about human behavior. Adding to the problem is the fact that many people have a vested interest in a public that is either without evaluative skills or that believes there is no way to evaluate psychological claims. The latter view, sometimes called the "anything goes" outlook, is one of the fallacies discussed in this book, and it is particularly costly to the public. Many pseudosciences are multi-million-dollar industries that depend on the lack of public awareness that claims about human behavior can be tested. The general public is also unaware that many of the claims made by these pseudosciences (for example, astrology, psychic surgery, speed reading, biorhythms, subliminal weight loss, and psychic detectives) have been tested and proved false. The existence of the pseudoscience industry, which is discussed in this book, increases the media's tendency toward the sensationalistic reporting of science. This tendency is worse in psychology than in other sciences, and understanding the reasons why this is so is an important part of learning how to think straight about psychology. This book, then, is directed not at potential researchers in psychology, but at a much larger group: the consumers of psychological information. The target audience is the beginning psychology student and the general reader who have encountered information on psychological issues in the general media and have wondered how to go about evaluating its validity.

This book is not a standard introductory psychology text. It does not outline a list of facts that psychological research has uncovered. Indeed, telling everyone to take an introductory psychology course at a university is probably not the ultimate solution to the inaccurate portrayal of psychology in the media. There are many laypeople with a legitimate interest in psychology who do not have the time, money, or access to a university to pursue formal study. More important, as a teacher of university-level psychology courses, I am forced to admit that my colleagues and I often fail to give our beginning students a true understanding of the science of psychology. The reason is that lower-level courses often do not teach the critical analytical skills that are the focus of this book. As instructors, we often become obsessed with "content"—with "covering material." Every time we stray a little from the syllabus to discuss issues such as psychology in the media, we feel a little guilty and begin to worry that we may not "cover all the topics" before the end of the term.

Consider the average introductory psychology textbook. Many now contain between 600 and 800 multi-columned pages and reference literally hundreds of studies in the published literature. Of course, there is nothing wrong with such books containing so much material. It simply reflects the increasing knowledge base in psychology. There are, however, some unfortunate side effects. Instructors are often so busy trying to cram their students full of dozens of theories, facts, and experiments that they fail to deal with some of the fundamental questions and misconceptions that students bring with them to the study of psychology. The instructors (and the introductory textbook authors), rather than dealing directly with these misconceptions, often hope that if students are exposed to enough of the empirical *content* of psychology, they will simply *induce* the answers to their questions. In short, the instructors hope that students will recognize the implicit answers to these questions in the discussions of empirical research in several content areas. All too often this hope is frustrated. In a final review session— or in office hours at the end of the term—instructors are often shocked and discouraged by questions and comments that might have been expected on the first day of the course, but not after 14 weeks: "But psychology experiments aren't real life; what can they tell us?"; "Psychology just can't be a *real* science like chemistry can it?"; "But I heard a therapist on TV say the opposite of what our textbook said"; "I think this theory is stupid—my brother behaves just the opposite of what it says"; "Psychology is nothing more than common sense"; "Everyone knows what anxiety is—why bother defining it?"; "Psychology is just a matter of opinion, isn't it?" For many students, such questions are *not* implicitly answered merely by a consideration of the content of psychology. In this book, I deal explicitly with the confusions that underlie questions and comments such as these.

Unfortunately, research supports the idea that the average introductory psychology course does very little to correct the many misconceptions about the discipline that are held by entering students (Best, 1982; McKeachie, 1960; Vaughan, 1977). One researcher stated, "I must conclude that the [introductory] course has little influence on their erroneous beliefs" (Vaughan, 1977, p. 140) and, further, drew the conclusion that "there is little evidence for a generally heightened skepticism, which might lead students to question statements about which they have received no additional information" (p. 140). Vaughan's latter conclusion touches on the basic purpose of this book. Psychology, probably more than any other science, requires critical thinking skills that enable students to separate the wheat from the chaff that accumulates around all sciences. These are the critical thinking skills that students will need to become independent evaluators of psychological information. Years after students have forgotten the *content* of an introductory psychology course, they will still use the fundamental principles covered in this book to evaluate psychological claims. Long after Erikson's stages of development have been forgotten, students will be using the "thinking tools" introduced in this text to evaluate new psychological information encountered in the media. Once acquired, these skills will serve as lifelong tools that will aid in the evaluation of knowledge claims. First, they provide the ability to conduct an initial gross assessment of plausibility. Second, these skills provide some criteria for assessing the reliability of "expert" opinion. Because the need to rely on expert opinion can never be eliminated in a complex society, the evaluation of an expert's credibility becomes essential to knowledge acquisition. Although these critical thinking skills can be applied to any discipline or body of knowledge, they are particularly important in the area of psychology because the field is so often misrepresented by the general media.

Many psychologists are pessimistic about any effort to stem the tide of misinformation about their discipline. While this pessimism is, unfortunately, often justified, this "consumer's guide" to psychology was motivated by the idea that psychologists must not let this problem become a self-fulfilling prophecy.

While I have welcomed the opportunity to prepare several editions of *How to Think Straight About Psychology*, it is unfortunately true that the reasons for the book's existence are just as applicable today as they were when I wrote the first edition. Media presentations of psychology are just as misleading as they ever were, and students in introductory psychology courses enter with as many misconceptions as they ever did.

Thus, the goals of all subsequent editions remain the same. They are shared by an increasing number of psychology instructors. Stanford University psychologist Roger Shepard (1983) echoed all the concerns that motivated the writing of the first edition of this text:

> Although most undergraduate psychology students may not go on to scientific careers, one hopes that they acquire some facility for the critical evaluation of the incomplete, naive, confused, or exaggerated reports of social science "findings" to which they will continue to be exposed by the popular media . . . Widespread notions that human behavior and

mental phenomena can be adequately understood through unaided common sense or, worse, by reference to nonempirical pseudosciences, such as astrology, present us with a continuing challenge. (p. 855)

The goal of the book remains what it always was: to present a short introduction to the critical thinking skills that will help students to better understand the subject matter of psychology and to better understand events in the world in which they live.

ACKNOWLEDGMENTS

This book has benefited from the contributions of many people. Helpful suggestions were received from reviewers Christopher Bauer of the University of New Hampshire; Albert Heldt of Grand Rapids Junior College; George Howard of the University of Notre Dame; Michael O'Boyle of Iowa State University; Blaine Peden of the University of Wisconsin, Eau Claire; Paul Solomon of Williams College; and Carol Wade of the College of Marin. Richard F. West of James Madison University read the manuscript and contributed much to the development of the book. A humane scholar and a true friend, his intellectual and emotional support was much appreciated.

In addition to these individuals, several other scholars have provided valuable feedback on earlier editions. These include Wayne Bartz of American River College; Virginia Blankenship, University of Northern Arizona; Anne Cunningham of the University of Washington; William Graziano of Texas A&M University; Gordon Hammerle of Adrian College; Randy Hansen of Oakland University; George Heise of Indiana University; Bernie Koenig of Fanshawe College; P. A. Lamal, University of North Carolina, Charlotte; Edward Morris, University of Kansas; Dean Purcell of Oakland University; Michael Ross of the University of Waterloo; Frank Schieber of Oakland University; David Shantz of Oakland University; Norman Silverman of the University of Illinois, Chicago; Larry Vandervert of Spokane Falls Community College; Barbara Wanchisen, Baldwin-Wallace College. The insights from many discussions about teaching methodology with Ted Landau and Larry Lilliston of Oakland University, and Sam Rakover of the University of Haifa, were incorporated into the book.

Finally, I wish to thank Paula J. Stanovich for more than just the "emotional support" that is routinely alluded to in acknowledgments. Her concern for all human beings, particularly those less fortunate, is an inspiration to all those who know her. A view we both share is that every human being should have the opportunity to utilize their full potential. This book attests to the fact that I have had such an opportunity. Paula works to speed the day when this opportunity will be fully extended to all handicapped individuals.

Keith E. Stanovich

Chapter 1

Psychology Is Alive and Well (and Doing Fine Among the Sciences)

The Freud Problem

Stop 100 people on the street and ask them to name a psychologist, either living or dead. Record the responses. Of course, Joyce Brothers and other "media psychologists" would certainly be named. If we leave out the media and pop psychologists, however, and consider only those who have made a recognized contribution to psychological knowledge, there would be no question about the outcome of this informal survey. Sigmund Freud would be the winner hands down. B. F. Skinner would probably finish a distant second. No other psychologist would get enough recognition to even bother about. Thus Freud, along with the pop psychology presented in the media, largely defines psychology in the public mind.

The notoriety of Freud has greatly affected the general public's conceptions about the field of psychology and has contributed to many misunderstandings. For example, many introductory psychology students are surprised to learn that, if all the members of the American Psychological Association who were concerned with Freudian psychoanalysis were collected together, they would make up less than 10 percent of the membership. In another large organization of psychology, the American Psychological Society, they would make up considerably less than 5 percent.

Modern psychology is not obsessed (as are the media and some humanities disciplines) with the ideas of Sigmund Freud. Nor is it largely defined by them. Freud's work is an extremely small part of the varied set of issues, data, and theories that are the concern of modern psychologists. This larger body of research and theory encompasses the work of four recent Nobel prize winners (David Hubel, Torsten Wiesel, Herbert Simon, and Roger Sperry) and a former director of the National Science Foundation (Richard Atkinson), all of whom are virtually unknown to the public.

The notoriety of Freud represents a significant obstacle to the public's understanding of psychology. It is bad enough that Freud's importance to modern psychology is vastly exaggerated. What makes the situation worse is that Freud's methods of investigation are completely unrepresentative of how modern psychologists conduct their inquiries (recall that Freud began his seminal work roughly a hundred years ago). The study of Freud's methods gives an utterly misleading impression of psychological research. For example, Freud did not make use of controlled experimentation, which, as we shall see in Chapter 6, is the most potent weapon in the modern psychologist's arsenal of methods. Freud thought that case studies could establish the truth or falsity of theories. We shall see in Chapter 4 why this idea is mistaken. Finally, a critical problem with Freud's work concerns the connection between theory and behavioral data. As we shall see in Chapter 2, for a theory to be considered scientific, the link between the theory and behavioral data must meet some minimal requirements. Freud's theories often do not meet these criteria. To make a long story short, Freud built an elaborate theory on a database (case studies and introspection) that was not substantial enough to support it. Freud concentrated on building complicated theoretical structures, but he did not, as modern psychologists do, ensure that they would rest on a database of reliable, replicable behavioral relationships. Many scholars who have attempted to trace the early history of psychology, including Howard Gardner (1985), have pointed to Freud's style of work as a significant impediment to the development of the discipline:

> While many scholars were intrigued by Freud's intuitions, they felt that no scientific discipline could be constructed on the basis of clinical interviews and retrospectively constructed personal histories; moreover, they deeply resented the pretense of a field that did not leave itself susceptible to disconfirmation. (p. 15)

In this chapter, we shall attempt to deal with the Freud problem in two ways. First, when we illustrate the diversity of modern psychology, the rather minor position occupied by Freud will become clear. Second, we shall discuss what features are common to psychological investigations across a wide variety of domains. A passing knowledge of Freud's work has obscured from the general public what is the only unifying characteristic of modern psychology: the quest to understand behavior by using the methods of science.

The Diversity of Modern Psychology

There is, in fact, a great diversity of content and perspective in modern psychology. This diversity drastically reduces the coherence of psychology as a discipline. Henry Gleitman (1981), winner of the American Psychological Foundation's Distinguished Teaching Award, characterized psychology as "a loosely federated intellectual empire that stretches from the domains of the biological sciences on one border to those of the social sciences on the other" (p. 774). William Bevan (1982) captured the diversity of psychology quite explicitly by terming the field "a domain that encompasses the functioning of all organisms in all settings" (p. 1312).

Understanding that psychology is composed of an incredibly wide and diverse set of investigations is critical to an appreciation of the nature of the discipline. Simply presenting some of the concrete indications of this diversity will illustrate the point. The American Psychological Association (APA) has 48 different divisions, each representing either a particular area of research and study or a particular area of the practice of psychology. These 48 divisions are listed in Table 1.1. From the table, you can see the range of subjects studied by psychologists, the range of settings involved, and the different aspects of behavior studied. The other large organization of psychologists—the American Psychological Society—is just as diverse. Actually, Table 1.1 understates the diversity within psychology because it gives the impression that each division is a specific specialty area. In fact, each of the 48 divisions listed in the table is a broad area of study that contains a wide variety of subdivisions! In short, it is difficult to exaggerate the diversity of the topics that fall within the field of psychology.

Implications of Diversity

Students often come to the study of psychology hoping to learn the one grand psychological theory that unifies and explains all aspects of human behavior and consciousness. Such students are often disappointed, for they find not one grand theory, but many different theories, each covering a limited aspect of behavior. The diversity of psychology guarantees that the task of theoretical unification will be immensely difficult. Indeed, many psychologists would argue that such a unification is impossible. Others, however, are searching for greater unification within the field (Anderson, 1991; Gibson, 1994; Kimble, 1990, 1994; Newell, 1990). No matter what their position on the issue, all psychologists agree that theoretical unification will be extremely difficult and that such a unification will occur years in the future if it is to occur at all.

The lack of theoretical integration in psychology not only disappoints some students but also leads many others to denigrate the scientific progress that psychology has made. Such criticism often arises from the mistaken notion that all true sciences must have a grand, unifying theory. It is a mistaken notion because many other sciences also lack a unifying conceptualization. Harvard psychologist William Estes (1979) emphasized this point:

> The situation in which the experimental psychologists find themselves is not novel, to be sure, nor peculiar to psychology. Physics during the early twentieth century subdivided even at the level of undergraduate teaching into separate disciplines. Thus I was introduced to that science through separate university courses in mechanics, heat, optics, acoustics, and electricity. Similarly, chemistry has branched out, evidently irreversibly, into inorganic, organic, physical, and biochemical specialties, among which there may be no more communication than among some of the current subdisciplines of psychology. In both cases, unity has reemerged only at the level of abstract mathematical theory. Medicine has similarly fragmented into specialties, but is like psychology in that there has been no appearance of a new unity. (pp. 661–662)

TABLE 1.1
DIVISIONS OF THE AMERICAN PSYCHOLOGICAL ASSOCIATION

1. General Psychology
2. Teaching of Psychology
3. Experimental Psychology
5. Evaluation, Measurement, and Statistics
6. Physiological and Comparative Psychology
7. Developmental Psychology
8. Personality and Social Psychology
9. Psychological Study of Social Issues
10. Psychology and the Arts
12. Clinical Psychology
13. Consulting Psychology
14. Industrial and Organizational Psychology
15. Educational Psychology
16. School Psychology
17. Counseling Psychology
18. Psychologists in Public Service
19. Military Psychology
20. Adult Development and Aging
21. Applied Experimental and Engineering Psychology
22. Rehabilitation Psychology
23. Consumer Psychology
24. Theoretical and Philosophical Psychology
25. Experimental Analysis of Behavior
26. History of Psychology
27. Community Psychology
28. Psychopharmacology
29. Psychotherapy
30. Psychological Hypnosis
31. State Psychological Association Affairs
32. Humanistic Psychology
33. Mental Retardation and Developmental Disabilities
34. Population and Environmental Psychology
35. Psychology of Women
36. Psychology of Religion
37. Child, Youth, and Family Services
38. Health Psychology
39. Psychoanalysis
40. Clinical Neuropsychology
41. Psychology and Law
42. Psychologists in Independent Practice
43. Family Psychology
44. Psychological Study of Lesbian and Gay Issues
45. Psychological Study of Ethnic Minority Issues
46. Media Psychology
47. Exercise and Sport Psychology
48. Peace Psychology
49. Group Psychology and Group Psychotherapy
50. Addictions

Note: There are no Divisions 4 or 11.

It is also important to understand that what a discipline considers within its province is in part historical accident. One contributing factor is the often arbitrary way that universities partition the range of human knowledge into "departments," which may have administrative convenience but which should not be viewed as unchangeable categories. Indeed, William Bevan, a past president of the APA, said that the fragmentation within the discipline of psychology is so great that psychology departments exist only as an administrative convenience, so members can get their mail from the same bank of mailboxes. In their sociological and historical analysis of American higher education, Christopher Jencks and David Riesman (1968) stated, "A discipline is at bottom nothing more than an administrative category. The various subdisciplines within biology or history or psychology, for example, have only the most limited intellectual relationship to one another, and the same is true in every other field" (p. 523).

Indeed, it is not difficult to imagine a university disbanding its psychology department and integrating its members into other departments (Gardner, 1985; Scott, 1991; Spence, 1987). Physiological psychologists could go into biology departments; many social psychologists could go into sociology departments and business schools; cognitive and perceptual psychologists could go into interdisciplinary departments of cognitive science (Gardner, 1985); organizational and industrial psychologists could go into business schools; clinical and counseling psychologists could go into departments of social work, human resources, and education; developmental psychologists might go to departments of education, cognitive science, or human resources; and so on. Few psychologists would notice any difference in the intellectual interchange with their new colleagues. Actually, many would experience greater camaraderie with their new colleagues than with the old ones in "psychology." Modern psychology, in terms of content, simply does not hang together as a coherent set of topics. One must look to a more general level to find anything that unifies the discipline.

Once we acknowledge the implications of the social and historical factors that determine the structure of disciplines, we can recognize that it is illogical to demand that all fields be unified. Indeed, it has been suggested that the term *psychological studies,* rather than *psychology,* would more accurately reflect the diversity of the discipline. The use of this new term would also make it less surprising to the student that the different areas within the discipline have been characterized by vastly different rates of scientific progress. Some have made impressive progress in the explanation and prediction of behavior, while others have progressed hardly at all. The term *psychology* does not convey this state of affairs. Instead, it implies a coherence of subject matter that is simply not characteristic of the discipline.

If we wish to find any unity in the subject of psychology, we must not look for connections among the topics that psychologists study. We must instead address the methods that psychologists use to advance knowledge. Here is the only place that we have any hope of finding common cause among psychologists. But here, in the domain of the methods psychologists use to advance knowledge, is where we also find some of the greatest misunderstandings of the discipline.

UNITY IN SCIENCE

Any coherence that the discipline of psychology does display stems from its quest to understand behavior by using the methods of science. Indeed, any claim to uniqueness that psychology has resides in its adherence to using the full range of scientific methods to understand behavior. Simply to say that psychology is "concerned with human behavior" does not distinguish it from other disciplines. Many other professional groups and disciplines—including economists, philosophers, novelists, the law, sociology, history, political science, anthropology, and literary studies—are, in part, "concerned with human behavior." Psychology is not unique in this respect.

Practical applications do not establish any uniqueness for the discipline of psychology either. For example, many college students decide to major in psychology because they have the laudable goal of wanting to "help people." But "helping people" is an applied part of an incredibly large number of fields, including social work, education, nursing, occupational therapy, physical therapy, police science, human resources, speech therapy, and many others. Similarly, "helping people" by "counseling" them is a routine part of the fields of education, social work, police work, nursing, pastoral work, occupational therapy, and many others. The goal of training applied specialists to "help people" by "counseling" them does not demand that we have a discipline called *psychology*.

The two things that justify psychology as an independent discipline are that it studies the full range of human and nonhuman behavior with the techniques of science and that applications that derive from this knowledge are scientifically based. Were this not true, there would be no reason for psychology to exist. As previously noted, plenty of other fields are "concerned with behavior," and there is no shortage of "therapies" to "help people" that come from disciplines outside psychology.

Psychology is, however, somewhat different from other behavioral fields in that it attempts to give the public two guarantees. One is that the conclusions about behavior that it produces derive from scientific evidence. The second is that practical applications of psychology have been derived from and tested by scientific methods. Does psychology ever fall short of these goals? Yes, quite often (see Dawes, 1994). This book is about how we might better attain them. But in principle, these are the goals that justify psychology as an independent field. If psychology ever decides that these goals are not worth pursuing, then it might as well fold its tent and let its various concerns devolve to other disciplines, as outlined above, because it would be a totally redundant field of intellectual inquiry.

Clearly, then, the first and most important step that anyone must take in understanding psychology is to realize that its defining feature is that it is the data-based scientific study of behavior. Comprehending all of the implications of this fact will occupy us for the rest of this book because it is the primary way that we develop the ability to think straight about psychology. Conversely, the primary way that people get confused in their thinking about psychology is that they fail to realize that it is a scientific discipline. For example, it is quite common to hear people outside the discipline voice the opinion that psychology is not a science. Why is this a common occurrence?

Attempts to convince the public that psychology cannot be a science stem from a variety of sources. As will be discussed in later chapters, much confusion about the actual discipline of psychology is deliberately fostered by purveyors of bogus psychology. There has grown up in our society a considerable industry of pseudoscientific belief systems that have a vested interest in convincing the public that anything goes in psychology and that there are no rational criteria for evaluating psychological claims. This is the perfect atmosphere in which to market such offers as "Lose weight through hypnosis," "Develop your hidden psychic powers," and "Learn French while you sleep," along with the many other parts of the multi-million-dollar self-help industry that either are not based on scientific evidence or, in many cases, are actually contradicted by much available evidence.

Another source of resistance to scientific psychology stems from the tendency to oppose the expansion of science into areas where unquestioned authorities and "common sense" have long reigned. History provides many examples of initial public resistance to the use of science rather than philosophical speculation, theological edict, or folk wisdom to explain the natural world. Each science has gone through a phase of resistance to its development. Learned contemporaries of Galileo refused to look into his new telescope because the existence of the moons of Jupiter would have violated their philosophical and theological beliefs. For centuries, the understanding of human anatomy progressed only haltingly because of lay and ecclesiastical prohibitions against the dissection of human cadavers. Charles Darwin was repeatedly denounced. Paul Broca's Society of Anthropology was opposed in France because knowledge about human beings was thought to be subversive to the state.

Each scientific step to greater knowledge about human beings has evoked opposition. This opposition eventually dissipated, however, when people came to realize that science does not defile humanity by its investigations but instead contributes to human fulfillment by widening the sphere of knowledge. Who now believes that astronomy's mapping of the galaxies and intricate theories about the composition of distant stars destroy our wonder at the universe? Who would substitute the health care available in their community for that available before human cadavers were routinely dissected? An empirical attitude toward the stars or the human body has not diminished humanity. More recently, Darwin's evolutionary synthesis has laid the foundation for startling advances in genetics and biology. Nevertheless, as we get closer to the nature of human beings and their origins, vestiges of opposition remain. In the United States, religious extremists continue to advocate the teaching of creationism in the public schools, and surveys show that the scientific fact that humans evolved from lower organisms is not accepted by a large portion (in some surveys, a majority) of the public. If evolutionary biology, with its long and impressive record of scientific achievements, can still engender public opposition, is it any wonder that psychology, the most recent discipline to bring long-held beliefs about human beings under scientific scrutiny, currently provokes people to deny its validity?

Finally, many who deny psychology the status of a science are themselves quite confused about the nature of science. Every undergraduate psychology instructor has encountered the freshman or sophomore student who has chosen to major in psychology "because I don't like science." The instructor is, of course, prepared for the student's astonishment when informed that psychology is indeed a member of the sciences ("I can't believe I have to take statistics!"). When the instructor asks, "Have you taken much biology or chemistry since coming to the university?" the reply is very predictable: "Oh no, I've *always* avoided science." Note the irony here: The student knows nothing about the sciences but is absolutely certain that psychology is not one of them! Unfortunately this attitude characterizes many of psychology's critics.

What, Then, Is Science?

In order to understand what psychology is, we must understand what science is. What, then, is science? We can begin by dealing first with what science is not. In this way we can rid ourselves of the vast majority of common misconceptions. First, science is not defined by subject matter. Any aspect of the universe is fair game for the development of a scientific discipline. This includes all aspects of human beings, including their behavior and brain functions. We cannot divide the universe into "scientific" and "nonscientific" topics. Although strong forces throughout history have tried to place human beings outside the sphere of scientific investigation, they have been unsuccessful, as we shall see. The reactions against psychology as a scientific discipline probably represent the modern remnants of this ancient struggle. A claim that human behavior cannot be studied scientifically—which would rule psychology out of the sciences by definition—should not be accepted as a given but should be viewed as a hypothesis that can be evaluated. Actually the hypothesis has been evaluated. It is false.

Science is also not defined by the use of particular experimental apparatus. It is not the test tube, the computer, the electronic equipment, or the investigator's white coat that defines science. These are the trappings of science but are not its defining features. (If this were the case, there would be no question about psychology's status because psychology departments in all major universities are full of computers, chemicals, and electronic equipment of all types.) Science is, rather, a way of thinking about and observing the universe that leads to a deep understanding of its workings.

In the remainder of this chapter, we shall discuss three important and interrelated features that define science: (1) the use of systematic empiricism; (2) the production of public knowledge; and (3) the examination of solvable problems. Although we shall examine each feature separately, remember that the three connect to form a coherent general structure. (For a more detailed discussion of the general characteristics of a science, see the works of Bronowski, Popper, Cournaud, and Medawar in the references section of this book.)

Systematic Empiricism

If you look up the word *empiricism* in any dictionary, you will find that it means "the practice of relying on observation." Although this seems clear enough, there is an even simpler way of defining empiricism. The empirical attitude in science can be summarized by the phrase "Let's take a look." Scientists find out about the world by examining it. The fact that this may seem obvious to you is an indication of the spread of the scientific attitude in the past couple of centuries. In the past it has not always seemed so obvious. Recall the refusal to look into Galileo's telescope. It was long thought that the way to know about the world was through pure thought and argument or appeal to authority. Galileo claimed to have seen moons around the planet Jupiter. Another astronomer, Francesco Sizi, attempted to refute Galileo, not with observations, but with the following argument:

There are seven windows in the head, two nostrils, two ears, two eyes and a mouth; so in the heavens there are two favorable stars, two unpropitious, two luminaries, and Mercury alone undecided and indifferent. From which and many other similar phenomena of nature such as the seven metals, etc., which it were tedious to enumerate, we gather that the number of planets is necessarily seven. . . . Besides, the Jews and other ancient nations, as well as modern Europeans, have adopted the division of the week into seven days, and have named them from the seven planets; now if we increase the number of planets, this whole system falls to the ground. . . . Moreover, the satellites are invisible to the naked eye and therefore can have no influence on the earth and therefore would be useless and therefore do not exist. (Holton & Roller, 1958, p. 160)

The point is not that the argument is laughably idiotic, but that it was seen as a suitable rebuttal to an actual observation! We laugh now because we have the benefit of hindsight. Three centuries of the demonstrated power of the empirical approach give us an edge on poor Sizi. Take away those years of empiricism, and many of us may have been there nodding our heads and urging him on. No, the empirical approach is not necessarily obvious, which is why we often have to teach it, even in a society that is dominated by science.

Empiricism pure and simple is not enough, however. Note that the heading for this section is "*Systematic* Empiricism." Observation is fine and necessary, but pure, unstructured observation of the natural world will not lead to scientific knowledge. Write down every observation you make from the time you get up to the time you go to bed on a given day. When you finish, you will have a great number of facts, but you will not have a greater understanding of the world. Scientific observation is termed *systematic* because it is structured so that the results of the observation reveal something about the underlying nature of the world. Scientific observations are usually theory-driven; they test different explanations of the nature of the world. They are structured so that, depending on the outcome of the observation, some theories are supported and others rejected.

Publicly Verifiable Knowledge: Replication and Peer Review

Scientific knowledge is public in a special sense. By *public,* we do not mean that the results of scientific observations are posted on community-center bulletin boards. Instead, we refer to the fact that scientific knowledge does not exist solely in the mind of a particular individual. In an important sense, scientific knowledge does not exist at all until it has been submitted to the scientific community for criticism and empirical testing. Knowledge that is considered "special"—the province of the thought processes of a particular individual, immune from scrutiny and criticism by others—can never have the status of scientific knowledge.

Science makes the idea of public verifiability concrete via the procedure of *replication.* In order to be considered in the realm of science, a finding must be presented to the scientific community in a way that enables other scientists to attempt the same experiment and obtain the same results. When this occurs, we say that the finding has been replicated. Scientists use replication to define the idea of public knowledge. It ensures that a particular finding is not due simply to the errors or biases of a particular investigator. In short, for a finding to be accepted by the scientific community, it must be possible for someone other than the original investigator to duplicate it. When a finding is presented in this way, it becomes public. It is no longer the sole possession of the original researcher; it is instead available for other investigators to extend, criticize, or apply in their own ways.

John Donne, in his most famous devotion, told us that "no man is an island." In science, no researcher is an island. Each investigator is connected to the scientific community and its knowledge base. It is this interconnection that enables science to grow cumulatively. Researchers constantly build on previous knowledge in order to go beyond what is currently known. This is possible only if previous knowledge is stated in such a way that any investigator can use it to build on.

By *publicly verifiable knowledge,* then, we mean findings presented to the scientific community in such a way that they can be replicated, criticized, or extended by anyone in the community. This is a most important criterion not only for scientists but also for the layperson, who, as a consumer, must evaluate scientific information presented in the media. As we shall see in Chapter 11, one important way to distinguish charlatans and practitioners of pseudoscience from legitimate scientists is that the former often bypass the normal channels of scientific publication and instead go straight to the media with their "findings." One ironclad criterion that will always work for the public when presented with scientific claims of uncertain validity is the question: Have the findings been published in a recognized scientific journal that uses some type of peer review procedure? The answer to this question will almost always separate pseudoscientific claims from the real thing.

Peer review is a procedure in which each paper submitted to a journal is critiqued by several scientists who then submit their criticisms to an editor (usually a scientist with an extensive history of work in the specialty area covered by the journal), who decides whether the weight of opinion warrants publication of the paper, publication after further experimentation and statistical analysis, or rejection because the research is flawed or trivial. Most journals carry a statement of editorial policy in each issue, so it is easy to check whether a journal is peer-reviewed.

Not all information in peer-reviewed scientific journals is necessarily correct, but at least it has met a minimal criterion of peer criticism and scrutiny. It is a minimal criterion, not a stringent one, because most scientific disciplines publish many different journals of varying quality. Most scientific ideas can get published somewhere in the legitimate literature if they meet some rudimentary standards. The idea that only a narrow range of data and theory can get published in science is false. This is an idea often suggested by purveyors of bogus remedies and therapies who try to convince the media and the public that they have been "shut out" of scientific outlets by a conspiracy of "orthodox science." But consider for a minute just how many legitimate outlets there are in a field like psychology. Table 1.2 (pp.13–15) lists the names of only a fraction (there are dozens of others) of the journals from which articles are summarized in the publication *Psychological Abstracts.* Most of the journals listed in the table are peer-reviewed. Virtually all halfway legitimate theories and experiments can find their way into this vast array of publication outlets.

Again, this is not to suggest that all ideas published in the journals summarized in *Psychological Abstracts* are necessarily good or correct. To the contrary, I emphasized above that this is only a *minimal* criterion. However, the point to be emphasized is that the failure of an idea, theory, claim, or therapy to have adequate documentation in the peer-reviewed literature of a scientific discipline is very diagnostic. Particularly when the lack of evidence is accompanied by a media campaign to publicize the claim, *it is a sure sign that the idea, theory, or therapy is bogus.*

The mechanisms of peer review vary somewhat from discipline to discipline, but the underlying rationale is the same. Peer review is one way (replication is another) that science institutionalizes the attitudes of objectivity and public criticism. Ideas and experimentation undergo a honing process in which they are submitted to other critical minds for evaluation. Ideas that survive this critical process have begun to meet the criterion of public verifiability. The peer review process is far from perfect, but it is really the only consumer protection that we have. To ignore it (or not to be aware of it) is to leave ourselves at the mercy of the multi-million-dollar pseudoscience industries that are so good at manipulating the media to their own ends (see Chapter 11). In subsequent chapters, we shall discuss in much more detail the high price we pay for ignoring the checks and balances inherent in the true scientific practice of psychology.

Empirically Solvable Problems: Scientists Seek Testable Theories

Science deals with solvable, or specifiable, problems. This means that the types of questions that scientists address are potentially answerable with currently available empirical techniques. If a problem is not solvable or a theory is not testable with the empirical techniques that scientists have at hand, then scientists will not attack it. For example, the question "Will 3-year-old children given structured language stimulation during day care be ready for reading instruction at an earlier age than children not given such extra stimulation?" represents a scientific problem. It is answerable by currently available empirical methods. The question "Are human beings inherently good or inherently evil?" is not an empirical question and thus is simply not in the realm of science. Likewise, the question "What is the meaning of life?" is not an empirical question and so is outside the realm of science.

Science advances by positing theories to account for particular phenomena in the world, deriving predictions from the theory, testing the predictions empirically, and modifying the theory based on the tests (the sequence is typically theory > prediction > test > modification). So what a scientist often means by the term *solvable problem* is "*testable* theory. "What makes a theory testable? The theory must have specific implications for observable events in the natural world; this is what is meant by *empirically testable.* This criterion for testability is often termed the *falsifiability criterion,* and it is the subject of Chapter 2.

You should be aware of two important misunderstandings of the idea that science deals only with a certain class of problem: the kind that is empirically solvable. First, scientists are often caricatured as believing that questions in the realm of science are the only important questions. This not necessarily true. Scientists do focus on a certain class of problem, but there is no implied denigration of nonscientific problems in this natural division of labor. Scientists are not concerned that the expert on Charles Dickens does not set aside a day once in a while to study DNA. On the other hand, it is similarly wrong to infer that the solid-state physicist who does not devote time to the study of Tennyson's *Idylls of the King* is denying the importance of literature and poetry. In short, just because scientists do not address nonscientific questions in their professional work, it does not follow that they are unconcerned about such questions. Informed artists are often concerned about current developments in science; so, too, scientists recognize the importance of the artistic and literary developments that affect our culture.

By saying that scientists tackle empirically solvable problems, we also do not mean to imply that different classes of problems are inherently solvable or unsolvable and that this division is fixed forever. Quite the contrary: Some problems that are currently unsolvable may become solvable as theory and empirical techniques become more sophisticated. This is how science in general has developed and how new sciences have come into existence. There is always ample room for disagreement about what is currently solvable. Scientists themselves often disagree on this point as it relates to current problems of ambiguous status. Thus, while all scientists agree on the solvability criterion, they may disagree on its specific applications. Nobel laureate Peter Medawar titled one of his books *The Art of the Soluble* (1967) to illustrate that part of the creativity involved in science is finding the problem on the furthest edge of the frontier of human knowledge that will yield to empirical techniques.

Psychology itself provides many good examples of the development from the unsolvable to the solvable. There are many questions (such as, "How does a child learn to speak the language of his or her parents?"; "Why do we forget things we once knew?"; "How does being in a group change a person's behavior and thinking?") that had been the subjects of speculation for centuries before anyone recognized that they could be addressed by empirical means. As this recognition slowly developed, psychology coalesced as a collection of problems concerning behavior in a variety of domains. Psychological issues gradually became separated from philosophy, and a separate empirical discipline developed.

Psychology and Folk Wisdom: The Problem with "Common Sense"

We all have implicit theories of human behavior that govern our interactions and our thoughts about ourselves and other people. Indeed, some social, personality, and cognitive psychologists study the nature of these implicit psychological theories. Rarely do we state our theories in a clear, logical form. Instead, we usually become aware of them only when attention is drawn to them or when we find them challenged in some way. In fact, most of us do not adhere to coherent theories at all. Instead, we have a ragbag of general principles, homilies, and clichés about human behavior that we draw on when we feel that we need an explanation. The problem with this commonsense knowledge about human behavior is

TABLE 1.2
PARTIAL LIST OF PUBLICATIONS WHOSE ARTICLES ARE
SUMMARIZED IN *PSYCHOLOGICAL ABSTRACTS*

Academic Psychology Bulletin

Acta Psychologica

Addictive Behaviors

Adolescence

Advances in Behavioral Pediatrics

Advances in Behavior Research and Therapy

Aging and Work

American Behavioral Scientist

American Journal of Art Therapy

American Journal of Clinical Biofeedback

American Journal of Clinical Hypnosis

American Journal of Community Psychology

American Journal of Family Therapy

American Journal of Mental Retardation

American Journal of Psychology

American Journal of Psychotherapy

American Psychologist

Animal Learning and Behavior

Annual of Animal Psychology

Applied Cognitive Psychology

Applied Psycholinguistics

Applied Psychological Measurement

Behavioral and Brain Sciences

Behavioral Assessment

Behavioral Disorders

Behavioral Engineering

Behavioral Science

Behavior Modification

Behavior Research and Therapy

Behavior Therapy

Biological Psychology

Brain and Language

Brain, Behavior and Evolution

British Journal of Clinical Psychology

British Journal of Developmental Psychology

British Journal of Educational Psychology

British Journal of Mathematical and Statistical Psychology

British Journal of Social Psychology

Canadian Journal of Behavioral Science

Canadian Journal of Experimental Psychology

Canadian Psychology

Child Behavior Therapy

Child Development

Clinical Neuropsychology

Clinical Psychologist

Cognition

Cognition and Emotion

Cognitive Psychology

Cognitive Science

Cognitive Therapy and Research

Contemporary Educational Psychology

Counseling Psychologist

Current Directions in Psychological Science

Developmental Psychobiology

Developmental Psychology

Developmental Review

Educational and Psychological Measurement

Educational Psychologist

Environment and Behavior

European Journal of Social Psychology

Genetic Psychology Monographs

Health Psychology

Hormones and Behavior

Human Development

Human Factors

Infant Behavior and Development

Intelligence

continued

Table 1.2—*Continued*

International Journal of Aging and Human Development

International Journal of Behavioral Development

International Journal of Eating Disorders

International Journal of Group Psychotherapy

International Journal of Psycholinguistics

International Journal of Psychology

International Journal of Sport Psychology

International Review of Applied Psychology

Journal for the Theory of Social Behavior

Journal of Abnormal Child Psychology

Journal of Abnormal Psychology

Journal of Affective Disorders

Journal of Applied Behavioral Science

Journal of Applied Developmental Psychology

Journal of Applied Psychology

Journal of Behavioral Assessment

Journal of Behavioral Medicine

Journal of Black Psychology

Journal of Child Psychology and Psychiatry

Journal of Child Psychotherapy

Journal of Clinical Child Psychology

Journal of Clinical Psychology

Journal of Community Psychology

Journal of Comparative and Physiological Psychology

Journal of Consulting and Clinical Psychology

Journal of Contemporary Psychotherapy

Journal of Counseling Psychology

Journal of Cross-Cultural Psychology

Journal of Economic Psychology

Journal of Educational Psychology

Journal of Environmental Psychology

Journal of Experimental Child Psychology

Journal of Experimental Psychology: Animal Behavior Processes

Journal of Experimental Psychology: Human Perception and Performance

Journal of Experimental Psychology: Learning, Memory and Cognition

Journal of Experimental Social Psychology

Journal of General Psychology

Journal of Genetic Psychology

Journal of Individual Psychology

Journal of Instructional Psychology

Journal of Mathematical Psychology

Journal of Memory and Language

Journal of Mental Imagery

Journal of Mind and Behavior

Journal of Motor Behavior

Journal of Nonverbal Behavior

Journal of Occupational Psychology

Journal of Pediatric Psychology

Journal of Personality

Journal of Personality and Social Psychology

Journal of Personality Assessment

Journal of Psychohistory

Journal of Psycholinguistic Research

Journal of Psychological Anthropology

Journal of Psychology

Journal of Psychology and Theology

Journal of Research in Personality

Journal of School Psychology

Journal of Sport Psychology

Journal of the American Psychoanalytic Association

Journal of the Experimental Analysis of Behavior

Journal of Transpersonal Psychology

Law and Human Behavior

Law and Psychology Review

Learning and Individual Differences

Learning and Motivation

continued

TABLE 1.2—*Continued*

Managerial Psychology	*Psychological Research*
Memory and Cognition	*Psychological Review*
Merrill-Palmer Quarterly	*Psychological Science*
Motivation and Emotion	*Psychology in the Schools*
Multivariate Behavioral Research	*Psychology of Music*
Neuropsychologica	*Psychology of Women Quarterly*
New Directions for Methodology of Social and Behavioral Science	*Psychometrika*
	Psychonomic Bulletin and Review
Organizational Behavior and Human Decision Processes	*Psychophysiology*
	Quarterly Journal of Experimental Psychology: Comparative and Physiological Psychology
Perception	
Perception and Psychophysics	*Quarterly Journal of Experimental Psychology: Human Experimental Psychology*
Personality and Individual Differences	
Personality and Social Psychology Bulletin	*Rehabilitation Psychology*
Personality Study and Group Behavior	*Representative Research in Social Psychology*
Personnel Psychology	*Scandinavian Journal of Behavior Therapy*
Physiological Psychology	*Scandinavian Journal of Psychology*
Physiology and Behavior	*School Psychologist*
Political Psychology	*School Psychology Review*
Professional Psychology	*Sensory Processes*
Psychological Bulletin	*Social Behavior and Personality*
Psychological Inquiry	*Social Psychology Quarterly*
Psychological Medicine	*Theory and Psychology*
Psychological Record	*Vision Research*

that much of it contradicts itself and is therefore unfalsifiable (the principle of falsifiability is the topic of the next chapter).

Often a person uses some folk proverb to explain a behavioral event even though on an earlier occasion this same person used a directly contradictory folk proverb to explain the same type of event. For example, most of us have heard or said, "Look before you leap." Now there's a useful, straightforward bit of behavioral advice—except that I vaguely remember admonishing on occasion, "He who hesitates is lost." And "Absence makes the heart grow fonder" is a pretty clear prediction of an emotional reaction to environmental events. But then what about "Out of sight, out of mind"? And if "haste makes waste," why does "time wait for no man"? How could the saying "Two heads are better than one" not be true? Except that "too many cooks spoil the broth." If I think, "It's better to be safe than sorry," why do I also believe, "Nothing ventured, nothing gained"? And if "opposites attract," why do "birds of a feather flock together"? I have counseled many students "never to put off until tomorrow what you can do today." But I hope my last advisee has never heard me say this because I just told him, "Cross that bridge when you come to it."

The enormous appeal of clichés like these is that, taken together as implicit "explanations" of behavior, they cannot be refuted. No matter what happens, one of these "explanations" will be cited to cover it. No wonder we all think we are such excellent judges of human behavior and personality. We have an explanation for anything and everything that happens.

Also contributing to our feeling of expertise in explaining human behavior is a phenomenon that psychologist Baruch Fischhoff (1975, 1977; Slovic & Fischhoff, 1977) has studied extensively and has labeled the "I-knew-it-all-along" or "hindsight effect." It seems that when we are given new information, we immediately incorporate it into what we already know. Thus it becomes very difficult to discern how much of new information we previously knew and how much we have only recently learned. In most cases people vastly overestimate how much they knew in advance. Thus, when presented with factual information that they could not have produced by themselves in advance, people still think that they knew it all along. People do not realize how much of their ability to "explain" the behavior of others is due to hindsight; namely, their knowledge that the behavior has already happened. We fail to realize that we would not have been able to predict the behavior in advance. Given a different outcome, we would have explained it just as easily and would have concluded that what actually happened was virtually inevitable, given what we "know" about human behavior. The discovery of the hindsight effect by psychologists has important practical consequences because, for example, physicians have been found to display a hindsight bias (Arkes, Wortmann, Saville, & Harkness, 1981), but their judgment can be improved by training in avoiding the bias (Arkes, Faust, Guilmette, & Hart, 1988).

The hindsight phenomenon even affects people's memory of their own attitudes and behavior. Researcher Greg Marcus (1986) conducted a longitudinal study of people's political attitudes from 1973 to 1982. When, in 1982, people had to indicate what their attitudes had been in 1973, their memories were distorted in a very specific way. They tended to think that their attitudes in 1973 were more similar to their present attitudes than they had really been. In fact, people's memories of their attitudes in 1973 were more similar to their present (1982) attitudes than they were to their *actual* attitudes in 1973. In short, people have a hard time remembering that they didn't always have the attitudes that they currently have.

So sometimes our implicit psychological theories can't be refuted. We will see in the next chapter why this inability to be refuted makes such theories not very useful. However, a further problem occurs even in cases where our folk beliefs do have some specificity, that is, even when they are empirically testable. The problem is that psychological research has shown that, when many common cultural beliefs are subjected to empirical test, they turn out to be false (see Kohn, 1990). Take, for example, common beliefs about the value of work experience to teenage high-school students. Most adult Americans think that the current trend toward the employment of greater numbers of teenagers in the work force while they attend school is a good thing because (1) they will be earning money to help pay for their further education and for family expenses; (2) they will develop a "work ethic" that will make them more responsible employees in later life; (3) they will develop a greater respect for our economy; and (4) they will be more motivated students because they are integrated into the economy.

Developmental psychologists have conducted extensive studies of the effect of working on the behavior, attitudes, and educational achievement of high-school students (Bachman & Schulenberg, 1993; Greenberger & Steinberg, 1986; Steinberg, Fegley, & Dornbusch, 1993). They have found that virtually every one of our cultural beliefs about teenage employment is false. Only an extremely small amount of the money that teenagers earn goes to help with family expenses or to further their education. The vast majority of earnings are spent on luxury items that convey social status or for which television advertising has created a "need." Working while in high school has strong harmful effects on the students' education and educational experiences. And most interesting of all, work experience makes teenagers more cynical and less respectful of work and its value in our economy. In one study, working teenagers were more likely to endorse statements like "People who work harder at their jobs than they have to are a little bit crazy" and "There's no such thing as a company that cares about its employees" than were nonworking teenagers (Greenberger & Steinberg, 1986). Finally, from a review of the research in this area, Greenberger and Steinberg concluded that "working appears to promote, rather than deter, some forms of delinquent behavior" (p. 6). It appears that we have developed a substantial cultural myth about the value of work for young people. The common rhetoric about "building character" and "learning the value of money" is false. These clichés are "folktales" of the type that anthropologists are fond of studying in "underdeveloped" countries—tales that make us feel good and that justify current cultural practices but that have no basis in reality.

It is not difficult to generate other instances of folk beliefs (or "common sense") that are wrong. Take, for example, the idea that children who excel academically or who read a lot are not socially or physically adept ("bookworms" are "sissies" or are "not sociable"). This idea still circulates in our society even though it is utterly false. There is voluminous evidence that, contrary to "commonsense" folk belief, readers and academically inclined individuals are more physically robust and are more socially involved than are people who do not read (Gage & Berliner, 1984, pp. 18–19; Market Facts, 1984; Zill & Winglee, 1990). For example, children high in scholastic achievement are more likely to be accepted by their peers than children low in achievement (Gage & Berliner, 1984). People who read a lot are more likely to play sports, jog, camp, hike, and do car repair than are people who do not read very much (Zill & Winglee, 1990). The results of one major study were summarized as follows:

> Book readers are often portrayed in films or on stage as solitary, somewhat aloof, self-absorbed personalities whose devotion to their books seems to take the place of interaction with the rest of the world. This study, however, proves this stereotype to be nothing more than a myth. Far from being introverted or social out-

casts, book readers emerge as well-rounded individuals active in a wide range of social and cultural activities. On the contrary, in many ways they are more active than nonbook readers. (Market Facts, 1984, p. 71)

Many folk beliefs are perpetuated without any attempt at their evaluation. This often occurs even in cases where the claim could be easily tested. For example, in the United States, group homes for mentally handicapped individuals have often been opposed by neighbors who use the argument "My property value will decline." From our previous discussion, you should immediately recognize that the argument is an empirically solvable problem. Perhaps it will be easier to see if we put the statement in the form of a question: Do property values in a neighborhood decline after the introduction of a group home for mentally handicapped individuals? Two researchers have conducted an extensive empirical study of this question. By analyzing the sale prices of 525 houses at various distances from 13 different group homes, Ryan and Coyne (1985) were able to determine that the introduction of group homes did not adversely affect neighborhood property values. This finding has been replicated by other investigators (Gelman, Epp, Downing, Twatrk, & Eyerly, 1989).

There are other common examples of the perpetuation of incorrect folk beliefs without attempts to get easily collectible empirical evidence. For instance, in the rush to make the public aware of the condition of dyslexia (unexplained reading failure), the media and other groups have perpetuated the myth that a host of famous individuals, such as Albert Einstein, Auguste Rodin, George Patton, and Woodrow Wilson, were dyslexic. This folk myth continues to be spread even though a cursory knowledge of the psychological definition of dyslexia and the reading of a standard biography of any of these individuals would reveal the inaccuracy of the claim. Einstein, for example, was reading Kant at age 13 (see Adelman & Adelman, 1987; Coles, 1987), a performance hardly representative of individuals who are currently labeled dyslexic (Aaron & Joshi, 1992; Maughan, Hagell, Rutter, & Yule, 1994; Spreen, 1988; Stanovich & Siegel, 1994). Nevertheless this "fact" has become "common knowledge" among millions of Americans.

Folk beliefs are not always immune to evidence. Sometimes, when the contradictory evidence becomes too widely known, they do change. For example, years ago one widely held cliché about children was "Early ripe, early rot" (Fancher, 1985, p. 141). The cliché reflected the belief that childhood precocity was associated with adult abnormality, a belief sustained by many anecdotes about childhood prodigies who came to ruin in later life. In this case the psychological evidence documenting the inaccuracy of the cliché has been absorbed into the general culture, and one almost never hears this bit of folk "wisdom" anymore.

This last example also carries a warning by reminding us to beware today's "common sense"—because it is not difficult to show that yesterday's "common sense" has often turned into today's "nonsense." After all, "common sense" is what "everybody knows," right? Right. Well, everybody knows that women shouldn't be able to vote, right? Everybody knows that black Americans shouldn't be taught to read, right? Everybody knows that handicapped individuals should be institutionalized out of the sight of society, right? In fact, 150 years ago, all of these beliefs were what "everybody knew." Of course, we now recognize this "common sense" of the past as nonsense, as prejudiced beliefs based on unverified assumptions. But in these examples we can see the critical role that psychology plays, vis-à-vis "common sense." Psychology tests the empirical basis of the assumptions that "common sense" rests on. Sometimes the assumptions do not hold up when tested, as we saw in many of the previous examples. From the examples discussed above—and many more could be cited—we can see that psychology's role as the empirical tester of much folk wisdom often brings it into conflict with many widely held cultural beliefs. Psychology is often the bearer of the "bad tidings" that comfortable folk beliefs do not stand up to the cold light of day. Perhaps it is not surprising that many people would like not only to ignore the message but also to do away with the messenger.

PSYCHOLOGY AS A YOUNG SCIENCE

There has always been opposition to an empirically based psychology. Just 100 years ago, Cambridge University refused to establish a psychophysics laboratory because the study of such a topic would "insult religion by putting the human soul on a pair of scales" (Hearst, 1979, p. 7). Psychology's battle to establish its problems as empirically solvable has only recently been won. As psychology has been able to demonstrate that many problems about human behavior can be scientifically studied and solved, the battle over the status of the field as a whole has receded, to be replaced by skirmishes over specific issues.

Psychologists will continue to address more problems that are the subject of strongly held beliefs about human beings because many of these problems are empirically testable. Psychologists now study topics such as the development of moral reasoning, the psychology of romantic love, the nature of racial prejudice, and the psychological and social determinants of religious beliefs. Some people object to empirical investigation in these areas; yet there has been scientific progress in each of them.

Perhaps you have already noted the inconsistency of many of the criticisms leveled at psychology. On one hand, some people object to calling psychology a science and deny that psychologists can establish empirical facts about human behavior. On the other hand, there are those who object to the investigation of certain areas of human behavior and beliefs because of what psychologists may discover about them. Skinnerian psychologists regularly deal with these contradictory criticisms. For instance, critics have argued that the laws of reinforcement formulated by behaviorists do not apply to human behavior. At the same time, other critics are concerned that the laws will be used for the rigid and inhumane control of people. Thus the behaviorists are faced with some critics who deny that their laws can be applied and others who charge that their laws can be applied too easily!

A similar example of inconsistency occurred in the mid-1970s when Wisconsin Senator William Proxmire singled out for public criticism the work of social psychologists who were studying human love and attachment. In one statement Proxmire argued that human love could not be studied scientifically, but in the next breath he argued that most people want to leave topics like this a mystery, that they do not want the answer to the question of why people are attracted to each other because the answer might be disturbing (see Shaffer, 1977). Again, we have the same confusion that we saw in criticisms of behaviorism. The two arguments, used by the same individual in this case, are logically inconsistent: Proxmire argued that human love could not be studied empirically, but he also argued that people would be disturbed by the empirical facts that scientific study of the topic would reveal!

Examples like this arise because the relatively new science of psychology has just begun to uncover facts about aspects of human behavior that have previously escaped study. The relative youth of psychology as a science explains partially why its status as an empirical discipline is inadequately appreciated, since the public's regard for any science corresponds to its having become acceptable at some distant point in the past. In this context, the confusion surrounding psychology seems a little easier to comprehend, although it is still lamentable. Another result of psychology's relatively recent emergence is that many of its areas of study are in their infancy and have barely begun to yield significant facts and powerful theories. Nevertheless, during the past four decades, psychology has become firmly established in the interconnecting structure of knowledge that we call science.

In summary, we have demonstrated that psychology is an incredibly diverse discipline. The field has many different subareas, and the record of progress of these subareas is very mixed, as one would expect of a young discipline. Nevertheless, like other sciences, psychology is characterized by the use of systematic empiricism to uncover knowledge about behavior, by the quest to produce publicly verifiable knowledge that is open to scrutiny and criticism, and by a focus on empirically solvable problems and testable theories. In the next chapter we focus on this last characteristic: How do we tell whether a theory is testable or not?

Chapter 2

FALSIFIABILITY

A Discourse on How to Foil
Little Green Men in the Head

In 1793 a severe epidemic of yellow fever struck Philadelphia. One of the leading doctors in the city at the time was Benjamin Rush, a signer of the Declaration of Independence. During the outbreak Rush was one of the few physicians who were available to treat literally thousands of yellow fever cases. Rush adhered to a theory of medicine that dictated that illnesses accompanied by fever should be treated by vigorous bloodletting. He administered this treatment to many patients, including himself when he came down with the illness. Critics charged that his treatments were more dangerous than the disease. However, following the epidemic, Rush became even more confident of the effectiveness of his treatment, even though several of his patients had died. Why?

One writer summarized Rush's attitude this way: "Convinced of the correctness of his theory of medicine and lacking a means for the systematic study of treatment outcome, he attributed each new instance of improvement to the efficacy of his treatment and each new death that occurred despite it to the severity of the disease" (Eisenberg, 1977, p. 1106). In other words, if the patient got better, this improvement was taken as proof that bloodletting worked. If the patient died, it merely meant that the patient had been too ill for any treatment to work. We now know that Rush's critics were right: his treatments were as dangerous as the disease. In this chapter we will discuss how Rush went wrong. His error illustrates one of the most important principles of scientific thinking, one that is particularly useful in evaluating psychological claims.

In this chapter we focus in more detail on the third general characteristic of science that we discussed in Chapter 1: scientists deal with solvable problems. What scientists most often mean by a "solvable problem" is a "testable theory." The way scientists make sure they are dealing with testable theories is by ensuring that their theories are falsifiable—that they have implications for actual events in the natural world. In this chapter we will see why what is termed the *falsifiability criterion* is so important in psychology.

THEORIES AND THE FALSIFIABILITY CRITERION

Benjamin Rush fell into a fatal trap when assessing the outcome of his treatment. His method of evaluating the evidence made it impossible to conclude that his treatment did not work. If the recovery of a patient meant confirmation of his treatment (and hence his theory of medicine), then it only seems fair that the death of a patient should have meant disconfirmation. Instead, he rationalized away these disconfirmations. By interpreting the evidence as he did, Rush violated one of the most important rules regarding the construction and testing of theories in science: he made it impossible to falsify his theory.

Scientific theories must always be stated in such a way that the predictions derived from them can potentially be shown to be false. Thus the methods of evaluating new evidence relevant to a particular theory must always include the possibility that the data will falsify the theory. This principle is often termed the *falsifiability criterion,* and its importance in scientific progress has been most forcefully articulated by Karl Popper, a philosopher of science whose writings are read widely by working scientists (Magee, 1985).

The falsifiability criterion states that, for a theory to be useful, the predictions drawn from it must be specific. The theory must go out on a limb, so to speak, because in telling us what *should* happen, the theory must also imply that certain things will *not* happen. If these latter things do happen, then we have a clear signal that something is wrong with the theory: it may need to be modified, or we may need to look for an entirely new theory. Either way, we shall end up with a theory that is nearer to the truth. In contrast, if a theory does not rule out any possible observations, then the theory can never be changed, and we are frozen into our current way of thinking, with no possibility of progress. Thus a successful theory is not one that accounts for every possible happening because such a theory robs itself of any predictive power.

Because we shall often refer to the evaluation of theories in the remainder of this book, we must clear up one common misconception surrounding the term *theory.* The misconception is reflected in the commonly used phrase, "Oh, it's only a theory." This phrase captures what laypersons often mean when they use the term *theory:* an unverifiable hypothesis, a mere guess, a hunch. This is most definitely *not* the way the term *theory* is used in science. When scientists refer to theories, they do not mean unverifiable guesses.

A theory in science is an interrelated set of concepts that is used to explain a body of data and to make predictions about the results of future experiments. *Hypotheses* are specific predictions that are derived from theories, which are more general and comprehensive. Currently viable theories are those that have had a lot of their hypotheses confirmed. The theoretical structures of such theories are thus consistent with a large number of observations. However, when the database begins to contradict the hypotheses derived from a theory, scientists begin trying to construct a new theory that will provide a better interpretation of the data. Thus the theories that are under scientific discussion are those that have been verified to some extent and that do not make many predictions that are contradicted by the available data. They are not mere guesses or hunches.

The difference between the layperson's and the scientist's use of the term *theory* was exploited in the 1980s by some religious Fundamentalists who wanted creationism taught in the public schools. Their argument was "After all, evolution is only a theory." This statement suggests the layperson's usage of the term *theory* to mean "only a guess." The theory of evolution by natural selection is a theory, but in the scientific sense. It is a conceptual structure that is supported by a large and varied set of data (Berra, 1990). It is not a mere guess, equal to any other mere guess.

The Theory of Knocking Rhythms

A hypothetical example will show how the falsifiability criterion works. A student knocks at my door. A colleague in my office with me has a theory that makes predictions about the rhythms that different types of people use to knock. Before I open the door, my colleague predicts that the person behind it is a female. I open the door and, indeed, the student is a female. Later I tell my colleague that I am impressed, but only mildly so because he had a 50 percent chance of being correct even without his "theory of knocking rhythms." He says he can do better. Another knock comes. My colleague tells me it is a male under 22 years old. I open the door to find a male student whom I know to be just out of high school. I comment that I am somewhat impressed since our university has a considerable number of students over the age of 22. Yet I still maintain that, of course, young males are quite common on campus. Thinking me hard to please, my colleague proposes one last test. After the next knock, my colleague predicts, "Female, 30 years old, 5 feet 2 inches tall, carrying a book and a purse in the left hand and knocking with the right." After opening the door and confirming the prediction completely, I have quite a different response. I say that, assuming my colleague did not play a trick and arrange for these people to appear at my door, I am now in fact extremely impressed.

Why the difference in my reactions? Why do my friend's three predictions yield three different responses, ranging from "So what?" to "Wow"? The answer has to do with the specificity and precision of the predictions. The more specific predictions made a greater impact when they were confirmed. Notice, however, that the specificity varied directly with the falsifiability. The more specific and precise the prediction was, the more potential observations there were that could have falsified it. For example, there are a lot of people who are *not* 30-year-old females who are 5 feet 2 inches tall.

Good theories, then, make predictions that expose themselves to falsification. Bad theories do not put themselves in jeopardy in this way. They make predictions that are so general that they are almost bound to be true (for example, the next person to knock on my door will be less than 100 years old) or are phrased in such a way that they are completely protected from falsification (the Benjamin Rush example). In fact, a theory can be so protected from falsifiability that it is simply no longer considered scientific at all. Indeed, it was Popper's attempt to define the criteria that separate science from nonscience that led him to emphasize the importance of the falsifiability principle. There is a direct link here to psychology and to our discussion of Freud in Chapter 1.

Freud and Falsifiability

In the early decades of this century Popper was searching for the underlying reasons that some scientific theories seem to lead to advances in knowledge and others lead to intellectual stagnation (Magee, 1985). Einstein's general relativity theory, for example, led to startlingly new observations (for instance, that the light from a distant star bends when it passes near the sun) precisely because its predictions were structured so that many possible events could have contradicted them and thus falsified the theory.

Popper reasoned that this was not true of stagnant theories and pointed to Freudian psychoanalysis as an example. Freudian theory uses a complicated conceptual structure that explains human behavior after the fact but does not predict things in advance. It could explain everything. But, Popper argued, it was precisely this property that made it scientifically useless. It made no specific predictions. Adherents of psychoanalytic theory spent much time and effort in getting the theory to explain every known human event, from individual quirks of behavior to large-scale social phenomena, but their success in making the theory a rich source of after-the-fact explanation robbed it of any scientific utility. Freudian psychoanalytic theory currently plays a much larger role as a spur to the literary imagination than it does as a theory in contemporary psychology. Its demise within psychology can be traced in part to its failure to satisfy the falsifiability criterion.

A good example of this legacy is the field known as *psychohistory*, which consists largely of attempts to explain the behavioral patterns of well-known individuals by examining the critical "psychic events" in their lives, particularly those that took place in childhood. Such psychobiographies almost always have a ring of truth and a general air of plausibility. The childhood reconstruction used in such biographies gives a sense of inevitability to the later events in the person's life. Robert Liebert's review of David Abrahamsen's psychobiography of Richard Nixon, *Nixon vs. Nixon: An Emotional Tragedy* (1977), amply illustrates the pitfalls of this type of post hoc analysis. In classic psychoanalytic style Abrahamsen explained Watergate by referring to Nixon's unconscious Oedipal need to fail. Liebert (1977) contended that the case of Nixon clearly illustrates the problem with this type of analysis:

> The danger in Abrahamsen's kind of post hoc analysis is this: had Nixon, after rising from the ashes in 1968, died of natural causes after ending the war in Vietnam and opening relations with China, but before Watergate, would Abrahamsen have concluded that Nixon's life and career was [sic] an example of a man driven by an Oedipal need for failure? Or, could one have said that given his extraordinarily successful career, he was a man driven by an Oedipal need to triumph, and then reconstructed the case accordingly? (p. 69)

In short, the style of such theorizing invites the spinning of endless webs of rational-sounding conjectures, but the theory's very generativity is in fact its

Achilles' heel. And this Achilles' heel can lead to disastrous consequences. As an eminent critic has argued, "Incorrect but widely dispersed ideas about the mind inevitably end by causing social damage. Thanks to the once imposing prestige of psychoanalysis, people harboring diseases or genetic conditions have deferred effective treatment while scouring their infantile past for the sources of their trouble" (Crews, 1993, p. 65).

Take, for example, the history of Gilles de la Tourette syndrome. This is a disorder characterized by physical tics and twitches that may involve any part of the body, as well as vocal symptoms such as grunts and barks, echolalia (involuntary repetition of the words of others), and coprolalia (compulsive repetition of obscene words). Tourette syndrome is an organically based disorder of the central nervous system and is now successfully treated by administering the drug haloperidol (Bower, 1990). Throughout history, individuals with Tourette syndrome have been persecuted—earlier as witches by religious authorities, and in more modern times by being subjected to exorcisms (Hines, 1988). Importantly, understanding of the cause and treatment of the disorder was considerably hampered from 1921 to 1955, when explanations and treatments for Tourette syndrome were dominated by psychoanalytic conceptualizations (see Shapiro, Shapiro, Bruun, & Sweet, 1978). Author after author presented unfalsifiable psychoanalytic explanations for the syndrome. The resulting array of vague explanations created a conceptual sludge that obscured the true nature of the syndrome and probably impeded scientific progress toward an accurate understanding of it. For example, according to one author, Tourette syndrome is

> a classic example of the retrogressive effect of psychoanalysis on the investigation of brain disease. La Tourette had attributed the disease to a degenerative process of the brain. After Freud's theories became fashionable in the early decades of the present century, attention in such conditions was deflected from the brain. . . . The consequence of this retrograde movement was that patients tended to be referred to psychiatrists (usually of a psychoanalytic persuasion) rather than to neurologists, so that physical examinations and investigation were not performed. (Thornton, 1986, p. 210)

Shapiro et al. (1978) described one psychoanalyst who thought that his patient was "reluctant to give up the tic because it became a source of erotic pleasure to her and an expression of unconscious sexual strivings." Another considered the tics "stereotyped equivalents of onanism. . . . The libido connected with the genital sensation was displaced into other parts of the body." A third considered the tic a "conversion symptom at the anal-sadistic level." A fourth thought that a person with Tourette syndrome had a "compulsive character, as well as a narcissistic orientation" and that the patient's tics "represent[ed] an affective syndrome, a defense against the intended affect." The summary by Shapiro et al. of the resulting theoretical situation demonstrates quite well the harmful effects of ignoring the falsifiability criterion:

> Psychoanalytic theorizing of this kind in effect leaves no base untouched. Tics are a conversion symptom but not hysterical, anal but also erotic, volitional but also compulsive, organic but also dynamic in origin. . . . These psychological labels, diagnoses, and treatments were unfortunately imposed on patients and their families,

usually with little humility, considerable dogmatism, and with much harm. . . . These papers, because of their subsequent widespread influence, had a calamitous effect on the understanding and treatment of this syndrome. (pp. 39–42, 50, 63)

Progress in the treatment and understanding of Tourette syndrome began to occur only when researchers recognized that the psychoanalytic "explanations" were useless. These explanations were enticing because they *did* explain things. In fact, they explained everything, after the fact. However, the explanations they provided created only the illusion of understanding. By attempting to explain everything after the fact, they barred the door to any advance. Progress occurs only when a theory does not predict *everything* but instead makes specific predictions that tell us—in advance—something specific about the world. The predictions derived from such a theory may be wrong, of course, but this is a strength, not a weakness.

The Little Green Men

It is not difficult to recognize unfalsifiable conceptualizations when one is detached from the subject matter and particularly when one has the benefit of historical hindsight (as in the Benjamin Rush example). It is also easy to detect unfalsifiable conceptualizations when the instance is obviously concocted. For example, it is a little known fact that I have discovered the underlying brain mechanism that controls behavior. You will soon be reading about this discovery (in the *National Enquirer,* available at your local supermarkets). In the left hemisphere of the brain, near the language areas, reside two tiny green men. They have the power to control the electrochemical processes taking place in many areas of the brain. And, well, to make a long story short, they basically control everything. There is one difficulty, however. The green men have the ability to detect any intrusion into the brain (surgery, X rays, etc.), and when they do sense such an intrusion, they tend to disappear. (I forgot to mention that they have the power to become invisible.)

I have no doubt insulted your intelligence by using an example more suitable to junior-high-school students. However, consider this. As an instructor in psychology, I am often confronted by students who ask me why I have not lectured on all the startling new discoveries in extrasensory perception (ESP) and parapsychology that have been made in the past few years. I have to inform these students (whose beliefs are not atypical; several surveys have shown that a majority of the American public believes that ESP has been scientifically demonstrated) that most of what they have heard about these subjects has undoubtedly come from the general media, rather than from scientifically respectable sources. In fact, some scientists have looked at these claims and have not been able to replicate the findings. I remind these students, who not uncommonly have already completed a methodology course, that replication of a finding is critical to its acceptance as an established scientific fact and that this is particularly true in the case of results that contradict either previous data or established theory.

I further admit that many scientists have lost patience with ESP research. Although one reason is undoubtedly that the area is tainted by fraud, charlatanism, and media exploitation, perhaps the most important reason for scientific disenchantment is the existence of what Martin Gardner, in his column in *Scientific American,* once called the Catch-22 of ESP research.

It works as follows: A "believer" (someone who accepts the existence of ESP phenomena before beginning an investigation) claims to have demonstrated ESP in the laboratory. A "skeptic" (someone who doubts the existence of ESP) is brought in to confirm the phenomena. Often, after observing the experimental situation, the skeptic calls for more controls, and though these are sometimes resisted, well-intentioned believers often agree to them. When the controls are instituted, the phenomena cannot be demonstrated (see Alcock, 1981, 1990; Druckman & Swets, 1988; Frazier, 1981; M. Gardner, 1981; Gilovich, 1991; Hines, 1988; Hyman, 1992; Kurtz, 1987). The skeptic, who correctly interprets this failure as an indication that the original demonstration was due to inadequate experimental control and thus cannot be accepted, is often shocked to find that the believer does not regard the original demonstration as invalid. Instead, the believer invokes the Catch-22 of ESP: psychic powers, the believer maintains, are subtle, delicate, and easily disturbed. The "negative vibes" of the skeptic were probably responsible for the disruption of the "psi powers." The powers will undoubtedly return when the negative aura of the skeptic is removed.

Now comes the surprise. My student does not chuckle at this but says, "Yeah, it makes sense. I can see how the skeptic might give off negative interferences that would mess up ESP." Slightly stunned but maintaining my composure, I gently remind the student of the funny example of the little green men I used in class a few weeks ago. I point out that, although the whole class thought my argument about the little green men was ridiculous, the believer's argument is logically analogous. ESP operates just as the little green men do. It's there as long as you don't intrude to look at it carefully. When you do, it disappears. If we accept this explanation, it will be impossible to demonstrate the phenomenon to any skeptical observers. It appears only to believers. Of course, this position is unacceptable in science. We do not have magnetism physicists and nonmagnetism physicists (those for whom magnetism does and does not work). At this point, the student looks a little sheepish. He or she mumbles agreement with me, then usually quickly leaves the room. I, of course, never know whether the agreement is an indication of true understanding or the result of embarrassment and a wish to escape the situation. Perhaps it is a little of both, for the student has been asked to do one of the most difficult things in the world: confront a strongly held belief with contradictory evidence. It can be quite disconcerting to rigorously apply the criteria of scientific explanation to long-held beliefs. But this is just what a psychologist must do. No one ever said it would be easy.

Not All Confirmations Are Equal

The principle of falsifiability has important implications for the way we view the confirmation of a theory. Many people think that a good scientific theory is one that has been repeatedly confirmed. They assume that the amount of confirming evidence is critical in the evaluation of a theory. But falsifiability implies that the number of times a theory has been confirmed is not the critical element. The reason is that, as our example of the "theory of knocking rhythms" illustrated, not all confirmations are equal. Confirmations are more or less impressive depending on the extent to which the prediction exposes itself to potential disconfirmation. One confirmation of a highly specific, potentially falsifiable prediction (for instance, a female, 30 years old, 5 feet 2 inches tall, carrying a book and a purse in the left hand and knocking with the right) has a greater impact than the confirmation of 20 different predictions that are all virtually unfalsifiable (for instance, a person less than 100 years old).

Thus we must look not only at the quantity of the confirming evidence, but also at the quality of the confirming instances. Using the falsifiability criterion as a tool to evaluate evidence will help the research consumer resist the allure of the nonscientific, all-explaining theory that inevitably hinders the search for a deeper understanding of the nature of the world and the people who inhabit it. Indeed, such theoretical dead ends are often tempting precisely because they can never be falsified. They are islands of stability in the shifting ocean of the modern world.

Popper often made the point that "the secret of the enormous psychological appeal of these theories lay in their ability to explain everything. To know in advance that whatever happens you will be able to understand it gives you not only a sense of intellectual mastery but, even more important, an emotional sense of secure orientation in the world" (Magee, 1985, p. 43). However, the attainment of such security is not the goal of science, because intellectual security is purchased at the cost of intellectual stagnation. Science is a mechanism for continually challenging previously held beliefs by subjecting them to empirical tests in such a way that they can be shown to be wrong. This characteristic often puts science—particularly psychology—in conflict with so-called folk wisdom or common sense.

Falsifiability and Folk Wisdom

Psychology is a threat to the comfort that folk wisdom provides because, as a science, it cannot be content with explanations that cannot be refuted. The goal of psychology is to test empirically alternative behavioral theories in order to rule out some of them. Aspects of folk wisdom that are explicitly stated and that do stand up to empirical testing are, of course, welcomed, and many have been incorporated into psychological theory. However, psychology does not seek the comfort of explanatory systems that account for everything after the fact but predict nothing in advance. It does not accept systems of folk wisdom that are designed never to be changed and that end up being passed on from generation to generation. It is self-defeating to try to hide this fact from students or the public. Unfortunately, some psychology instructors and popularizers are aware that psychology's threat to folk wisdom disturbs some people, and they sometimes seek to soothe such feelings by sending a false underlying message that implies, "You'll learn some interesting things, but don't worry—psychology won't challenge things you believe in strongly." This is a mistake, and it contributes to confusion both about what science is and about what psychology is.

Science *seeks* conceptual change. Scientists try to describe the world as it really is, as opposed to what our prior beliefs dictate it should be. The dangerous trend in modern thought is the idea that people must be shielded from the nature of the world, that a veil of ignorance is necessary to protect a public unequipped to deal with the truth. Biologist Michael Ghiselin (1989) reflected the views of most scientists in writing:

> Often people feel disoriented when it may be necessary to revise their beliefs— even learning the truth about Santa Claus can be upsetting. Much of the resistance to intellectual change has been based upon the assumption that traditional beliefs are the expedient way to control those whom we treat as our inferiors, be they children, women, or the poor. The trouble here is that children mature, and to control their behavior by lying ill prepares them for dealing with the truth as adults. As to women and the poor, one might question the propriety of disadvantaging such persons by denying them knowledge. (p. 204)

Psychology is thus like other sciences in rejecting the idea that people need to be shielded from the truth.

Ghiselin (1989) argued further that we all lose when knowledge is not widespread:

> We are better off if we have healthy neighbors, and it would be utter folly to monopolize the supply of medicine in order to be more healthy than they are. So too with knowledge. Our neighbor's ignorance is as bad for us as his ill health, and may indeed be the cause of it. Industry and all the rest of us benefit from a supply of skilled labor. We rely upon others for their skill and expertise. (p. 192)

Psychologists feel, like Ghiselin, that we all lose when we are surrounded by others who hold incorrect views of human behavior. Our world is shaped by public attitudes toward education, crime, health, industrial productivity, child care, and many other critical issues. If these attitudes are the products of incorrect theories of human behavior, then we are all harmed.

The Freedom to Admit a Mistake

Scientists have found that one of the most liberating and useful implications of the falsifiability principle is that, in science, making a mistake is not a sin. One of Karl Popper's most influential books has a title that is a beautiful short summary of how science progresses: *Conjectures and Refutations* (1963). According to Popper, the most useful theoretical predictions (conjectures) are those with very specific implications, those that expose themselves to falsification (refutations). But of course, such predictions will in fact sometimes *be* falsified. Thus we can say that the falsified hypotheses are mistakes in the sense that they do not reflect the way the world is, but the correcting of such mistakes ultimately brings us closer to the truth. The reason is that falsified hypotheses provide information that scientists use to adjust their theories so that they accord more closely with the data. By this continual process of adjusting theory when data do not accord with it, scientists eventually arrive at theories that better reflect the nature of the world. Falsification is a mechanism of theoretical change, not to be avoided as it is in everyday life.

In fact our way of operating in "everyday life" might be greatly improved if we could use the falsifiability principle on a personal level. This is why the word *liberating* was used in the opening sentence of this section. It has a personal connotation that was specifically intended, for the ideas developed here have implications beyond science. We would have many fewer social and personal problems if we could only understand that, when our beliefs are contradicted by evidence in the world, it is better to adjust our beliefs than to deny the evidence and cling tenaciously to dysfunctional ideas. Physicist J. Robert Oppenheimer argued:

> There's a point in anybody's train of reasoning when he looks back and says "I didn't see this straight." Men in other walks of life need the ability to say without shame, "I was wrong about that." Science is a method of having this happen all the time. You notice a conflict or some oddity about a number of things you've been thinking about for a long time. It's the shock that may cause you to think another thought. That is the opposite of the worldly man's endless web of rationalization to vindicate an initial error. (Dos Passos, 1964, pp. 150–151)

How many times have you been in a hot argument with someone when right in the middle—perhaps just as you were giving a heated reply and defending your point of view—you realized ("Oh, my God") that you were wrong about some critical fact or piece of evidence. What did you do? Did you back down and admit to the other person that you had assumed something that wasn't true and that the other person's interpretation now seemed more correct to you? Probably not. If you are like most of us, you engaged in an "endless web of rationalization to vindicate an initial error." You tried to extricate yourself from the argument without admitting defeat. The last thing you would have done was admit that you were wrong. Thus, both you and your partner in the argument became a little more confused about which beliefs more closely tracked the truth. If refutations never become public (as they do in science), if both true and false beliefs are defended with equal vehemence, and if the correct feedback about the effects of argument is not given (as in this example), there is no mechanism for getting beliefs more reliably in sync with reality. This is why so much of our private and public discourse is confused and why the science of psychology is a more reliable guide to the causes of behavior than is "common sense."

Many scientists have attested to the importance of understanding that making errors in the course of science is normal, and that the real danger to scientific progress is the natural human tendency to avoid exposing our beliefs to situations where they might be shown to be wrong. Peter Medawar (1979) wrote:

> Though faulty hypotheses are excusable on the grounds that they will be superseded in due course by acceptable ones, they can do grave harm to those who hold them because scientists who fall deeply in love with their hypotheses are proportionately unwilling to take no as an experimental answer. Sometimes instead of exposing a hypothesis to a cruelly critical test, they caper around it, testing only subsidiary implications, or follow up sidelines that have an indirect bearing on the hypothesis without exposing it to the risk of refutation. . . . I cannot give any scientist of any age better advice than this: *the intensity of the conviction that a hypothesis is true has no bearing on whether it is true or not.* (p. 39; italics in the original)

Thoughts Are Cheap

Our discussion of the idea of testing folk wisdom leads us to another interesting corollary of the falsifiability principle: Thoughts are cheap. What we mean here, of course, is that certain *kinds* of thoughts are cheap. Biologist and science writer Stephen J. Gould (1987) illustrated this point:

> Fifteen years of monthly columns have brought me an enormous correspondence from nonprofessionals about all aspects of science. . . . I have found that one common misconception surpasses all others. People will write, telling me that they have developed a revolutionary theory, one that will expand the boundaries of science. These theories, usually described in several pages of single-spaced typescript, are speculations about the deepest ultimate questions we can ask—what is the nature of life? the origin of the universe? the beginning of time? But thoughts are cheap. Any person of intelligence can devise his half dozen before breakfast. Scientists can also spin out ideas about ultimates. We don't (or, rather, we confine them to our private thoughts) because we cannot devise ways to test them, to decide whether they are right or wrong. What good to science is a lovely idea that cannot, as a matter of principle, ever be affirmed or denied? (p. 18)

The answer to Gould's last question is "No good at all." The type of thoughts that Gould is saying are cheap are those that we referred to earlier in our discussion of Karl Popper's views: grand theories that are so global, complicated, and "fuzzy" that they can be used to explain anything—theories constructed more for emotional support ("an emotional sense of secure orientation in the world" to quote Popper again) because they are not meant to be changed or discarded. Gould was telling us that theories like this are useless for scientific purposes, however comforting they may be. Science is a creative endeavor, but the creativity involves getting conceptual structures to fit the confines of empirical data. This is tough. These types of thoughts—those that explain the world as it actually is—are not cheap. Probably this is why good scientific theories are so hard to come by and why unfalsifiable pseudoscientific belief systems pervade our society.

James Gleick, author of a popular 1988 book on chaos theory in mathematics and science, wrote about how, after the publication of his book, he was inundated with letters from purveyors of "cheap thoughts": unfalsifiable grand theories of the universe. In an article titled "Uh-oh, Here Comes the Mailman" (1990) Gleick wrote, "Many of my correspondents these days have conceived completely new cosmologies. It seems that when you write about science, you quickly get onto an international mailing list for psychic discoveries, mathematical proofs, stock market, and grand theories of everything" (p. 1).

Gleick viewed this response as an indicator of the public's misunderstanding of how science works:

> What's going on here? We're supposed to be living in an era of sophistication about science, an era of universal education, of public-television science specials, of daily newspaper science pages. . . . Still, whether they are sadly crackpot or wholesomely curious, some people seem to need something different. False knowledge is remarkably durable. . . . Otherwise intelligent people believe in ESP and parapsychology. . . . Newspaper and book publishers who should know better have no qualms about feeding their readers' hunger for horoscopes. (p. 32)

Gleick speculated that the reason for this sad state of affairs is that people do not fully understand that certain types of ideas are cheap. As Gould said, any verbally fluent and intelligent person can come up with an unfalsifiable "theory of the universe." Scientific theories, on the other hand, do not come cheap. Gleick (1990) suggested that so many pseudoscientific beliefs exist among the public because

> science is hard. It is imperfect. People find it easier to absorb weird ideas from science than to understand the process that leads to the ideas. The grand theories and themes sound magical sometimes; but real scientists have to sweat their way through piles of real data from a night at the big telescope or a day in the laboratory. When they make a theory they can't afford to indulge a taste for voodoo. They are about to be proved right or wrong. Another pile of data is on the way. (p. 32)

In this passage Gleick reinforced Gould's point in the earlier quote: Theories in science make contact with the world. They are falsifiable. They make specific predictions. But I think that Gleick was wrong in one respect. Yes, doing science is hard. Actually coming up with the theories that are truly scientific explanations is a prodigious task. But understanding the general logic by which science works is *not* so difficult. Indeed, there are books about the logic of scientific thinking that have been written for children (Kramer, 1987). So while science may be hard for *scientists,* there is at least one sense in which it should not be so hard for the general public. The public, however, must be willing to learn a few general principles—no more than the few principles in this book. But the catch is that these principles must be well learned. So let's get on with it.

Errors in Science: Getting Closer to the Truth

In the context of explaining the principle of falsifiability, we have outlined a simple model of scientific progress. Science advances by conjectures and refutations. Theories are put forth and hypotheses derived from them. The hypotheses are tested by a variety of techniques that we shall discuss in the remainder of this book. If the hypotheses are confirmed by the experiments, then the theory receives some degree of corroboration. If the hypotheses are falsified by the experiments, then the theory must be altered in some way, or it must be discarded for a better theory.

Of course, saying that knowledge in science is tentative and that hypotheses derived from theories are potentially false does not mean that everything is up for grabs. There are many relationships in science that have been confirmed so many times that they are termed *laws* because it is extremely doubtful that they will be overturned by future experimentation. It is highly unlikely that we shall find one day that blood does not circulate or that the earth does not orbit the sun. These mundane facts are not the type of hypotheses that we have been talking about. They are of no interest to scientists precisely because they are so well established. Scientists are interested only in those aspects of nature that are on the fringes of what is known, that is, those things that are not so well confirmed that there is no doubt about them.

This aspect of scientific practice—that scientists gravitate to those problems on the fringes of what is known and ignore things that are well confirmed (so-called laws)—is very confusing to the general public. It seems that scientists are always emphasizing what they don't know rather than what is known. This is true, and there is a very good reason for it. To advance knowledge, scientists must be at the outer limits of what is known. Of course, this is precisely where things are uncertain. But science advances by a process of trying to reduce the uncertainty at the limits of knowledge. Psychologist Robert McCall (1988) discussed the public misunderstanding that results from this characteristic of science:

> Scientists are taught to question, even to quibble, and to ruminate over the solidity of evidence and the interpretation of findings that appear contradictory in the hope of discerning a nugget of truth. . . . Although such quibbling is an essential part of the scientific process, it can make scientists look indecisive and incompetent to journalists and to the public. What society and some reporters fail to understand is that by definition, professionals on the edge of knowledge do not know what causes what. Scientists, however, are privileged to be able to say so, whereas business executives, politicians, and judges, for example, sometimes make decisions in audacious ignorance while appearing certain and confident. (p. 88)

It should also be emphasized that, when scientists talk of falsifying a theory based on observation and about replacing an old, falsified theory with a new one, they do not mean that all the previous facts that established the old theory are thrown out (we shall talk about this at great length in Chapter 8). Quite the contrary, the new theory must explain all of the facts that the old theory could explain *plus* the new facts that the old theory couldn't explain. So the falsification of a theory does not mean that scientists have to go back to square one. Science writer Isaac Asimov illustrated the process of theory revision very well in a very readable essay titled "The Relativity of Wrong" (1989), where he wrote about how we have refined our notions of the earth's shape. First, he warned us not to think that ancient belief in a flat earth was stupid. On a plain (where the first civilizations with writing developed), the earth looks pretty flat, and Asimov urged us to consider what a quantitative comparison of different theories would reveal. First, we could express the different theories in terms of how much curvature per mile they hypothesized. The flat-earth theory would say that the curvature is 0 degrees per mile. This theory is wrong, as we know. But in one sense it is close. As Asimov (1989) wrote:

> About a century after Aristotle, the Greek philosopher Eratosthenes noted that the sun cast a shadow of different lengths at different latitudes (all the shadows would be the same length if the earth's surface were flat). From the difference in shadow length, he calculated the size of the earthly sphere and it turned out to be 25,000 miles circumference. The curvature of such a sphere is about 0.000126 per mile, a quantity very close to 0 per mile, as you can see. . . . The tiny difference between 0 and 0.000126 accounts for the fact that it took so long to pass from the flat earth to the spherical earth. Mind you, even a tiny difference, such as that between 0 and 0.000126 can be extremely important. The difference mounts up. The earth cannot be mapped over large areas with any accuracy at all if the difference isn't taken into account and if the earth isn't considered a sphere rather than a flat surface. (pp. 39–40)

But science, of course, did not stop with the theory that the earth was spherical. As we discussed earlier, scientists are always trying to refine their theories as much as possible and to test the limits of current knowledge. For example, Newton's theories of gravitation predicted that the earth should not be perfectly spherical, and indeed this prediction has been confirmed. It turns out that the earth bulges a little at the equator and that it is a little flat at the poles. It is something called an *oblate spheroid*. The diameter of the earth from North Pole to South Pole is 7,900 miles, and the equatorial diameter is 7,927 miles. The curvature of the earth is not constant (as in a perfect sphere); instead, it varies slightly from 7.973 inches to 8.027 inches to the mile. As Asimov noted, "The correction in going from spherical to oblate spheroidal is much smaller than going from flat to spherical. Therefore, although the notion of the earth as a sphere is wrong, strictly speaking, it is not as wrong as the notion of the earth as flat" (p. 41). Asimov's example of the shape of the earth illustrates for us the context in which scientists use such terms as *mistake, error,* or *falsified*. Such terms do not mean that the theory being tested is wrong in every respect, only that it is incomplete. So when scientists emphasize that knowledge is tentative and may be altered by future findings, they are referring to a situation like this example. When scientists believed that the earth was a sphere, they realized that, in detail, this theory might someday need to be altered. However, the alteration from spherical to oblate spheroidal preserves the "roughly correct" notion that the earth is a sphere. We do not expect to wake up one day and find that it is a cube.

Chapter 3

OPERATIONISM AND ESSENTIALISM
"But, Doctor, What Does It Really Mean?"

Do physicists really know what gravity is? I mean *really*. What is the real *meaning* of the term *gravity?* What is the underlying essence of it? What does it ultimately mean even to speak of *gravity?* When you get down to rock bottom, what is it all about?

Questions such as these reflect a view of science that philosopher Karl Popper called *essentialism*. This is the idea that the only good scientific theories are those that give ultimate explanations of phenomena in terms of their underlying essences or their essential properties. People who hold this view usually also believe that any theory that gives less than an ultimate explanation of a phenomenon is useless. It does not reflect the true underlying situation, the essence of the way the world is. In this chapter we shall discuss why science does not answer essentialist questions and why, instead, science advances by developing *operational definitions* of concepts.

WHY SCIENTISTS ARE NOT ESSENTIALISTS

Scientists, in fact, do not claim to acquire the type of knowledge that the essentialist seeks. The proper answer to the questions raised above is that physicists *don't* know what gravity is in this sense. Scientists do not claim to produce perfect knowledge (the unique strength of science is not that it is an error-free process, but that it provides a way of eliminating the errors that are part of our knowledge base) or to answer "ultimate" questions about the universe. Peter Medawar (1984) wrote that there exist

> questions that science cannot answer and that no conceivable advance of science would empower it to answer. These are the questions that children ask—the "ultimate questions." . . . I have in mind such questions as: How did everything begin? What are we all here for? What is the point of living? (p. 66)
>
> [However,] the failure of science to answer questions about first and last things does not in any way entail the acceptance of answers of other kinds; nor can it be taken for granted that because these questions can be put they can be answered. So far as our understanding goes, they can not. (p. 60)

[Finally, however,] there is no limit upon the ability of science to answer the kind of questions that science *can* answer. . . . Nothing can impede or halt the advancement of scientific learning except a moral ailment such as the failure of nerve. (p. 86)

Stephen J. Gould (1987) echoed Medawar's point that science does not answer metaphysical questions about "first and last things" and that "science is not speculation about unattainable ultimates; it is a way of knowing based upon laws now in operation and results subject to observation and inference. We acknowledge limits in order to proceed with power and confidence" (p. 16).

Thus one reason that scientists are suspicious of claims that some person, theory, or belief system provides absolute knowledge about ultimate questions is that scientists consider questions about "ultimates" to be unanswerable. Furthermore, claims of perfect or absolute knowledge tend to choke off inquiry. Since a free and open pursuit of knowledge is a prerequisite for scientific activity, scientists are always skeptical of claims that the ultimate answer has been found. Some of the most embarrassing moments in science have occurred when an investigator has announced that the scope of knowledge in a certain area was complete, so further research was unnecessary. In a speech delivered in 1894, the renowned physicist Albert Michelson declared that "the more important fundamental laws and facts of physical science have all been discovered, and these are now so firmly established that the possibility of their ever being supplanted in consequence of new discoveries is exceedingly remote" (Gardner, 1983, p. 327). The irony of this statement is that it preceded by only a few years the astonishing period in physics during which the theories of relativity and quantum mechanics were developed.

Essentialists Like to Argue About the Meaning of Words

A common indication of the essentialist attitude is an obsessive concern about defining the meaning of terms and concepts before the search for knowledge about them begins. "But we must first define our terms" is a frequent essentialist slogan. "What does that theoretical concept *really* mean?" The idea seems to be that, before a word can be used as a concept in a theory, we must have a complete and unambiguous understanding of all the underlying language problems involved in its usage. In fact, this is exactly the opposite of the way scientists work. Before they begin to investigate the physical world, physicists do not engage in debates about how to use the word *energy* or whether the word *particle* really captures the essence of what we mean when we talk about the fundamental constituents of matter.

The meaning of a concept in science is determined *after* extensive investigation of the phenomena the term relates to, not before such an investigation. The refinement of conceptual terms comes from the interplay of data and theory that is inherent in the scientific process, not from debates on language usage. Writer Bryan Magee (1985) summarized Popper's view this way:

If one wanted to be provocative one might assert that the amount of worthwhile knowledge that comes out of any field of enquiry (except of course language studies) tends to be in inverse proportion to the amount of discussion about the meaning of words that goes on in it. Such discussion, far from being necessary to clear thinking and precise knowledge, obscures both, and is bound to lead to endless argument about words instead of about matters of substance. (p. 49)

Consider the example provided by the biological concept *living*. Two distinguished biologists summarized the situation in this way:

A great many nonbiologists believe that animated and contentious discussions of the definition of "life" are a principal preoccupation of institutes and university departments of biology. In reality, the subject is not mentioned at all, except perhaps to disparage the rather simple-minded people who believe that an agreed-upon definition of life will lead to a better comprehension of biology. Biologists already have a working understanding of "life" that is good enough for present purposes; we do not believe that any current research enterprise is at all impeded by the lack of a more formal definition.

Situations do certainly arise in real life in which a definition of "life" . . . is genuinely important. Consider, for instance, the decision whether or not to use for grafting the kidney or other organ of a potential donor whose heart may still be beating. Such a decision turns upon a number of technical evaluations that belong to a world far removed from the entries in a sematological dictionary: the assessment of brain function especially, and the question of whether the condition of the possible donor is reversible or not. These are factual, empirical questions that reference to a dictionary will not help to answer.

A hunger for definitions is very often a manifestation of a deep-seated belief . . . that all words have an inner meaning. . . . Indeed, amateurs will sometimes put a question about definition in a form which reveals their enslavement to this illusion: "What is the true meaning of the word 'life'?" they ask. There is no true meaning. There is a usage that serves the purposes of working biologists well enough, and it is not the subject of altercation or dispute. (Medawar & Medawar, 1983, pp. 66–67)

In short, the explanation of phenomena, not the analysis of language, is the goal of the scientist. The key to progress in all the sciences has been to abandon essentialism and to adopt operationism, our topic of inquiry in this chapter. Nowhere is this more evident than in psychology. Psychologist George Mandler (1984) urged his colleagues to get on with the study of behavior and give up essentialist arguing about language because

such a position also vitiates the game playing that is so attractive in science—the erection and destruction of hypotheses with a claim to better and better approximations of reality, but not a claim to ultimate truth. To assert that such a truth is available by a proper examination of our phenomenal selves or by the proper analysis of language is, at least, a hindrance, at worst, a wall that keeps us from playing that most productive game—science. (p. 7)

In his book, which is on the psychology of emotion, Mandler advised researchers in this area that

just as the psychologies of memory, perception, or thought concentrate on processes rather than definitions, so a psychology of emotion should stress the underlying psychological processes and mechanisms that produce the sort of events that we call emotions. Such an approach not only avoids the question "What is an emotion?" . . . but actually denies its psychological relevance. (p. 12)

Operationists Link Concepts to Observable Events

Where, then, does the meaning of concepts in science come from if not from discussions about language? What are the criteria for the appropriate use of a scientific concept? To answer these questions, we must discuss operationism, an idea that is crucial to the construction of theory in science and one that is especially important for evaluating theoretical claims in psychology.

Although there are different forms of operationism, it is most useful for the consumer of scientific information to think of it in the most general way. *Operationism* is simply the idea that concepts in scientific theories must in some way be grounded in, or linked to, observable events that can be measured. Linking the concept to an observable event is the operational definition of the concept and makes the concept public. The operational definition removes the concept from the feelings and intuitions of a particular individual and allows it to be tested by anyone who can carry out the measurable operations.

For example, defining the concept *hunger* as "that gnawing feeling I get in my stomach" is not an operational definition since it is related to the personal experience of a "gnawing feeling" and thus is not accessible to other observers. In contrast, definitions that involve some measurable period of food deprivation or some physiological index such as blood sugar levels are operational because they involve observable measurements that anyone can carry out. Similarly psychologists cannot be content with a definition of *anxiety,* for example, as "that uncomfortable, tense feeling I get at times" but must define the concept by a number of operations such as questionnaires and physiological measurements. The former definition is tied to a personal interpretation of bodily states and is not replicable by others. The latter puts the concept in the public realm of science.

It is important to realize that a concept in science is defined by a *set* of operations, not by just a single behavioral event or task. Instead, several slightly different tasks and behavioral events are used to converge on a concept (we will talk more about the idea of *converging operations* in Chapter 8). For example, educational psychologists define a concept such as *reading ability* in terms of performance on a standardized instrument such as the Woodcock Reading Mastery Tests (Woodcock, 1987). The total reading ability score on the Woodcock Reading Mastery instrument comprises indicators of performance on a number of different subtests that test slightly different skills but are all related to reading, for example, reading a passage and thinking of an appropriate word to fill in a blank in the passage, coming up with a synonym for a word, pronouncing a difficult word correctly in isolation, and several others. *Collectively* performance on all of these tasks defines the concept *reading ability*.

The link between concepts and observable operations varies greatly in its degree of directness or indirectness. Some scientific concepts are defined almost entirely by observable operations in the real world. Although some philosophers and scientists (in psychology, for example, the behaviorists) have argued that theoretical concepts in science should be defined solely by such direct associations, most recognize the need for concepts that are defined only partially by these direct links. For example, the use of some concepts is determined by both a set of operations and the particular concept's relationship to other theoretical constructs. Finally, there are concepts that are not directly defined by observable operations, but linked to other concepts that are.

For example, much research has been done on the so-called type A behavior pattern because it has been linked to the incidence of coronary heart disease (Dembroski & Costa, 1987). We will discuss the type A behavior pattern in more detail in Chapter 8. The important point to illustrate here, however, is that the type A behavior pattern is actually defined by a *set* of subordinate *concepts:* a strong desire to compete, a potential for hostility, time-urgent behavior, an intense drive to accomplish goals, and several others (Dembroski & Costa, 1987). However, each one of one these defining features of the type A behavior pattern (a strong desire to compete, etc.) is *itself* a concept in need of operational definition. Indeed, considerable effort has been expended in operationally defining each one (Dembroski & Costa, 1987). The important point for our present discussion is that the concept of the type A behavior pattern is a complex concept that is not *directly* defined by operations. Instead, it is linked with other concepts, which, in turn, have operational definitions. The type A behavior pattern provides an example of a concept with an indirect operational definition.

Thus, although theoretical concepts differ in how closely they are linked to observations, all concepts acquire their meaning partially through their link to such observations.

Scientific Concepts Evolve

It is important to realize that the definition of a scientific concept is not fixed but constantly changing as the observations that apply to the concept are enriched. If the original operational definition of a concept turns out to be theoretically unfruitful, it will be abandoned in favor of an alternative set of defining operations. Thus concepts in science are continually evolving and can increase in abstractness as the knowledge concerning them increases. For example, at one time the electron was thought of as a tiny ball of negative charge circling the nucleus of an atom. Now it is viewed as a probability density function having wavelike properties in certain experimental situations.

In psychology the development of the concept of intelligence provides a similar example. At first, the concept had only a strict operational definition: Intelligence is what is measured by tests of mental functioning. As empirical evidence accumulated relating intelligence to scholastic achievement, learning, brain injury, and other behavioral and biological variables, the concept was both enriched and expanded (see Sternberg, 1982). It now appears that intelligence is best conceptualized as a higher order construct defined by several more specific information-processing operations. These hypothesized processes, in turn, have more direct operational definitions stated in terms of measurable performance.

The concepts in theories of human memory have likewise evolved. Psychologists now rarely use global concepts like *remembering* or *forgetting;* instead, they test the properties of more specifically defined memory subprocesses, such as short-term acoustic memory, iconic storage, semantic memory, and episodic memory. The older concepts of *remembering* and *forgetting* have been elaborated with more specifically operationalized concepts.

Thus the usage of theoretical terms evolves from scientific activity rather than from debates about the meaning of words. This is one of the most salient differences between the operational attitude of science and the essentialist quest for absolute definition. Neurologist Norman Geschwind (1985) characterized this difference as follows: "I think that one of the things you learn in the history of medicine is that many people think that the way to study a problem is to define the problem and then study it. That turns out again and again to be wrong because you discover the only way to define the problem properly is to know the answer" (p. 15).

Computer scientist John McCarthy (1983) succinctly emphasized the idea that concepts in science derive meaning not from language definitions, but from observations and other concepts to which they are related: "In general, we cannot give definitions, because the concepts form a system that we fit as a whole to phenomena. Similarly, the physicist doesn't give a definition of electron or quark. Electron and quark are terms in a complicated theory that predicts results of experiments" (p. 47).

Philosopher Paul Churchland (1984) argued the same point:

> To fully understand the expression "electric field" is to be familiar with the network of theoretical principles in which that expression appears. Collectively, they tell us what an electric field is and what it does. This case is typical. Theoretical terms do not, in general, get their meanings from single, explicit definitions stating conditions necessary and sufficient for their application. They are implicitly defined by the network of principles that embed them. Such casual "definitions" as one does find given (for example, "The electron is the unit of electricity") usually give only a small part of the term's significance, and are always subject to falsification in any case. (p. 56)

As scientific concepts evolve, they often become enmeshed in several different theoretical systems and acquire alternative operational definitions. There is not necessarily anything wrong with the concept when this happens. For example, many believe that psychology is discredited by the fact that many of its important theoretical constructs, such as intelligence, are operationalized and conceptualized in more than one way (Sternberg, 1990). But such a situation is not unique to psychology and it is not a matter for despair or handwringing. In fact, it is a relatively common occurrence in science. Heat, for example, is conceptualized in terms of thermodynamic theory and in terms of kinetic theory. Physics is not scandalized by this state of affairs. Consider the electron. Many of its properties are explained by its being conceptualized as a wave. Other properties, however, are better handled if it is viewed as a particle. The existence of these alternative conceptualizations has tempted no one to suggest that physics be abandoned.

Operational Definitions in Psychology

Many people understand the necessity of operationism when they think about physics or chemistry. They understand that, if scientists are going to talk about a particular type of chemical reaction, or about energy, or about magnetism, they must have a way of measuring these things. Unfortunately, when people think and talk about psychology, they often fail to recognize the need for operationism. Why is it not equally obvious that psychological terms must be operationally defined, either directly or indirectly, in order to be useful explanatory constructs in scientific theories?

One reason is what has been termed the *preexisting bias* problem in psychology. We alluded to this problem in Chapter 1. People do not come to the study of geology with emotional beliefs about the nature of rocks. The situation in psychology is very different. We all have intuitive theories of personality and human behavior because we have been "explaining" human behavior to ourselves all our lives. All our personal psychological theories contain theoretical concepts (for example, *smart, aggressive, anxiety*), and we have all managed fine with our own particular use of them. Thus it is only natural to ask why we have to accept some other definition. Although this attitude seems reasonable on the surface, it is a complete bar to any scientific progress in understanding human behavior and is the cause of much public confusion about psychology.

One of the greatest sources of lay misunderstanding and one of the biggest impediments to the accurate presentation of psychological findings in the media is the fact that many technical concepts in psychology are designated by words used in everyday language. This everyday usage opens the door to a wide range of misconceptions. The layperson seldom realizes that, when psychologists use words such as *intelligence, anxiety, aggression,* and *attachment* as theoretical constructs, they do not necessarily mean the same thing that the general public does.

The nature of this difference should be apparent from the previous discussion of operationism. When terms such as *intelligence* or *anxiety* are used in psychological theories, their direct or indirect operational definitions determine their correct usage. These definitions are often highly technical, usually fairly specific, and often different from popular usage in many ways. For example, many people, when hearing the phrase "the first principal component of the factor analysis of a large sampling of cognitive tasks," may not recognize it as part of the operational definition of the term *intelligence*. Similarly, in lay usage, the term *depression* has come to mean something like "feeling down in the dumps." In contrast, the technical definition of depressive disorders takes up over a dozen pages in the *Diagnostic and Statistical Manual of Mental Disorders* (American Psychiatric Association, 1980) and means something quite different from being "down in the dumps." A clinical psychologist's *depression* is not the same as the layperson's *depression*. Other sciences also have this problem, although perhaps in a less severe form than psychology. Recall the previous discussion of the concept *life*. As Medawar and Medawar (1983) pointed out, "The trouble is that 'life,' like many other technical terms in science, has been pirated from the vernacular and is used in scientific contexts far removed from those that might arise in common speech" (p. 66).

Thus, when the psychologist and the layperson use the same word to mean different things, they often misinterpret each other. Such confusion would be less prevalent if new words had been coined to represent psychological constructs. On occasion such words have been coined. Just as physicists have their *erg* and *joule,* psychology has its *dissonance* and *encoding,* words that are not actually coined but are uncommon enough to prevent confusion.

"But," the layperson may object, "why do psychologists inflict this on us? New jargon, highly technical definitions, uncommon uses of words. Why do we need them? Why is my idea of 'intelligence' not an acceptable idea to talk about?"

We come here to the crux of the problem. The first step in resolving it is to emphasize a point from our earlier discussion: Operationism is not unique to psychology. It is characteristic of all sciences. Most of the time we accept it readily, recognizing its obvious nature. If a scientist is investigating radioactivity, we take it for granted that he or she has to have some observable way of measuring the phenomenon, a method that another investigator can use to obtain the same results. This method is what makes possible the public nature of science, one of its defining features. Two different scientists agree on the same operational definition so that it is possible for one to replicate the other's results. However, what seems obvious in other contexts is sometimes not so clear when we think about psychology. The necessity for operational definitions of concepts like *intelligence* and *anxiety* is often not recognized because we use these terms all the time, and after all, don't we all just "know" what these things mean?

The answer is "No, we don't." Or more accurately, our personal definitions are simply not consistent with those of other people.

Operationism as a Humanizing Force

The problem with relying on what we all just "know" is the same problem that plagues all intuitive (that is, nonempirical) systems of belief. What you "know" about something may not be quite the same as what Jim "knows" or what Jane "knows." How do we decide who is right? You may say, "But I feel strongly about this, so strongly that I know I'm right." What if Jim, who thinks somewhat differently, feels even more strongly than you do? Jim feels so strongly that he's sure that he's right. And then there's Jane, who thinks differently from you or Jim, claiming that she must be right because she feels even more strongly than Jim does.

This simple parody is meant only to illustrate a fundamental aspect of scientific knowledge, one that has been a major humanizing force in human history: The truth of a knowledge claim is not determined by the strength of belief of the individual putting forth the claim. The problem with all intuitively based systems of belief is that they have no mechanism for deciding between conflicting claims. When everyone knows intuitively, but the intuitive claims conflict, how do we decide who is right? History shows, sadly, that the result of such conflicts is usually a power struggle.

Some people mistakenly claim that an operational approach to psychology dehumanizes people and that instead we should base our views of human beings on intuition. Psychologist Donald Broadbent (1973) argued that the truly humane position is one that bases theoretical views of human beings on observable behavior rather than on the intuition of the theorizer:

> We can tell nothing of our fellow men except by seeing what they do or say in particular circumstances. If one dispenses with this procedure, and so claims to be treating other people as persons rather than machines, one is exposed to the dan-

ger of assuming that everybody should be the kind of person one is oneself. . . .
A proper sensitivity to others demands that we should take an interest in what
they actually do rather than what we think they do. The empirical method is a
way of reconciling differences. If one rejects it, the only way of dealing with a
disagreement is by emotional polemic. (p. 206)

Thus the humanizing force in science is that of making knowledge claims
public so that conflicting ideas can be tested in a way that is acceptable to all dis-
putants. Recall the concept of replication from Chapter 1. This allows a selection
among theories to take place without a power struggle. The public nature of science rests critically on the idea of operationism. By operationally defining concepts, we put them in the public realm, where they can be criticized, tested, improved, or perhaps rejected.

Psychological concepts cannot rest on someone's personal definition, which
may be uncommon, idiosyncratic, or vague. For this reason psychology must reject all personal definitions of concepts (just as physics, for example, rejects personal definitions of energy and meteorology rejects personal definitions of what a
cloud is) and must insist on publicly accessible concepts defined by operations
that anyone with proper training and facilities can perform. In rejecting personal
definitions, psychology is not shutting out the layperson but is opening up the
field—as all sciences do—to the quest for a common, publicly accessible knowledge that all can share.

Essentialist Questions and the
Misunderstanding of Psychology

Another reason many people seem to abandon the idea of operationism when
they approach psychology is that they seek essentialist answers to certain human
problems. Whether this is the result of psychology's relatively recent separation
from philosophy or of the public's more limited understanding of psychology
than of other sciences is unclear. In a sense, however, it does not matter. The net
result is the same. Psychology is expected to provide absolute answers to complex
questions in a way that other sciences are not.

Recall the questions at the beginning of this chapter: What is the real meaning
of the word *gravity?* What is the underlying essence of it? What does it ultimately
mean even to speak of *gravity?* Most people would recognize that these questions
require knowledge of the ultimate, underlying nature of a phenomenon and that
current theories in physics cannot provide answers to questions of this type.
Anyone familiar with popular writing about the progress of physical science in
the last few centuries will recognize that gravity is a theoretical construct of great
complexity and that its conceptual and operational relationships have been in
constant flux.

However, substitute the word *intelligence* for the word *gravity* in each of the
questions above, and suddenly, a miracle occurs. Now the questions are imbued
with great meaning. They seem natural and meaningful. They literally beg for an
ultimate answer. When the psychologist gives the same answer as the physicist—
that intelligence is a complex concept that derives meaning from the operations

used to measure it and from its theoretical relationships to other constructs—he or she is belittled and accused of avoiding the real issues.

One problem facing psychology, then, is that the public demands answers to essentialist questions that it does not routinely demand of other sciences. These demands often underlie many of the attempts to disparage the progress that has been made in the field. While these demands do not hinder the field itself, because psychologists, like other scientists, ignore demands for essentialist answers and simply go about their work, they *are* an obstacle to the public's understanding of psychology. The public becomes confused when an uninformed critic claims that there has been no progress in psychology. The fact that this claim so frequently goes unchallenged reflects the unfortunate truth of the major premise of this book: Public knowledge of the actual scientific achievements within psychology is distressingly meager. When examined closely, such criticisms usually boil down to the contention that psychology has not yet provided the ultimate answer to any of its questions. To this, psychology readily pleads guilty, as do all the other sciences. According to this criterion, there has been no scientific progress, period.

Some may find it discomforting to learn that no science, including psychology, can give answers to essentialist questions. Holton and Roller (1958) discussed the uneasiness that the layperson may feel when told that, to a physicist, the length of an object means, basically, "the difference between the two numbers stamped on a specific measuring stick at the two marks which coincide with the ends of the object." They pointed out that

> we are likely to have the uncomfortable feeling that such a definition of length merely shows us how to measure according to some man-made convention, and does not tell us what length "really is." Once more this is correct, and once more we must try to make our peace with the limitations of modern science; it does not claim to find out "what things really are." (pp. 219–220)

Holton and Roller discussed the phenomenon of radioactive decay in a similar manner. The number of atoms of a radioactive element that have decayed can be related to time via an exponential mathematical function. The function, however, does not explain why radioactive decay occurs. The solution to this problem will again probably involve a mathematical function, but it again will not answer the layperson's question of what radioactive decay *really* is. As science writer Robert Wright (1988) explained:

> There was something bothersome about Isaac Newton's theory of gravitation. . . . How, after all, could "action at a distance" be realized? . . . Newton sidestepped such questions. . . . Ever since Newton, physics has followed his example. . . . Physicists make no attempt to explain why things obey laws of electromagnetism or of gravitation. (p. 61)

Those who seek essentialist answers to questions concerning human nature are destined to be disappointed if they are looking to psychology. Psychology is not a religion. It is a broad field that seeks a scientific understanding of all aspects of human behavior. Therefore, psychology's current explanations are temporary theoretical constructs that account for behavior better than alternative explanations. These constructs will certainly be superseded in the future by superior theoretical conceptualizations that are closer to the truth.

Operationism and the Phrasing of Psychological Questions

The idea of an operational definition can be a very useful tool in evaluating the falsifiability of a psychological theory. The presence of concepts that are not directly or indirectly grounded in observable operations is an important clue to recognizing a nonfalsifiable theory. These concepts are usually intended to rescue such a theory from disconfirmation after the data have been collected. Thus the presence of loose concepts, those for which the theorist cannot provide direct or indirect operational links, should be viewed with suspicion.

A strong grasp of the principle of operationism will also aid in the recognition of problems or questions that are scientifically meaningless. For example, I have in my files a wire service article, from United Press International, entitled "Do Animals Think?" The article describes recent experimentation in animal behavior. There is nothing wrong with the research described in the article, but it is clear that the title is merely a teaser. The question in the title is scientifically meaningless unless some operational criteria can be specific for the term *think,* and none are given in the article. A similar problem concerns the many recent newspaper articles that have asked, "Can computers think?" Without some operational criteria, this question is also scientifically meaningless, even though it is infinitely useful as grist for cocktail party conversation.

Actually it is instructive to observe people debating this last question because such a debate provides an opportunity to witness quite concretely the preexisting bias problem in psychology that we discussed earlier. Most people are strongly biased toward not wanting a computer to be able to think. Why? For a variety of reasons the layperson's concept *think* has become so intertwined with the concept *human* that many people have an emotional reaction against the idea of non-human things thinking (for example, computers or extraterrestrial life forms that look nothing like the humans on our planet).

However, despite their strong feelings against the idea of thinking computers, most people have not thought about the issue very carefully and are at a loss to come up with a definition of thinking that would include most humans (babies, for example) and exclude all computers. It is sometimes humorous to hear the criteria that people who are unfamiliar with current work in artificial intelligence come up with, for they invariably choose something that computers can do. For example, many people propose the criterion "ability to learn from experience," only to be told that many artificial intelligence systems running on computers have fulfilled this criterion (Boden, 1987; Caudill & Butler, 1990; Johnson, 1986; Quinlan, 1991). The strength of preexisting bias can be observed in this situation. Is the person's response "Oh, I didn't know. Well, since the criterion for thinking that I put forth is met by computers, I will have to conclude that at least those computers think"? Usually this intellectually honest response is not the one that is given. More commonly the person begins groping around for another criterion in the hope that computers cannot meet it.

Usually the second choice is something like "creativity" ("coming up with something that people judge as useful that no person has thought of before "—we will ignore the question of whether most *humans* would meet this criterion). When told that most experts agree that computers have fulfilled this criterion (Boden, 1987; Johnson, 1986; McCorduck, 1979), the person still does not admit the possibility of thinking machines. Often the person abandons the attempt to derive an operational definition at this point and instead attempts to argue that computers could not possibly think because "humans built them and programmed them; they only follow their programs."

Although this argument is one of the oldest objections to thinking machines (Evans, 1980; McCorduck, 1979), it is actually fallacious. Preexisting bias prevents many people from recognizing that it is totally irrelevant to the question at issue. Almost everyone would agree that thinking is a process taking place in the natural world. Now notice that we do not invoke the "origins" argument for other natural processes. Consider the process of heating food. Consider the question: Do ovens heat? Do we say, "Ovens don't really heat, because ovens are built by *people*. Therefore it only makes sense to say that *people* heat. Ovens don't *really* heat"? Or what about lifting? Do cranes lift? Is our answer "Cranes don't really lift because cranes are built by *people*. Therefore it only makes sense to say that *people* lift. Cranes don't *really* lift"? Of course not. The origin of something is totally irrelevant to its ability to carry out a particular process. The process of thinking is just the same. Whether or not an entity thinks is independent of the origins of the entity. If we use the "origins" argument, it is actually unclear whether *people* think. Why?

> In one technical and boring sense, of course, it's perfectly true that computers always follow their programs, since a program is nothing but a careful specification of all the relevant processes inside the machine. That, however, doesn't prove anything because a similar point might be made about us. Thus, assuming there were a "careful specification" of all the relevant processes in our brains . . . it would be equally easy to say: "We—or rather our brain parts—always act only as specified." But, obviously, no such fact could show that we are never creative or free—and the corresponding claim about computers is no more telling. (Haugeland, 1985, p. 9)
>
> The common slogan, "A computer can only do what you tell it to do" may be misleading. . . . If it is taken to mean either that the programmer can foresee everything the program will do or that the program will do all and only what the programmer intended it to do, then it is false. (Boden, 1987, p. 7)
>
> Much the same applies to a brain: it, too, must come equipped with sets of programs which cause it to run through its repertoire. . . . No one can dispute that all aspects of our intelligence evolve from preexisting programs and the background experiences of life. (Evans, 1980, pp. 186, 187)

The failure to think rationally about the possibility of thinking machines was one reason that the computer scientist Alan Turing developed his famous test of whether computers think. What is important to our discussion is that the test Turing devised is an *operational* test. Turing began his famous article "Computing Machinery and Intelligence" (1950) by writing, "I propose to consider the question 'Can machines think.' " Not wanting discussion of the issue to descend to the usual circular cocktail-party chatter or endless essentialist arguments about what we mean by *think,* Turing proposed a strict operational test of whether a computer could think. His proposal was that it would be reasonable to grant a computer thinking powers if it could carry on an intelligent conversation.

The creativity in the Turing proposal was that he proposed a way to operationalize the question while at the same time guarding against the *preexisting bias* problem. Turing strictly specified the logistics of the test of whether the computer could carry on an intelligent conversation. It was *not* to be done by simply wheeling a computer terminal into a room, having a tester interact with the computer via keyboard and screen, and then having the tester judge whether the computer had, in fact, carried on an intelligent conversation. Turing did *not* propose this type of test because he was concerned about the preexisting bias problem. Turing was sure that, once the person sat down before a keyboard and screen, something obviously a *machine,* she or he would deny it thinking capabilities no matter *what* it did. Therefore he proposed a test that controlled for the irrelevant external characteristics of the thinking device. His well-known proposal was to have the tester engage in conversation via two keyboards—one connected to a computer and the other to a human, both out of sight—and then to decide which was which. If the tester could not identify the human with greater than chance accuracy, then one reasonable inference was that the conversational abilities—the operational definition of thinking—of the computer were equal to those of a human.

Turing's key insight was the

> same insight that inspires the practice among symphony orchestras of conducting auditions with an opaque screen between the jury and the musician. What matters in a musician, obviously, is musical ability and only musical ability: such features as sex, hair length, skin color, and weight are strictly irrelevant. . . . Turing recognized that people might be similarly biased in their judgments of intelligence by whether the contestant had soft skin, warm blood, facial features, hands and eyes—which are obviously not themselves essential components of intelligence. (Dennett, 1985, p. 123)

Turing's test teaches us the necessity of operational definitions if we are to discuss psychological concepts rationally, that is, in a principled way rather than merely as a reflection of our own biases about the question at issue.

The intellectual style revealed when we observe people discussing the issue of artificial intelligence illustrates well the difference between scientific and nonscientific styles of thinking. The scientific approach is to develop an operational definition that seems reasonable and then to see what conclusions about thinking, computers, and humans it leads to. In contrast, preexisting bias dominates the thinking of most people. They have already arrived at certain conclusions and are not interested in what is actually known about the relative contrasts between computer and human performance. Instead, with minds made up, their intellectual energies are spent in a desperate juggling of words that will protect their prior beliefs from change. What we see, then, is a combination of preexisting bias and nonoperational essentialist attitudes that fuel the assumption that people "just know" what thinking "really" is without any necessity of operational criteria. Such attitudes are what make most people's intuitive psychological theories unfalsifiable and, hence, useless.

Chapter 4

Testimonials and Case Study Evidence
Placebo Effects and the Amazing Randi

Cut to the *Phil Donahue Show*, one of the most popular audience participation television talk shows of the 1980s. Today's guest is Dr. Alfred Pontificate, director of the Oedipus Institute of Human Potential. Our host Phil darts among the audience, eliciting questions about the doctor's provocative new Theory of Birth Order, which is based on the idea that the course of one's life is irrevocably set by family interactions that are determined by birth order. The discussion inevitably turns from theoretical concerns to requests for explanations of personal events of importance to members of the audience. The doctor complies without much prodding.

For example, "Doctor, my brother is a self-destructive workaholic. He ignores his wife and family and places work-related problems above everything else. He has an ulcer and a drinking problem that he refuses to acknowledge. His family hasn't been on a real vacation in two years. He's headed for divorce and doesn't seem to care. Why has he chosen such a self-destructive course?"

To which the doctor replies, "What is his birth order, my dear?"

"Oh, he is the oldest of the children."

"Yes," the doctor says, "this is quite common. We see it often in the clinic. The underlying dynamics of a situation like this arise because parents transfer their life hopes and frustrations to their firstborn child. Through a process of unconscious wish-transference the child absorbs these hopes and frustrations, even if the parents never articulate them. Then, through the unconscious process that I call the dynamic expectation spiral, the aspirations of the parents become manifest as a pathological need for achievement in the child."

Although the audience on the Donahue show often asks hostile questions when the guest challenges their beliefs, this rarely happens when a behavioral "expert" seems to confirm conventional wisdom. Once in a while, however, the show is animated by an audience member who questions the evidence behind the guest's declarations. In this case, an eager, forthright questioner is in the studio. "But wait a minute, Doctor," the questioner begins. "My brother is a first-born, too. My parents sent the bum to Harvard and told me to go to a two-year school to be a dental hygienist. So, this great brain of theirs drops out after one year, goes to some mountaintop in Colorado, and the last time we saw him he was weaving baskets! I don't understand what you're saying about firstborns."

The audience tenses for the confrontation, but, alas, the doctor always wins in the end: "Oh, yes, I have seen many cases like your brother. Yes, I often meet them in my practice. They are people for whom the dynamic expectation spiral has short-circuited, creating an unconscious desire to thwart wish transference. Thus the individual's life develops in such a way as to reject conventional achievement aspirations." A hushed pause follows, then on we go to the next "case."

Of course, we are dealing with something quite familiar here. This is another example of the Benjamin Rush problem. This "theory" of birth order is structured so that no observation can disconfirm it. Because it is an unfalsifiable theory, the confirmations put forth to prove it are meaningless because nothing is ruled out by the theory.

However, our concern here is not with the theory itself, but with the nature of the evidence that is presented to support it. When pressed for evidence, Dr. Pontificate presents his own "clinical experience" or "case studies" as proof. This is an extremely common occurrence in the realm of media psychology. Talk shows and paperback book racks are full of psychological theories based on the clinical experience of the originator. Many of the therapies presented to the public through these outlets are backed by nothing more than the testimonials of individuals who have undergone them and consider themselves improved or cured. In this chapter, we shall develop a principle of great use to consumers of psychological information: Case studies and testimonials are virtually worthless as evidence for the evaluation of psychological theories and treatments. In this chapter, we will demonstrate why this is true, and we will also discuss the proper role of the case study in psychology.

STAGES OF SCIENTIFIC INVESTIGATION

The usefulness of case study information is strongly determined by how far scientific investigation is advanced in a particular area. The insights gained from case studies or clinical experience may be quite useful in the early stages of the investigation of certain problems, as indicators of which variables deserve more intense study. Case studies have played a prominent role in opening up new areas of study in psychology. Two examples are the theories of Freud and of Jean Piaget.

However, when we move from the early stages of scientific investigation, where case studies may be very useful, to the more mature stages of theory testing, the situation changes drastically. Case studies and testimonials are not useful at the later stages of scientific investigation because they cannot be used as confirming or disconfirming evidence in the test of a particular theory. The reason is that case studies and testimonials are isolated events that lack the comparative information necessary to rule out alternative explanations.

The idea of alternative explanations is critical to an understanding of theory testing. The goal of experimental design is to structure events so that support of one particular explanation simultaneously disconfirms other explanations. Scientific progress can occur only if the data that are collected rule out some explanations, as discussed in Chapter 2. Science sets up conditions for the natural selection of ideas. Some survive empirical testing and others do not. Those that remain are closer to the truth. This is the honing process by which ideas are sifted so that those that contain the most truth are found. But there must be selection in this process: data collected as support for a particular theory must not leave many other alternative explanations as equally viable candidates. For this reason, scientists construct control or comparison groups in their experimentation. These groups are formed so that, when their results are compared with those from an experimental group, some alternative explanations are ruled out. How this is done will be a main topic in several later chapters.

Case studies and testimonials stand as isolated phenomena. They lack the comparative information necessary to prove that a particular theory or therapy is superior. It is thus wrong to cite a testimonial or a case study as support for a *particular* theory or therapy. Those who do so mislead the public if they do not point out that such evidence is open to a wide range of alternative explanations. In short, the isolated demonstration of a phenomenon may be highly misleading. This can be illustrated more specifically by considering the example of placebo effects.

WHY TESTIMONIALS ARE WORTHLESS: PLACEBO EFFECTS

Virtually every therapy that has ever been devised in medicine and psychology has garnered supporters and has been able to produce individuals who will testify sincerely to its efficacy. Medical science has documented testimonials to the curative powers of swine teeth, crocodile dung, powdered Egyptian mummy, and many other even more imaginative remedies (Shapiro, 1960). In fact, it has long been known that the mere suggestion that treatment is being administered is enough to make many people feel better.

The tendency of people to report that any treatment has helped them, regardless of whether or not it has a real therapeutic element, is known as the *placebo effect*. The concept of the placebo effect was well illustrated in the movie *The Wizard of Oz*. The wizard did not *actually* give the tin man a heart, the scarecrow a brain, and the lion courage, but they all felt better nevertheless. In fact, because it is only in the last hundred years or so that medical science has developed a substantial number of treatments that actually have therapeutic efficacy, it has been said that "prior to this century, the whole history of medicine was simply the history of the placebo effect" (Postman, 1988, p. 96).

We can illustrate the concept of a placebo effect by considering biomedical research, where all studies of new medical procedures must include controls for placebo effects. Typically, if a new drug is being tested on a group of patients, an equivalent group will also be formed and given a pill that does not contain the drug (a placebo). Neither group will know what they are receiving. Thus, when the two groups are compared, the placebo effect—that is, the tendency to feel better when any new treatment is introduced—is controlled for. It would not be sufficient merely to show that a percentage of patients receiving the new drug report relief from their symptoms, because in the absence of a control group it would be impossible to know what percentage is reporting relief due to a placebo effect rather than the efficacy of the drug itself. One study (see Bok, 1974) of patients with a variety of ailments indicated that about 35 percent reported satisfactory relief after receiving a placebo. Placebo effects can be very powerful, so much so that there have even been reports of people who have become addicted to placebo pills (Bok, 1974), needing more and more to maintain their state of health!

Placebo effects illustrate quite well the problem of relying on testimonial evidence. If testimonials accumulate around virtually every therapy tried, how can they be used to support one specific remedy? All the competing remedies also have supporting testimonials. What we want to know, of course, is which remedy is *best*. We cannot determine this by using testimonial evidence.

Placebo effects are implicated in all types of psychological therapy. Many people with psychological problems of mild to moderate severity report improvement after receiving psychotherapy. However, controlled studies have demonstrated that some proportion of this recovery rate is due to a combination of placebo effects and the mere passage of time, often termed *spontaneous remission*. Most therapeutic treatments are some unknown combination of an active therapeutic component and a placebo effect.

A study by psychologist Anthony Greenwald and his colleagues (Greenwald, Spangenberg, Pratkanis, & Eskenazi, 1991) illustrates the importance of including placebo controls in experimental tests of therapeutic efficacy. In this study, the authors tested the usefulness of subliminal self-help audiotapes (tapes that use messages below hearing threshold), which are commonly advertised in magazines and on television. They tested one tape program designed to improve memory and another designed to improve self-esteem. After taking memory and self-esteem tests, the subjects listened to the tape they were given each day for a month (the amount of time that the advertisers of the tapes said was sufficient to produce the advertised effects). Some subjects were given a self-esteem tape labeled as "self-esteem tape," and other subjects were given the memory tape labeled as "memory tape." Importantly, however, two more groups of subjects were tested: one that was given a tape labeled "self-esteem tape" but had the *content* of the memory tape and another that was given a tape labeled "memory tape" but had the *content* of the self-esteem tape. These two conditions served as placebo controls. For example, if it was the *content* of the tape that mattered, then people who got the memory content labeled "self-esteem" should have scored as high on memory tests as the people who got the memory content on the tape labeled "memory tape," and they should have scored lower on self-esteem tests than the two other groups that got the self-esteem tape. This is not what happened. Instead, it was the *label* on the tape that was important, not the content. Both groups that got a tape labeled "self-esteem" scored higher on the posttest of self-esteem (even though one group had received *memory* content), and both groups that got a tape labeled "memory" scored higher on the posttest of memory (even though one group had received *self-esteem* content). Thus, any effectiveness that subliminal self-help tapes have is simply due to a placebo effect. The specific content of the tapes has no effects on human behavior.

In studies of psychotherapy effectiveness, it is often difficult to determine exactly how to treat the placebo control group, but these complications should not concern us here. Instead, it is important to understand why researchers are concerned about separating true therapeutic effects from placebo effects and spontaneous remission. A study of therapeutic effectiveness by Gordon Paul (1966, 1967) provides an example of what the outcomes of such investigations reveal. Paul studied groups of students who suffered from maladaptive anxiety in public-speaking situations. Of an experimental group that received desensitization therapy specific to their speech anxiety problem, 85 percent showed significant improvement. A placebo group received a pill that they were told was a potent tranquilizer but that was actually a bicarbonate capsule. Of this group, 50 percent displayed significant improvement. Of a third group that did not receive any therapy at all, 22 percent also displayed significant improvement. Thus it appears that the spontaneous remission rate was 22 percent for this particular problem, that an additional 28 percent of the subjects displayed improvement due to generalized placebo effects (50 percent minus 22 percent), and that the desensitization therapy did have a specific effect over and above that of the placebo (85 percent compared to 50 percent).

As in the Paul study, other research has shown that psychotherapies do have a positive effect over and above what would be expected purely as the result of a placebo (Landman & Dawes, 1982; Lipsey & Wilson, 1993; Prioleau, Murdock, & Brody, 1983; Smith, Glass, & Miller, 1980). But experiments using placebo controls have demonstrated that merely citing the overall percentage of people who report improvement vastly overestimates the degree of improvement that is uniquely due to the particular treatment. Thus the statements of a group of patients testifying that they were helped are not sufficient to justify belief in a particular therapy. Instead, it must be shown that the placebo effect has been accounted for.

The problem is essentially that testimonials are incredibly easy to generate. Cornell University psychologist Thomas Gilovich (1991) noted that, "with the body so effective in healing itself, many who seek medical assistance will experience a positive outcome even if the doctor does nothing beneficial. Thus, even a worthless treatment can appear effective when the base-rate of success is so high" (p. 128). As Peter Medawar (1967) described the situation, "If a person a) is poorly, b) receives treatment intended to make him better, and c) gets better, then no power of reasoning known to medical science can convince him that it may not have been the treatment that restored his health" (p. 14). In short, placebo effects are potentially occurring whenever a therapeutic intervention is undertaken, *regardless of the efficacy of the intervention.* The problem is that placebo effects are so potent that, no matter how ludicrous the therapy one uses, if it is administered to a large group of people it is easy to find a few who will be willing to give a testimonial to its efficacy (the early-morning whack-on-the-head therapy—use it every day and you'll feel better! Send $10.95 for your special, medically tested rubber hammer).

But we really should not joke about such a serious matter. Unwarranted reliance on testimonials and case study evidence may have disastrous consequences. Members of a research team that contributed to the modern conceptualization of Tourette syndrome as an organically based disorder (Shapiro et al., 1978; see Chapter 2) pointed out that inappropriate reliance on case study evidence helped to perpetuate the unfalsifiable psychoanalytic explanations of the syndrome that impeded true scientific progress in investigating the nature of the disorder:

> Unfortunately, these theories, invested with strong emotional feelings, then lead to specific recommendations for treatment. . . . Those investigators interested in studying psychological factors should be encouraged to do so. Judgments about the results of such investigations, however, should be based on established principles of scientific investigation, or, in our opinion, on a data oriented approach. *Data from single case study or clinical impressions should be acknowledged as opinion or hypotheses for future investigation.* (p. 363; italics added)

The "Vividness" Problem

It is fine to point out how the existence of placebo effects renders testimonials useless as evidence, but we must recognize another obstacle that prevents people from understanding that testimonials cannot be accepted as proof of a claim. Social and cognitive psychologists have studied what is termed the *vividness effect* in human memory and decision making (see Nisbett & Ross, 1980). When faced with a problem-solving or decision-making situation, people retrieve from memory the information that seems relevant to the situation at hand. Thus they are more likely to use the facts that are more accessible to solve a problem or make a decision. One factor that strongly affects accessibility is the vividness of information.

The problem is that there is nothing more vivid or compelling than sincere personal testimony that something has occurred or that something is true. The vividness of personal testimony often overshadows other information of much higher reliability. How often have we carefully collected information on different product brands before making a purchase, only to be dissuaded from our choice at the last minute by a chance recommendation of another product by a friend or an advertisement? Car purchases are a typical example (Nisbett & Ross, 1980). We may have read surveys of thousands of customers in *Consumer Reports* and decided on car X. After consulting the major automotive magazines and confirming that the experts also recommend car X, we feel secure in our decision—until, that is, we meet a friend at a party who knows a friend who knows a friend who bought an X and got a real lemon, spent hundreds on repairs, and would never buy another. Obviously, this single datum should not substantially affect our opinion, which is based on a survey of thousands of owners and the judgment of several experts. Yet how many of us could resist the temptation to overweight this evidence?

The auto purchase situation illustrates that the problems created by vivid testimonial evidence are not unique to psychology. For example, Stephen Budiansky (1984), Washington correspondent of the British science journal *Nature,* has summarized the situation in medicine with a statement that reinforces many of the points about science that we have discussed in previous chapters:

> Science eschews the personal. Although it is commonplace to ascribe this tendency to some fundamental coldness on the part of scientists, in fact it is really one of the great intellectual triumphs of the 20th century that scientists have learned to discount the experiences of individuals when searching for cause and effect in the natural world. The health sciences have had a particularly rough time of it; people tend to get sick for a variety of reasons (including psychosomatic ones) and people more often than not get better no matter what "cure" is prescribed. The apparently undying popularity of quack remedies, invariably supported by testimonials from satisfied customers, is vivid proof of how hard we find it to look beyond personal experience. (p. 7)

Instances of how vividness affects people's opinions are not hard to find. Attitudes about crime are strongly affected by particularly salient cases and by what is vividly presented on television, rather than by the actual statistical facts about human criminal behavior. For example, one survey indicated that 87 percent of a sample agreed with the statement that "too many murderers are using the insanity plea to keep from going to prison." It is highly likely that this opinion was strongly influenced by the publicity received by the insanity plea in certain highly publicized cases, like the assassination attempt on President Reagan by John Hinckley, Jr.

Jeffrey and Pasewark (1983) asked a group of college students and a group of community residents who were not students to estimate how many of the persons in their state who were charged with felonies punishable by more than one year in prison pleaded "not guilty by reason of insanity." They were then asked to estimate what percentage of the time the plea was successful. The students estimated that the insanity plea was used by 33 percent of the defendants (the figure for the community residents was 38 percent). Both groups of subjects estimated that the plea was successful 45 percent of the time. Actually, in that particular state, the insanity plea was used by less than 1 percent of the defendants. When used, it was successful only 4 percent of the time! Clearly the public's perceptions of the operation of the insanity plea in the legal arena are markedly inaccurate (Phillips, Wolf, & Coons, 1988), a misperception probably derived, as Jeffrey and Pasewark (1983) argued, "from publicity accorded by the public media to criminal cases of notoriety" (p. 38; see also Steadman & Cocozza, 1978). In short, the vividness of particular examples, rather than actual statistics, determines public opinion.

And the loser is the public. Consider another example well known to college admissions officers. A perennially popular media story is the "high cost of higher education." To make the story more "vivid," television reporters invariably seek out the private eastern college with the highest tuition in the country, multiply the sum by four years, and then present the resulting (usually astronomical) figure as "the soaring cost of a college education." This very vivid example probably frightens thousands of struggling families each year and probably discourages hundreds of high-school students from pursuing higher education. We certainly do know that high-school students markedly overestimate the cost of higher education. A survey conducted by the Gallup Organization ("*A Wealth,*" 1988) found that high-school students estimated that the average annual tuition and fees at a four-year state college was $6,841, four times higher than the actual cost ($1,566).

Reporter Haynes Johnson (1991) wrote of how Brigadier General John Hutton, a former doctor, found out that President Reagan "had not realized the seriousness of AIDS until July 1985, when he saw a news report disclosing that the actor Rock Hudson had died of the disease. This was more than five years after AIDS had been identified, thousands of Americans had been infected, and AIDS had been the subject of intense national publicity. When Reagan saw the news report about Hudson's death, he asked General Hutton to tell him about the disease" (p. 454). In short, the constant news reports and statistics on the increasing numbers of AIDS deaths had not attracted the president's attention, but the report of a single person who was known to him did.

Finally, imagine that you saw the following headline one Friday morning in your newspaper: "Jumbo Jet Crash: 413 Killed." Goodness, you might think, what a horrible accident. What a terrible thing to happen. Imagine though, that the following Thursday you got up and your newspaper said, "Another Jumbo Jet Disaster: 442 Die." My God, you might think. Not another disaster! How horrible. What in the world is wrong with our air traffic system. And then imagine—please imagine as best you can—getting up the following Friday and seeing in the paper: "Third Tragic Airline Crash: 431 Dead." Not only you but the nation would be beside itself. A federal investigation would be demanded. Flights would be grounded. Commissions would be appointed. Massive lawsuits would be filed. *Newsweek* and *Time* would run cover stories. It would be the lead item on television news programs for several days. Television documentaries would explore the issue. The uproar would be tremendous.

But this is not an imaginary problem. It is real. A jumbo jet *does* crash every week. Well, not one jet, but a lot of little jets. Well, not little jets really, but little transportation devices. These devices are called passenger automobiles. And approximately 457 people die in them *each week* in the United States (23,800 people each year—37,500 if we counted trucks and motorcycles; National Safety Council, 1990), enough to fill a jumbo jet.

A jumbo jet's worth of people die in passenger cars on our nation's highways every week, *yet we pay no attention*. The "Jumbo Jet's Worth of People Who Die" are not presented to us in a vivid way by the media. Hence the 457 people who die *each week* in passenger cars (plus the *additional* 263 who die *each week* in trucks and motorcycles) have no "vividness" for us. We don't talk about them at the dinner table as we do when a jet goes down and kills a lot of people. We do not debate the safety of the highways as we would the safety of the air traffic system if a jumbo jet crashed every week and killed 400 people. The 457 are not on the news because they are scattered all over the country and thus are a statistical abstraction to most of us. The media do not vividly present to us these 457 deaths because they do not happen in the same place. Instead, the media present to us (occasionally) a number (e.g., 457 per week). This *should* be enough to get us thinking, but it is not. Driving automobiles is an extremely dangerous activity, however it is measured (Lichtenstein, Slovic, Fischhoff, Layman, & Combs, 1978;

National Safety Council, 1990), yet there has never been a national debate about its risk relative to the benefits involved. Is this an acceptable toll for a suburban lifestyle that demands a lot of driving? We never ask the question because no problem is recognized. No problem is recognized because the cost is not presented to us in a vivid way, as is the cost of airline crashes.

Think of the absurdity of the following example. A friend drives you 20 miles to the airport where you are getting on a plane for a trip of about 750 miles. Your friend is likely to say, "Have a safe trip," as you part. This parting comment turns out to be sadly ironic, because your friend is *three times more likely to die in a car accident on the 20-mile trip back home than you are on your flight of 750 miles* (National Safety Council, 1990). It is the vividness problem that accounts for the apparent irrationality of person A's wishing person B safety, when it is person A who is in more danger.

Misleading personal judgments based on the vividness of media–presented images are widespread. One study (MacDonald, 1990) surveyed parents to see which risks to their children worried them the most. Parents turned out to be most worried about their children's being abducted, an event with a probability of 1 in 700,000. In contrast, the probability of their child's being killed in a car crash, which the parents worried about much less, is well over *100 times more likely* than their being abducted (Paulos, 1988). Of course, the "abduction" fears are mostly a media–created worry. The results actually suggest that, largely because of perceptions skewed by vividness effects, "American parents seem to worry about events that are least likely to happen" (MacDonald, 1990). One of the researchers lamented that this focus on worries that are "currently fashionable" misdirects the attention of parents and leads them to "ignore areas where they could have more impact, like school performance, television viewing habits, drug use and car safety" (MacDonald, 1990).

Writer Katherine Dunn (1993) recounted the fear she felt as a parent in the mid-1980s when stories of "abducted children" were sweeping the country. Rumors were spread that as many as 70,000 children had been snatched in malls and used by pornographers and/or tortured by strangers. Dunn reported tracking down the actual evidence by calling the FBI. It turned out that the number 70,000 referred not to abductions but to the number of runaways and children involved in custody disputes. Regarding children being abducted by strangers— which was the heart of the rumor sweeping the country—the FBI had recorded seven such cases nationwide. It was obviously not the number of these cases that had prompted such parental fears, but the vividness of the descriptions of the harm to the children. The vastly greater danger to any child in the passenger seat of an automobile (even when buckled up) was simply not as vivid.

The Overwhelming Impact of the Single Case

Psychologists have extensively studied the tendency for people's judgment to be dominated by a single, salient example when more accurate and representative statistical evidence is available. Borgida and Nisbett (1977) had college psychology majors indicate which psychology courses they were likely to take in the future. Before making their choices, some subjects were shown a statistical summary of the ratings given the courses by all the students taking them during the previous term. Another group of subjects merely witnessed a couple of students giving their opinions about the courses. Despite the extensiveness of the information in the statistical summary, future course choices were more strongly determined by the few students who had given their personal opinions to the subjects face to face. Thus a single opinion given to the subject face to face was more effective in changing attitudes than the much more accurate and reliable statistical information.

The tendency for statistical information to be overwhelmed by a single case presented directly to the subject has been demonstrated in many other ways. Hamill, Wilson, and Nisbett (1980) showed subjects a taped interview with a prison guard. Some subjects viewed interviews with a guard whose responses and manner suggested that he was a truly humane individual. Others viewed an interview with an extremely inhumane and disagreeable guard. The interviews modified opinions about guards in a positive or negative direction, depending on which interview had been viewed. More interesting was the fact that half the subjects received information indicating that the interview they had witnessed was a part of a large study of prison guards and that the guard they had seen was highly typical of all guards in the prison system. The other subjects were told that the guard they had viewed was highly atypical of all guards, and that his behavior and opinions were very extreme, either positively or negatively, depending on the interview. The information about whether the interview they had witnessed was typical or not had no effect on the subjects' opinions about prison guards. Knowledge of the statistical reliability of the interview was overwhelmed by the reactions to the interview itself.

Wilson and Brekke (1994) demonstrated how insidious the vividness problem is and also how it influences actual consumer behavior. They investigated how people were influenced by two different types of information about two different brands (brand A and brand B) of condom. One type of information was a survey and analysis in *Consumer Reports* magazine, and the other was the opinions of two university students about their preferences for condom brands. First, Wilson and Brekke surveyed a group of subjects on which type of information they would *want* to be influenced by. Over 85 percent of the subjects said that they would *want* to be more influenced by the *Consumer Reports* article than by the opinions of the two students. A similar group of subjects were then recruited for a study in which they were told that they would be given, free of charge, some condoms of their own choosing. The subjects were told that they could consult either or both of two types of information: a survey and analysis in *Consumer Reports* magazine and the opinions of two university students about their preferences. Even though less than 15 percent of a similar group of subjects *wanted* to be influenced by the opinions of the two students, 77 percent of the subjects requested both types of information. Apparently the subjects could not resist seeing the testimonials even though they did not believe that they should be affected by them. And they were indeed affected by them. When the subjects chose to see both types of information and the recommendations of the two sources of information differed, 31 percent of the subjects chose the brand of condom recommended in the student testimonials over the brand recommended by *Consumer Reports.*

John Paulos is the author of a popular 1988 book on innumeracy: "an inability to deal comfortably with the fundamental notions of number and chance" (p. 3). He argued that the tendency to be innumerate is tied up with overreliance on vivid examples and testimonial evidence: "Innumerate people characteristically have a strong tendency to personalize—to be misled by their own experiences, or by the media's focus on individuals and drama" (p. 6).

Another example of how people respond differently to vivid anecdotal information comes from the media coverage of the Vietnam war in the mid to late 1960s. As the war dragged on and the death toll of Americans killed continued without an end in sight, the media took to reporting the weekly number of American service personnel who had been killed that week. Week after week the figure varied between 200 and 300, and the public, seemingly, became quite accustomed to this report. However, one week a major magazine published a spread, running on for several pages, of the individual pictures of those persons who had died in the previous week. The public was now looking, concretely, at the approximately 250 individual lives that were being lost in a typical week. The result was a major outcry against the toll that the war was taking. The 250 pictures had an effect that weekly numbers had not had. But we, as a society, must overcome this tendency not to believe numbers—to have to *see* everything. Most of the complex influences on our society are abstractions that are accurately captured only by numbers. We must become numerate or else we shall have our opinions determined by whoever can get the best image in front of us. This is not the way to conduct public discourse on complex issues like war, economics, education, and child care.

When the United States deployed large forces in the Middle East in preparation for a possible war with Iraq in the fall of 1990, military officials laid out the following prohibitions to the press: "The visual and audio recordings of personnel in agony or severe shock are not authorized. Imagery of patients suffering from severe disfigurement or undergoing plastic-surgery treatments is not authorized" (*Newsweek,* January 14, 1991, p. 19). Military officials were quite worried that, if the public actually *saw* the agony entailed in real war injuries (as opposed to the Rambo-type fantasy images common in movies and television) and the unromantic aftermath of such serious injuries, public support for war would vanish. The military officials were probably right. Until the public learns to treat abstractions as seriously as images, public opinion will be as fickle as the latest image to flicker across the screen.

The Anecdote War

Research results like those obtained by Hamill et al. (1980) illustrate the unique conjunction of circumstances that makes testimonial and case study evidence especially misleading. This type of evidence provides an extremely inadequate empirical justification for any claim, yet it is vastly overweighted in decision-making situations in which other, more diagnostic, information is available. The potency of testimonials and anecdotes threatens to undermine the usefulness of any knowledge generated by any of the behavioral sciences.

The psychological research on the overwhelming potency of the single example is very important to our understanding of the nature and origin of our attitudes and opinions about social issues. Many of our social and political ideas are based on one or two particularly vivid examples and are often maintained in the face of more accurate statistical data that should modify our views. This particular aspect of human cognition is often exploited by opinion makers. In the long run, however, this is a dangerous tactic because it can easily steer opinion in any direction.

For example, President Reagan made a political career out of speeches peppered with particularly vivid, memorable, and therefore effective anecdotes that led his audiences to the political conclusions he wished them to draw (Green & MacColl, 1983). Images of "welfare queens" used by Reagan suggested vast waste in social service programs that the actual statistics did not confirm (Brown, 1987). However, months into his presidency, the Reagan White House became infuriated at the news media for focusing on individual cases of workers who had toiled in factories for years only to be laid off during the early-Reagan-era recession. One of the president's advisers complained, "Is it news that some fellow out in South Succotash some place has just been laid off, that he should be interviewed nationwide?" (*Time*, April 5, 1982). Thomas Griffith, writing in *Time* magazine (April 5, 1982) about this incident summarized quite well the problems inherent in attempting to decide important political issues by engaging in an "anecdote war":

> Perhaps because Ronald Reagan doesn't read all that much, he cares more about what television shows than what print says. He and television both know that facts are heavy, arguments confusing, charts boring; to grab the biggest audience, give your story the human touch. This is "for-example" journalism and politics, which frequently mislead. Reagan's homely anecdotes often prove to be factually wrong. TV commonly focuses its cameras on the glibbest or noisiest "man (or woman) in the street" to typify instant public reaction. . . . Argument by anecdote replaces real discussion. (p. 570)

Later that year, as the recession continued, the vivid images of soup kitchens across the nation became worrying to a White House that knew that a single well-chosen anecdote is worth a thousand statistics in the public mind. The president's adviser, Ed Meese, questioned the focus on hungry children in America and complained that "I've heard a lot of anecdotal stuff, but I haven't heard any authoritative figures." Live by the anecdote, die by the anecdote.

President Reagan's misleading use of the individual anecdote to sway opinion has led many to believe that it is an exclusive weapon of political conservatives. Liberals who lament that statistics indicating that abuse of the welfare system by recipients is small compared to other illegal activities such as tax evasion, for example, are overwhelmed when an individual meets or hears about a single food-stamp recipient in a grocery line with an expensive item. However, the power of anecdotes knows no political boundaries. Each side of the political spectrum can engage in, and has engaged in, this strategy. Political columnist Richard Reeves

(1986) wrote about how in 1986 the Democrats attempted to fight fire with fire. "The best way to fight the anecdotal president," concluded Illinois Senator Paul Simon, "is with better anecdotes." Reeves described how the Democrats effectively publicized the case of a 14-year-old autistic child from Maryland who received a public education because of a provision in special education law that was opposed by Republicans and supported by Democrats. Thus no side in the political debate has a lock on the use of the anecdote.

Psychologists have played a vital role in an important, but still limited, modern intellectual trend: the call for a truce in the anecdote war. While no one wishes to deny the literary power of the anecdote or its contribution to communication in some situations (where would cocktail parties be without it?), many do question whether the political discourse of our society should be dominated by them. The "anecdote problem" is not a liberal or conservative issue. It is a question of the choice between rational and irrational decision making. Consider the testimony of Vincent DeVita, the director of the National Cancer Institute (NCI), and Henry Pitot, the director of the cancer center at the University of Wisconsin, before Congress in 1981 (*Science*, June 5, 1981). Answering a question about studies of the apricot pit derivative laetrile, DeVita stated that the most recent NCI research had shown it to be ineffective. Senator Paula Hawkins of Florida then said, "I know of a person who had skin cancer, who was diagnosed as a terminal case. The person took laetrile and she's alive 2 years later." Perhaps grinding his teeth at the thought of basing national policy on multi-million-dollar medical research on a random anecdote, Pitot replied with the polite understatement, "Individual cases don't make a generality."

What to Do About the Vividness Problem

Even though we all are prone to overestimating the value of testimonial and other single-case evidence, we can become more self-aware and more conscious of when our opinions are being overwhelmed by personal testimony or particularly vivid single cases. A column by writer Remar Sutton (1987) illustrates quite well how becoming more aware of these influences can help. He wrote about the beginning of his attempt at a major weight loss by describing how "a diving buddy" recommended a popular book, *Fit for Life*. Sutton described seeing the authors on a talk show and mentioned that they "appeared awfully sincere, sounded authoritative, and attacked some traditional nutritional thinking." He recalled that "every time a critic attacked them, they rebutted effectively *with their own experiences* [italics added]. All of that, *and* the talk show host said he lost weight and felt better with their plan, too." In short, Sutton admitted in his column that he had become interested in the ideas in this book through his hearing of personal experiences and testimonials.

But fortunately Sutton had acquired the critical thinking skills that this book is trying to teach. He researched the information given in the book, looking for confirming evidence—not on talk shows and in popular magazines, but in the peer-reviewed scientific literature (see Chapters 1 and 11). He concluded that "too many ideas presented in the book were simply not backed up by long-term controlled scientific research that was statistically valid. Indeed, most of these ideas were counter to statistically valid research." Furthermore, in the course of his research, Sutton found out that the two authors had received their nutrition certificates from a "school" in Austin, Texas, that was nothing more than a post office box!

Sutton had the insight to realize that he had been close to being "sucked in" by the quackery in the book and to ask himself, "So why did I nearly fall for the *Fit for Life* approach?" His answer provides a good review of several of the pitfalls described previously. He admitted that he "trusted [his] diving friend's recommendation based on his personal experience." Sutton described that he liked the way the authors "presented *themselves* as much as their information" and that he "believed that television . . . and large numbers of book sales made the message of *Fit for Life* legitimate."

Sutton's conclusion is a nice summary statement for this chapter:

> Like it or not, personal testimonials and the sincerity of a person's presentation do not necessarily make any product or opinion accurate. Carefully designed, properly controlled, replicable studies which prove statistically valid over the long term are the only assurance any of us have that a diet or medical treatment . . . can benefit us.

Sutton ended by stating that he was still not hostile to new or innovative approaches to dieting, and he urged proponents of new approaches to write him; but he reminded them: "I'll be happy to present the opposite point of view on diet and fitness as long as the proponents of these views can point me to the reliable scientific studies that provide statistical validity for that position. Please do write, but don't forget those bibliographies."

In summary, the problems created by reliance on testimonial evidence are ever present. The vividness of such evidence often eclipses more reliable information and obscures understanding. Psychology instructors worry that merely pointing out the logical fallacies of reliance on testimonial evidence is not enough to provide a deep understanding of the pitfalls of this type of data. What else can be done? Is there any other way to get this concept across to people? Fortunately there is an alternative—an alternative somewhat different from the academic approach. The essence of this approach is to fight vividness with vividness. To hoist testimonials by their own petard! To let testimonials devour themselves with their own absurdity. A practitioner of this approach is the one, the only, the indubitable Amazing Randi!

The Amazing Randi: Fighting Fire with Fire

James Randi is a magician and jack-of-all-trades (he was given a MacArthur Foundation "genius" grant) who, for several years, has tried to teach the public some basic skills of critical thinking. The Amazing Randi (his stage name) has done this by exposing the fraud and charlatanism surrounding claims of "psychic" abilities. Although he has uncovered many magicians and conjurors masquerading as psychics, he is best known for exposing the trickery of Uri Geller, the psychic superstar of the 1970s. Bursting on the scene with his grand claims of psychic powers, Geller captivated the media to an extraordinary degree. He was featured in newspapers, on television shows, and in major news magazines on several continents. Randi detected and exposed the common and sometimes embarrassingly simple magic tricks that Geller used to perform his psychic "feats," which included bending keys and spoons, starting watches, and similar fare, mundane for a good magician. Since the Geller exposé, Randi has continued to use his considerable talents in the service of the public's right to know the truth in spite of itself by exposing the fallacies behind ESP, biorhythms, psychic surgery, extraterrestrials, levitation, and other pseudosciences, all marvelously detailed with great humor in his book *Flim-Flam* (1980). (See also his 1987 book *The Faith Healers,* in which he exposed several bogus religious "healers" as frauds.)

One of Randi's minor diversions consists of demonstrating how easy it is to garner testimonial evidence for any preposterous event or vacuous claim. His technique is to let people be swallowed up in a trap set by their own testimonials. Randi makes much use of that fascinating American cultural institution, the talk show, often appearing as a guest in the guise of someone other than himself. On a New York show a few years ago, he informed the audience that, while driving through New Jersey earlier in the day, he had seen a formation of V-shaped, orange objects flying overhead in a northerly direction. Within seconds, as Randi put it, "the station switchboard lit up like an electronic Christmas tree." Witness after witness called in to confirm this remarkable sighting. Unfortunately for them, the "sighting" was only a product of Randi's imagination. Callers provided many details that Randi had "omitted," including the fact that there had been more than one pass of the "saucers." This little "scam" illustrates how completely unreliable are individual reports that "something happened."

In Winnipeg, Canada, Randi appeared on a radio show as an "astrographologist." A week earlier, listeners had been told to send in their handwriting samples and birth dates. Three were chosen and were contacted so that Randi could assess the "readings" of their personalities. He was hugely successful, receiving ratings from the listeners of 9, 10, and 10 on a 1-to-10 scale of accuracy. Randi did eventually reveal the secret of his method to the radio listeners. He had read, word for word, the "readings" that astrologer Sydney Omarr had given to three members of the audience of a recent *Merv Griffin Show.*

On a different radio show, Randi demonstrated the basis for the popularity of another pseudoscience: biorhythms. One listener agreed to keep a day-by-day diary and compare it with a two-month biorhythm chart that had been prepared especially for her. Two months later, the woman called back to inform the audience that biorhythms should be taken very seriously because her chart was more than 90 percent accurate. Randi had to inform her of the silly mistake made by his secretary, who had sent someone else's chart to her, rather than her own. However, the woman did agree to evaluate the correct chart, which would be mailed to her right away, and to call back. A couple of days later, the woman called back, relieved. Her own chart was just as accurate—in fact, even *more* accurate. On the next show, however, it was discovered that, whoops, another error had been made. The woman had been sent Randi's secretary's chart, rather than her own! With a snort, the woman hung up.

Randi's biorhythm and "astrographologist" scams are actually examples of a phenomenon that has been termed the *P. T. Barnum effect* (Barnum, the famous carnival operator, coined the statement "There's a sucker born every minute"). This effect has been extensively studied by psychologists (e.g., Dickson & Kelly, 1985), who have found that the vast majority of individuals will endorse generalized personality summaries as accurate and specific descriptions of themselves. The Barnum effect makes it easier to generate testimonials and, of course, shows why they are worthless. There are certain sets of statements and phrases that most people see as applicable to themselves (many of these phrases have been studied by psychologists; see, e.g., Dickson & Kelly, 1985; Hyman, 1981; Marks & Kammann, 1980; Snyder, Shenkel, & Lowery, 1977). Anyone can feed them to a "client" as individualized psychological "analysis." The client is usually very impressed by the individualized accuracy of the "personality reading," not knowing that the same reading is being given to everyone. Of course, the Barnum effect is the basis of belief in the accuracy of palm readers and astrologists.

What Randi is trying to do in these little scams is to teach people a lesson about the worthlessness of testimonial evidence. He consistently demonstrates how easy it is to generate testimonials in favor of just about *any* bogus claim. For this reason, presenting a testimonial in support of a *particular* claim is meaningless. Only evidence from controlled observations (to be described in Chapter 6) is sufficient to actually *test* a claim.

Testimonials Open the Door to Pseudoscience

It is sometimes claimed that pseudosciences like the ones we have just discussed are simply a way to have a little fun, that they really do no harm. After all, why should we care? Isn't it just a case of a few people engaging in wishful thinking and a few others making a couple of bucks out of them?

A complete examination of the problem reveals, however, that the harm done to society by the prevalence of pseudosciences is more widespread than is generally believed. First, belief in pseudoscience leads to personal tragedies. Consider the case of Rhea Sullins, the 7-year-old daughter of the president of the American Natural Hygiene Society, whose tenets include the substitution of the consumption of fruits and vegetables for the use of drugs and conventional medical treatment. When Rhea became ill, "her father put her on a water-only fast for 18 days and then on a diet of fruit juice for 17 more" (Gilovich, 1991, p. 6). Sadly, his daughter subsequently died of malnutrition. Examples like this one are unfortunately not hard to find (Bulgatz, 1992; Gilovich, 1991; Hines, 1988; Randi, 1987).

In a complex, technological society, the influence of pseudoscience can be propagated by decisions that affect thousands of other people. That is, you may be affected by pseudoscientific beliefs even if you do not share those beliefs. For example, major banks and several Fortune 500 companies employ graphologists for personnel decisions (Sutherland, 1992, p. 167) even though voluminous evidence indicates that graphology is useless for this purpose (Ben-Shakhar, Bar-Hillel, Blui, Ben-Abba, & Flug, 1989; Neter & Ben-Shakhar, 1989). To the extent that pseudodiagnostic graphological cues lead employers to ignore more valid criteria, both economic inefficiency and personal injustice are the result. How would you like to lose your chance for a job that you really wanted because you had a particular little "loop" in your writing? Or alternatively, how would you feel if you·were denied a job because a "psychic" saw a disturbance in your "aura"? In fact, this is actually happening to some people. Some corporations are paying for "psychic readings" of individuals who are candidates for hiring. For example, Susan King is a so-called clairvoyant whom companies pay to give them "readings" to aid in personnel decisions. She claims that she doesn't even need to meet the applicant—that she can work from photos and first names—although "some clients call her in to observe short-listed candidates during final interviews and even at cocktail parties afterwards" (Kershaw, 1991). In tough and competitive economic times, is this how you want your employment opportunities to be determined?

These examples are unfortunately not rare (see Dawes, 1988; Sutherland, 1992). We are all affected in numerous ways when pseudoscientific beliefs permeate society—even if we do not subscribe to the beliefs. For example, police departments hire psychics to help with investigations (Marshall, 1980) even though research has shown that this practice has no effectiveness (Hines, 1988; Reiser, Ludwig, Saxe, & Wagner, 1979; Rowe, 1993). Programmers at the ABC television network hired a Hollywood psychic to help make decisions about the content of the most influential communications technology in our society (Auletta, 1992, p. 114). And most astonishingly, an astrologer was employed in the Reagan White House, her advice affecting the "timing of presidential speeches, appearances, meetings with heads of state, airplane travel schedules, and even discussion topics" (Johnson, 1991, p. 454).

Pseudosciences such as astrology are now large industries, involving newspaper columns, radio shows, book publishing, magazine articles, and other means of dissemination. The leading horoscope magazine has a circulation of one-quarter million, larger than that of many legitimate science magazines (Bastedo, 1981). The House of Representatives Select Committee on Aging has estimated that the amount wasted on medical quackery nationally now approaches $10 billion each year. The committee's report stated that

> quackery now invades nearly every aspect of our lives, and, at points, attracts adherents with near religious zeal. The easy to recognize and somewhat comic figure of pitchmen of the past has been supplanted by sophisticated and shrewd hucksters with a keen sense of the vulnerability of potential customers, the limitations of the law and the profitability of exploiting both. Quackery has become big business. . . . The modern quack's prime target is the senior citizen. His purview is chronic and incurable diseases. His approach is the illustrated brochure, the supermarket press, television commercials, "testimonial" ads, phony foundations providing "scientific" information and storefront clinics. (U.S. Congress, 1984, pp. 3–4)

In short, pseudoscience is a multi-million-dollar business, and the incomes of thousands of individuals depend on its public acceptance.

The topic of pseudoscience in the area of medicine is useful to consider, because medical associations have been more aggressive in attacking pseudoscience and dissociating legitimate medical practice from the illegitimate than has psychology. Consider the guidelines published by the Arthritis Foundation and cited by the Committee on Aging for spotting the unscrupulous promoter:

1. He may offer a "special" or "secret" formula or device for "curing" arthritis.
2. He advertises. He uses "case histories" and testimonials from satisfied "patients."
3. He may promise (or imply) a quick or easy cure.
4. He may claim to know the cause of arthritis and talk about "cleansing" your body of "poisons" and "pepping up" your health. He may say surgery, X-rays and drugs prescribed by a physician are unnecessary.
5. He may accuse the "medical establishment" of deliberately thwarting progress, or of persecuting him . . . but he doesn't allow his method to be tested in tried and proven ways. (U.S. Congress, 1984, p. 12)

This list could also serve as a guide for spotting fraudulent psychological treatments and claims. Note, of course, point 2, which is the focus of this chapter. But also note that points 1 and 5 illustrate the importance of something discussed earlier: science is public. In addition to putting forth testimonials as "proof," the practitioners of pseudoscience often try to circumvent the public verifiability criterion of science by charging that there is a conspiracy to suppress their "knowledge." They use this as justification for going straight to the media with their "findings" rather than submitting their work to the normal scientific publication processes. The ploy is usually more successful in the area of psychology than anywhere else because the media often show less respect for the normal scientific mechanisms of psychology than they do for those of other sciences. It is important to keep this bias in mind (it will receive an extended discussion in Chapter 11). Unverified claims that the media would never think of reporting if they occurred in the physical sciences are seen as legitimate topics of psychological reporting because journalists have been convinced by the purveyors of pseudoscience that "anything goes" in psychology. Thus the consumer must be aware that television and the print media will publicize virtually any outlandish claim in the area of psychology if they think there is an audience for it, no matter how much the claim is contradicted by the available evidence. The public ends up the loser.

Pseudoscience hurts society in other ways. For example, there is what economists call the *opportunity cost*: people waste time and money that they could have spent on something else, and they therefore "lose opportunities." Physicist Philip Morrison (1983) argued:

> The danger of pseudoscience is not to science, but to society. . . . It is primarily an opportunity cost, in the language of economics. Here we have all these people interested in the exciting and wonderful and amazing properties of the world who could be learning something real. Instead they are hearing from Uri Geller. They've turned themselves over to dependence on charlatans. They could be learning something different. (p. 56)

But there are costs more specific than the general learning-opportunity cost. For example, claims of miracle cures raise false hopes that can cause psychological damage when they are dashed. One of the most despicable examples in my files on this subject is an article from a grocery store tabloid entitled "Psychic Shows the Blind How to See Using ESP." People can fail to take advantage of the real knowledge available to them because they become involved in pseudosciences. Proponents of psychic surgery implicitly encourage people to spend money on bogus cures and to ignore traditional "nonpsychic" medical procedures that may help them. Reporter Richard Brenneman (1990) described how a bogus psychic surgeon had bilked cancer victims out of their money and had also delayed their eventual treatment by legitimate medical means. Similarly, at a civic meeting on health care fraud, the president of the Michigan Council Against Health Fraud displayed a brochure for a phony cancer cure which said that "this product cannot be used with any other cancer therapy" ("If It Sounds," 1990). The damage done in cases like this is simply incalculable.

Finally, at a time when the basic research infrastructure of the United States is deteriorating badly, it is a tragedy for resources to be poured down the drain by pseudosciences. Yet this is just what has happened. In 1979 James McDonnell, the chairman of the board of the McDonnell Douglas Aircraft corporation, awarded a $0.5-million grant to Washington University in St. Louis to establish a laboratory for psychical research.

Randi's direct warnings to the director of the lab, a physicist, about the essential controls in such experiments and the absolute necessity of having a skeptical conjuror present were ignored, as was Randi's offer to be in attendance. Instead, the investigators in this $0.5-million project proceeded to allow themselves to be duped by some of the most simple-minded magic tricks imaginable, performed by two magician friends of James Randi who had presented themselves to the lab posing as psychics. On many occasions the controls were so loose that the ingenuity and skill of the magicians were hardly challenged. For example, Randi warned the laboratory that, if attempts were made to demonstrate Geller-type "spoon-bending" tricks, it would be important that the table placed in front of the subject not be cluttered with objects. Despite this warning, during the testing the table was continually littered with various specimens that were to be "psychically" bent. The specimens were not permanently marked; instead, they had paper tags on them, so that it was easy for the magicians to switch tags and, by simple conjuring skill, give the appearance that the specimens had been bent by nonphysical means.

Another "feat" led the researchers to report in a leading parapsychology journal as follows:

> A target S. S. [one of the subjects] apparently influenced consisted of a lucite mold with a slot cut in it just large enough to accommodate a 1/16 inch metal rod. The rod can be touched but not so that one can physically influence it. S. S. was observed and videotaped stroking this rod on the top and apparently causing it to bow upward approximately 2.5 mm. (Phillips & Shafer, 1982, p. 145)

Randi (1983) wrote about what really happened:

> Steve was asked to stroke the metal with his finger and cause it to bend. He quickly discovered that the rod tilted up and out of the groove. He simply removed the rod unnoticed, bent it slightly, and re-inserted it into the groove, lying on its side, since the groove was wide enough to accommodate the bend. Then he stroked and rotated the rod 90 degrees to make it appear to bend up and out of the groove. (pp. 27–28)

Almost three years of similarly sloppy testing failed to uncover the fact that these two subjects had no psychic powers but were magicians practicing their craft right under the noses of the investigating scientists. Finally, Randi and his two friends blew the whistle on their little experiment, which they had dubbed Project Alpha, and unlike so many debacles surrounding the pseudoscience of parapsychology, this one did receive national publicity (the exposure of the fraudulent nature of a psychic claim is often deemed not "newsworthy" by the same media outlets that publicized the bogus claim in the first place).

There are two footnotes to Project Alpha. The first is that one of the magicians, Mike Edwards, had been covered in the *National Enquirer* and billed as "One of the World's Best Psychics." The second is that, during the Washington University experiments, the other magician, Steve Shaw, had been exposed in the journal *Skeptical Inquirer,* a journal devoted to the critical examination of "paranormal" claims, as a magician who was posing as a mind reader and psychic.

It is simply tragic to allow scarce scientific resources to disappear into the morass of pseudoscience, particularly at a time when, to cite only one example, great strides are being made in some biomedical areas where, unfortunately, research is very expensive to conduct. (See June Goodfield's 1981 book *An Imagined World,* for an account of a young researcher with some innovative ideas on the nature of Hodgkin's disease who was repeatedly frustrated in her investigations because of insufficient funding to carry out her research.)

Thus the spread of pseudoscience is quite costly. And nothing fosters the spread of pseudosciences more than confusion about what type of evidence does and does not justify belief in a claim about a phenomenon. Testimonials, by providing readily available support for virtually any claim and by the impact that they have when used, open the door to the development of and the belief in pseudosciences. There is no more important rule for the consumer of psychological information than to beware of them. In the next several chapters, we shall see what type of evidence *is* required to justify claims.

Chapter 5

CORRELATION AND CAUSATION
Birth Control by the Toaster Method

Several years ago, a large-scale study of the factors related to the use of contraceptive devices was conducted in Taiwan. A large research team of social scientists and physicians collected data on a wide range of behavioral and environmental variables. The researchers were interested in seeing what variables best predicted the adoption of birth control methods. After testing all the variables, they found that the one that was most strongly related to contraceptive use was the number of electrical appliances (toaster, fans, etc.) in the home (Li, 1975).

This result probably does not tempt you to propose that the teenage pregnancy problem should be dealt with by passing out free toasters in high schools. But why aren't you tempted to think this? The correlation between appliances and contraceptive use was indeed strong, and this variable was the single best predictor among the many variables that were measured. Your reply, I hope, will be that it is not the strength but the *nature* of the relationship that is relevant. Starting a free toaster program would imply the belief that toasters *cause* people to use contraceptives. The fact that we view this suggestion as absurd means that, at least in clear-cut cases such as this, we recognize that two variables may be associated without having a causal relationship.

In this example, we can guess that the relationship exists because contraceptive use and the number of electrical appliances in the home are linked through some other variable that relates to both. Education would be one likely candidate for a mediating variable. We know that educational level is related to both contraceptive use and socioeconomic status. All we need now is the fact that families at higher socioeconomic levels tend to have more electrical appliances in their homes, and we have the linkage. Of course, other variables may mediate this correlation. However, the point is that, no matter how strong the correlation is between the number of toasters and contraceptive use, the relationship does not indicate a causal connection.

The contraceptive example makes it very easy to understand the fundamental principle of this chapter: The presence of a correlation does not necessarily imply causation. However, the limitations of correlational evidence are not always so easy to recognize. When the causal link seems obvious to us, when we have a strong preexisting bias, or when our interpretations become dominated by our theoretical orientation, it is tempting to treat correlations as evidence of causation. The case of Karl Pearson provides a clear and ironic example.

PEARSON AND TUBERCULOSIS

Pearson was a British statistician of considerable eminence who lived at the turn of the century. He developed a mathematical formula to express the strength of the relationship between two variables. Scientists cannot be satisfied with the vague statement that two variables are correlated; they must have some way of measuring the strength of the correlation. Pearson provided one of the most useful formulas to calculate this strength, and this "correlation coefficient" now bears his name. However, the father of the correlation coefficient set a disastrous precedent, for he was one of the most blatant violators of the principle that correlation does not necessarily imply causation.

Pearson calculated the correlations between many biological variables. One of his findings was that the correlation between the tendency of a parent to contract tuberculosis and the tendency of the parent's children to contract the same disease was .50. (Correlation coefficients range from 0 to 1.0 in absolute value: higher numbers indicate stronger relationships; negative values indicate inverse relationships.) Now, for Pearson this was far from a neutral finding, for he was an extreme hereditarian, a leader in the growing eugenics movement of his day. Pearson thought that virtually every imaginable human characteristic was primarily a product of genetic influences and used this belief to justify his prejudices. He argued, for example, that Jews living in slums were "innately dirty" (see Blum, 1978). Thus he saw the parent-child tuberculosis correlation as evidence of a hereditary cause of the disease. He dismissed environmental explanations and argued against sanitation campaigns on the grounds that the hereditary nature of the disease made them futile.

Of course, the discovery of the tubercle bacillus and the reduction of the disease due to improved sanitary conditions have rendered a harsh historical judgment on Pearson's views. His example illustrates the difficulty of refraining from causal interpretations of correlational data when a preexisting bias is present. This example also points to the importance of maintaining the strictest standards for evaluating evidence when the issue at hand is one of pressing social importance. Incorrect beliefs have serious consequences. Those who endorse the attitude that anything goes in the field of psychology should take heed. Many of our current pressing social problems come within the domain of psychology. The abandonment or distortion of the empirical attitude toward social problems can have disastrous effects, as an examination of the history of hunger in America illustrates.

THE THIRD-VARIABLE PROBLEM: GOLDBERGER AND PELLAGRA

In the early 1900s thousands of Americans in the South suffered and died of (approximately 100,000 fatalities per year) a disease called *pellagra*. Characterized by dizziness, lethargy, running sores, vomiting, and severe diarrhea, the disease was thought to be infectious and to be caused by a living microorganism of "unknown origin" (Chase, 1977, p. 205). It is not surprising, then, that many physicians of the National Association for the Study of Pellagra were impressed by evidence that the disease was linked to sanitary conditions. It seemed that homes in Spartanburg, South Carolina, that were free of pellagra invariably had inside plumbing and good sewerage. This correlation coincided quite well with the idea of an infectious disease transmitted because of poor sanitary conditions via the excrement of pellagra victims.

One physician who doubted this interpretation was Joseph Goldberger, who, at the direction of the Surgeon General of the United States, had conducted several investigations of pellagra. Goldberger thought that pellagra was caused by inadequate diet—in short, by the poverty common throughout the South. Many victims had lived on high-carbohydrate, extremely low-protein diets, characterized by small amounts of meat, eggs, and milk and large amounts of corn, grits, and mush. Goldberger thought that the correlation between sewage conditions and pellagra did not reflect a causal relationship in either direction (much as in the toaster–birth-control example). Goldberger thought that the correlation arose because families with sanitary plumbing were likely to be economically advantaged. This economic discrepancy would also be reflected in their diets, which would contain more animal protein.

But wait a minute! Why should Goldberger get away with *his* causal inference? After all, both sides are just sitting there with their correlations, Goldberger with pellagra and diet and the other physicians with pellagra and sanitation. Why shouldn't the association's physicians be able to say that Goldberger's correlation was equally misleading? Why was he justified in rejecting the hypothesis that an infectious organism was transmitted through the excrement of pellagra victims because of inadequate sewage disposal? Well, the reason Goldberger was justified has to do with one small detail that I neglected to mention: Goldberger had eaten the excrement of pellagra victims.

Why Goldberger's Evidence Was Better

Goldberger had a type of evidence (a controlled manipulation, discussed further in the next chapter) that is derived when the investigator, instead of simply observing correlations, actually manipulates the critical variable. This approach often involves setting up special conditions that rarely occur naturally, and to term Goldberger's special conditions unnatural is an understatement.

Confident that pellagra was not contagious and not transmitted by the bodily fluids of the victims, Goldberger had himself injected with the blood of a victim. He inserted throat and nose secretions from a victim into his own mouth:

> Finally, he selected two patients—one with scaling sores and the other with diarrhea. He scraped the scales from the sores, mixed the scales with four cubic centimeters of urine from the same patients, added an equal amount of liquid feces, and rolled the mixture into little dough balls by the addition of four pinches of flour. The pills were taken voluntarily by him, by his assistants and by his wife. (Bronfenbrenner & Mahoney, 1975, p. 11)

Neither Goldberger nor the other volunteers came down with pellagra. In short, Goldberger had created the conditions necessary for the infectious transmission of the disease and nothing had happened.

Goldberger had now manipulated the causal mechanism suggested by others and had shown that it was ineffective, but it was still necessary to test his own causal mechanism. Goldberger got two groups of prisoners from a Mississippi state prison farm who were free of pellagra to volunteer for his experiment. One group was given the high-carbohydrate, low-protein diet that he suspected was the cause of pellagra, while the other group received a more balanced diet. Within five months, the low-protein group was ravaged by pellagra, while the other group showed no signs of the disease. After a long struggle, during which Goldberger's ideas were opposed by those with political motives for denying the existence of poverty and by others wishing to advance hereditarian explanations for illnesses, his hypothesis was eventually accepted because it matched the empirical evidence better than any other.

The history of pellagra illustrates the human cost of basing social and economic policy on mistaken inferences from correlational studies. This is not to say that we should never use correlational evidence. Quite the contrary. In many instances it is all we have to work with (see Chapter 8), and in some cases it is all we need (for instance, when prediction, rather than determination of cause, is the goal). Scientists often have to use incomplete knowledge to solve problems. The important thing is that we approach correlational evidence with a certain skepticism. Examples such as the pellagra-sewage case occur with considerable frequency in all areas of psychology. The example illustrates what is sometimes termed the *third-variable problem*: the fact that the correlation between the two variables—in this case, pellagra incidence and sewage conditions—may not indicate a causal path in either direction but may arise because both variables are related to a third variable—here, diet—that has not even been measured. Correlations like that between sewage and pellagra are often termed *spurious correlations*: correlations that arise not because a causal link exists between the two variables that are measured, but because both variables are related to a third variable.

Let's consider a more contemporary example. During the 1980s, debates raged over the relative efficacy of public and private schools. Some of the conclusions drawn in this debate vividly demonstrate the perils of inferring causation from correlational evidence. The question of the efficacy of private versus public schools is an empirical problem that can be attacked with the investigative methods of the social sciences. This is not to imply that it is an easy problem, only that it is a scientific problem, potentially solvable. All advocates of the superiority of private schools implicitly recognize this, because at the crux of their arguments is an empirical fact: student achievement in private schools exceeds that in public schools. This fact is not in dispute, since educational statistics are plentiful and largely consistent across various studies. The problem is the use of these achievement data to conclude that the education received in private schools *causes* the superior test scores.

The outcome of educational testing is a function of many different variables, all of which are correlated. In order to evaluate the relative efficacy of public schools and private schools, we need more complex statistics than merely the relationship between the type of school attended and school achievement. For example, educational achievement is related to many different indicators of family background, such as parental education, parental occupation, socioeconomic status, the number of books in the home, and other factors. These characteristics are also related to the probability of sending a child to a private school. Thus family background is a potential third variable that may affect the relationship between academic achievement and the type of school. In short, the relationship may have nothing to do with the effectiveness of private schools but may be the result of the fact that economically advantaged children do better academically *and* are more likely to attend private schools.

Fortunately there exist complex correlational statistics known as *multiple regression* and *path analysis* (statistics developed in part by psychologists; see Chapter 10) that were designed to deal with problems such as this one. These statistics allow the correlation between two variables to be recalculated after the influence of other variables is removed, or "partialed out." Using these more complex correlational techniques, Ellis Page and Timothy Keith (1981), two researchers at Duke University, analyzed a large set of educational statistics on high-school students that were collected under the auspices of the National Center for Educational Statistics. They found that, after variables reflecting the students' home backgrounds and general mental ability were factored out, there was virtually no relationship between school achievement and the type of school attended. Their results have been confirmed by other researchers (Jencks, 1985; Sassenrath, Croce, & Penaloza, 1984; Walberg & Shanahan, 1983; Wolfle, 1987).

Thus it appears that advocating private schools as a means of improving educational achievement is the same as arguing for birth control by the toaster method. Academic achievement is linked to private school attendance not because of any direct causal mechanism, but because the family background and the general cognitive level of students in private schools are different from those of children in public schools.

The complex correlational statistics that allow us to partial out the effects of a third variable do not always reduce the magnitude of the original correlation. Sometimes the original correlation between two variables remains even after the partialing out of the third variable, and this itself can be informative. Such an outcome indicates that the original correlation was not due to a spurious relationship with that particular third variable. Of course, it does not remove the possibility of a spurious relationship due to some other variable.

A good example of this is provided in the data analyzed by Thomas, Alexander, and Eckland (1979). These investigators found that the probability that a high-school student will attend college is related to the socioeconomic status of the student's family. This is an important finding that strikes at the heart of the merit-based goals of our society. It suggests that opportunities for success in life are determined by a person's economic class. However, before jumping to this conclusion, we must consider several other alternative hypotheses. That is, the correlation between college attendance and socioeconomic status should be examined closely for spuriousness. One obvious candidate for a third variable is academic ability. Perhaps this is related to both college attendance and socioeconomic status, and if it is partialed out, the correlation between the first two variables may disappear. The investigators calculated the appropriate statistics and found that the correlation between college attendance and socioeconomic status remained significant even after academic aptitude was partialed out. Thus the fact that children of higher economic classes are more likely to attend college is not entirely due to differences in academic aptitude. This finding, of course, does not rule out the possibility that some other variable leads to the relationship between the first two, but it is clearly important, both practically and theoretically, to be able to rule out a major alternative explanation such as academic aptitude.

Finally, recall the example of the research on the effects of teenagers' work experience described in Chapter 1. Developmental psychologists have found that more work experience is associated with poorer school achievement and higher delinquency (Bachman & Schulenberg, 1993; Greenberger & Steinberg, 1986; Steinberg & Dornbusch, 1993). However, this evidence, by itself, is merely correlational. It may be the case, for example, that teenagers who choose to work a lot have lower academic ability and/or different home backgrounds to begin with. Researchers have tested these possible third variables with the complex correlational statistics mentioned above and have found that the negative associations still remain after academic ability and other background variables have been controlled (Bachman & Schulenberg, 1993; Steinberg & Dornbusch, 1993).

THE DIRECTIONALITY PROBLEM: EYE MOVEMENTS AND READING

There is no excuse for making causal inferences on the basis of correlational evidence when it is possible to manipulate variables in a way that would legitimately justify a causal inference. Yet this is a distressingly common occurrence when psychological issues are involved, and the growing importance of psychological knowledge in the solution of social problems is making this tendency increasingly costly. A well-known example in the area of educational psychology illustrates this point quite well.

Since the beginning of the scientific study of reading about a hundred years ago, researchers have known that there is a correlation between eye movement patterns and reading ability. Poorer readers make more erratic movements, display more regressions (movements from right to left), and make more fixations (stops) per line of text. On the basis of this correlation, some educators hypothesized that deficient oculomotor skills were the cause of reading problems, and many "eye movement–training" programs were developed and administered to elementary-school children. These programs were instituted long before it was ascertained whether the correlation really indicated that erratic eye movements caused poor reading.

It is now known that the eye movement–reading-ability correlation reflects a causal relationship that runs in exactly the opposite direction. Erratic eye movements do not cause reading problems (Coles, 1987; Rayner, 1985). It is the other way around. Slow recognition of words and difficulties with comprehension lead to erratic eye movements. When children are taught to recognize words efficiently and to comprehend better, their eye movements become smoother. Training children's eye movements, however, does nothing to improve their reading comprehension.

Since the mid-1970s, research has clearly pointed to word decoding and a language problem in phonology as the sources of reading problems (Gough, Ehri, & Treiman, 1992; Joshi & Leong, 1993; Stanovich & Siegel, 1994). Very few cases of reading disability are due to difficulties in the area of eye movement patterns (Olson, Kleigl, & Davidson, 1983; Stanovich, 1986a, 1986b). Yet, if most school districts of at least medium size were to search diligently in their storage basements, they would find dusty "eye movement trainers" that represent thousands of dollars of equipment money wasted because of the temptation to see a correlation as proof of a causal hypothesis.

Our discussion thus far has identified the two major classes of ambiguity present in a simple correlation between two variables. One is called the *directionality problem* and is illustrated by the eye movement example. Before immediately concluding that a correlation between variable A and variable B is due to changes in A causing changes in B, we must first recognize that the direction of causation may be the opposite, that is, from B to A. The second problem is the third-variable problem, and it is illustrated by the pellagra example (and the toaster–birth-control and private-school–achievement examples). The correlation between the two variables may not indicate a causal path in either direction but may arise because both variables are related to a third variable.

SELECTION BIAS

There are certain situations in which the possibility of a spurious correlation is very likely: situations in which there is a high probability that selection bias has occurred. The term *selection bias* refers to the relationships between certain subject and environmental variables that may arise when people with different biological, behavioral, and psychological characteristics select different types of environments. Selection bias creates a spurious correlation between environmental characteristics and behavioral-biological characteristics.

Let's look at a straightforward example that illustrates the importance of selection factors in creating spurious correlations. If you would, quickly name the state with the highest incidence of deaths due to respiratory illness. The answer to this question is, of course, Arizona. What? Wait a minute! Arizona has clean air, doesn't it? Does the smog of Los Angeles spread that far? Has the urban sprawl of Phoenix got that bad? No, it can't be. Let's slow down a minute. Maybe Arizona *does* have good air. And maybe people with respiratory illnesses tend to move there. And then they die. There you have it. A situation has arisen in which, if we're not careful, we may be led to think that Arizona's air is killing people.

However, selection factors are not always so easy to discern. They are often overlooked, particularly when, as in Pearson's case, there is a preexisting desire to see a certain type of causal link. Tempting correlational evidence combined with a preexisting bias may deceive even the best of minds. Let's consider some specific cases.

The importance of considering selection factors was illustrated quite well in the national debate over the quality of American education that took place throughout most of the 1980s. During this debate, the public was inundated with educational statistics, but was not provided with corresponding guidance for avoiding the danger of inferring causal relationships from correlational data that are filled with misleading selection factors.

Throughout the continuing debate, many members of the Reagan administration, including the Secretary of Education, repeatedly attempted to provide evidence that educational quality is not linked to teacher salary levels. One set of findings put forth was the Scholastic Aptitude Test (SAT) results for each of the 50 states. The average scores on this test, taken by high-school students who intend to go to college, did indeed show little relation to teacher salaries. If anything, the trends seemed to run opposite to the expected direction. Several states that had very high average teacher salaries had very low average SAT scores, and many states at the bottom of the teacher salary rankings had very high average SAT scores. A close look at the data patterns provides an excellent lesson in how easily selection factors can produce spurious correlations.

Upon further examination, we see that Mississippi students, for example, score higher than California students on the SAT (Taube & Linden, 1989). In fact, the difference is considerable. The average Mississippi scores are over 100 points higher. Since Mississippi teachers' salaries are the lowest in the nation, this finding must have been cause for celebration in the White House. But wait. Is it really true that schools are better in Mississippi than in California, that the general state of education is superior in the former? Of course not. Virtually any other objective index would show that California schools are superior. But if this is true, what about the SAT?

The answer lies in selection factors. The SAT is not taken by *all* high-school students. Unlike much standardized testing that schools conduct, in which all children are uniformly tested, the SAT involves selection bias (Taube & Linden, 1989; Wainer, 1989). Only students hoping to go to college take the test. This factor accounts for some of the state-by-state variance in average scores on the test and also explains why some of the states with the very best educational systems have very low average SAT scores.

Selection factors operate on the SAT scores of states in two different ways. First, some state university systems require the ACT test scores rather than the SAT scores. Thus, the only students who take the SAT in these states are students planning to go to college out of state. It is more likely that these students are from advantaged backgrounds and/or have higher academic aptitude than the average student. This is what is happening in the Mississippi/California example. Only 3 percent of Mississippi high-school students take the SAT; whereas the figure in California is 42 percent (Taube & Linden, 1989).

The second selection factor operating is a bit more subtle. In states with good educational systems, many students intend to continue their education after high school. In such states, a high proportion of students take the SAT, including a greater number with lesser abilities. States with high drop-out rates and lower overall quality have a much smaller proportion of students who aspire to college.

The group of students who eventually take the SAT in such states represents only those best qualified to go to college. The resulting average SAT scores in these states naturally tend to be higher than those from states where larger proportions of students pursue further education.

The misuse of SAT scores also provides us with an unfortunate example of how hard it is to correct the misleading use of statistics as long as the general public lacks the simple methodological and statistical thinking skills taught in this book. I included an example of the misuse of SAT scores due to selection biases in the first edition of this book, written in 1983. As I write the fourth edition, in 1994, I am looking at an article by Brian Powell (1993), an Indiana professor, analyzing a column written by political columnist George Will in which Will—you guessed it—argued against public expenditures on education because states with high SATs do not have high expenditures on education. Powell (1993) pointed out that the states that Will singled out as having particularly high scores—Iowa, North Dakota, South Dakota, Utah, and Minnesota—have SAT participation rates of only 5 percent, 6 percent, 7 percent, 4 percent, and 10 percent, respectively, whereas more than 40 percent of all high-school seniors in the United States take the SAT. The reason is that in these states, the test required for admission to public institutions is the ACT test. Only students planning on studying out of state, "often at prestigious private schools" (Powell, 1993, p. 352) take the SAT. In contrast, in New Jersey, which Will used as an example of a state with low SAT scores and high expenditures, 76 percent of high-school seniors take the test. Obviously the students in North and South Dakota who take the SAT are a more select group than those in New Jersey, where three quarters of all students take the test.

In the journal *Educational Researcher,* psychometrician Howard Wainer (1993) analyzed an article in the June 22, 1993 *Wall Street Journal* which featured a study by the Heritage Foundation, an ideologically biased think tank, which argued against spending money on education because—you guessed it—SAT scores were lower in states where more money was spent on education. Wainer's (1993) article goes beyond merely showing how selection bias causes this result, however. Wainer (1993) demonstrated that, when a test that uses a representative sample rather than a self-selected sample is analyzed—the National Assessment for Educational Progress (NAEP)—the relationship reverses: states that spend more on education have higher scores. Readers are invited to help me correct this misuse of SAT scores in the media. Write to the media outlet that you detect using SAT scores to compare states, and inform them of how they are misusing statistics. Send me any responses that you receive.

An example from clinical psychology demonstrates how tricky and "perverse" the selection bias problem can sometimes be. It has been demonstrated that the cure rate for various addictive-appetite disorders such as obesity, heroin use, and cigarette smoking is *lower* for those who have *had* psychotherapy than for those who have not (Rzewnicki & Forgays, 1987; Schachter, 1982). The reason, you will be glad to know, is not that psychotherapy makes addictive behavior more resistant to change. It is that, among those who seek psychotherapy, the disorder is more intractable, and self-cures have been ineffective.

In short, the consumer's rule for this chapter is simple: Be on the lookout for instances of selection bias, and avoid inferring causation when data are only correlational. It is true that complex correlational designs do exist that allow limited causal inferences, and that some research problems are structured in such a way that correlational evidence allows one to choose between causal hypotheses. It is also true that correlational evidence is helpful in demonstrating convergence on a hypothesis (see Chapter 8). Nevertheless, it is probably better for the consumer to err on the side of skepticism than to be deceived by correlational relationships that falsely imply causation.

Chapter 6

GETTING THINGS
UNDER CONTROL
The Case of Clever Hans

This chapter starts with a quiz. Don't worry; it's not about what you read in the last chapter. In fact, it should be easy because it's about the observable motion of objects in the world, something with which we have all had much experience. There are just three questions in the quiz.

For the first, you will need a piece of paper. Imagine that a person is whirling a ball attached to a string around his or her head. Draw a circle that represents the path of the ball as viewed from about the person's head. Draw a dot somewhere on the circle and connect the dot to the center of the circle with a line. The line represents the string, and the dot represents the ball at a particular instant in time. Imagine that at exactly this instant the string is cut. Your first task is to indicate with your pencil the subsequent flight of the ball.

For your next problem, imagine that you are a bomber pilot flying toward a target at 500 miles per hour at a height of 20,000 feet. To simplify the problem, assume that there is no air resistance. The question here is, at which location would you drop your bomb: before reaching the target, directly over the target, or when you have passed the target? Indicate either a specific distance in front of the target, directly over the target, or a specific distance past the target.

Finally, imagine that you are firing a rifle from shoulder height. Assume that there is no air resistance and that the rifle is fired exactly parallel to the ground. If a bullet that is dropped from the same height as the rifle takes one-half second to hit the ground, how long will it take the bullet that is fired from the rifle to fall if its initial velocity is 2,000 feet per second?

And the answers—oh, yes, the answers. They appear later on in this chapter. But first, in order to understand what the accuracy of our knowledge about moving objects has to do with psychology, we need to explore more fully the nature of the experimental logic that scientists use. In this chapter we will discuss principles of experimental control and manipulation.

SNOW AND CHOLERA

In his studies of pellagra Joseph Goldberger was partially guided by his hunch that the disease was not contagious. But 70 years earlier, John Snow, in his search for the causes of cholera, bet the opposite way and also won (Goldstein & Goldstein, 1978). Many competing theories had been put forth to explain the repeated outbreaks of cholera in London in the 1850s. Many doctors believed that the exhalations of victims were inhaled by others who then contracted the disease. This was called the *effluvia theory*. In contrast, Snow hypothesized that the disease was spread by the water supply, which had become contaminated with the excrement of victims.

Snow set out to test his theory. Fortunately there were many different sources of water supply in London, each serving different districts, so the incidence of cholera could be matched with the different water supplies, which varied in degree of contamination. Snow realized, however, that such a comparison would be subject to severe selection biases (recall the discussion in Chapter 5). The districts of London varied greatly in wealth, so any correlation between water supply and geography could just as easily be due to any of the many other economically related variables that affect health, such as diet, stress, job hazards, and quality of clothing and housing. In short, the possibility of obtaining a spurious correlation was nearly as high as in the case of the pellagra-sewage example discussed in Chapter 5. However, Snow was astute enough to notice and to exploit one particular situation that had occurred.

In one part of London there happened to be two water companies that supplied a single neighborhood in an unsystematic manner. That is, on a particular street, a few houses were supplied by one company, then a few by the other, because in earlier days the two companies had been in competition. There were even cases in which a single house had water from a company different from the one supplying the houses on either side of it. Thus Snow had uncovered a case in which the socioeconomic status of the people supplied by two water companies was virtually identical, or at least as close as it could be in a naturally occurring situation like this. Such a circumstance would still not have been of any benefit if the water from the two companies had been equally contaminated. The essence of experimentation is to observe or, better yet, to create a single difference between two groups that are otherwise the same. Had the two water supplies been equally contaminated, Snow would have had no difference to associate with cholera incidence. Fortunately this was not the case.

After the previous London cholera epidemic, one company, the Lambeth Company, had moved upstream on the Thames to escape the London sewage. The Southwark and Vauxhall Company, however, had stayed downstream. Thus the probability was that the water of the Lambeth Company was much less contaminated than the water of the Southwark and Vauxhall Company. This Snow confirmed by chemical testing. All that remained was to calculate the cholera death rates for the houses supplied by the two water companies. The rate for the Lambeth Company was 37 deaths per 10,000 houses, compared to a rate of 315 per 10,000 houses for the Southwark and Vauxhall Company.

In this chapter, we will discuss how the Snow and Goldberger stories both illustrate the logic of scientific thinking. Without an understanding of this logic, the things scientists do can seem mysterious, odd, or downright ridiculous. In a society dominated by the achievements of basic and applied science, it is important for the public to have some understanding of why scientists do what they do. More important, given the particular concerns of this book, part of the widespread confusion surrounding the field of psychology is traceable to a general misunderstanding of scientific logic.

COMPARISON, CONTROL, AND MANIPULATION

Although many large volumes have been written on the subject of scientific methodology, it is simply not necessary for the layperson, who may never actually carry out an experiment, to become familiar with all the details and intricacies of experimental design. The most important characteristics of scientific thinking are actually quite easy to grasp. Scientific thinking is based on the ideas of comparison, control, and manipulation. To achieve a more fundamental understanding of a phenomenon, a scientist compares conditions in the world. Without this comparison, we are left with isolated instances of observations, and the interpretation of these isolated observations is highly ambiguous, as we saw in Chapter 4.

By comparing data patterns under different conditions, scientists rule out certain explanations and confirm others. They construct their comparisons so that the outcome will eliminate a number of alternative theories that may have been advanced as explanations. That is, they try to weed out the maximum number of incorrect explanations. They do this either by directly controlling the experimental situation or by observing the kinds of naturally occurring situations that allow them to test alternative explanations.

The latter situation was illustrated quite well in the cholera example. Snow did not simply pick any two water companies. He was aware that water companies might supply different geographic localities that had vastly different health-related socioeconomic characteristics. Merely observing the frequency of cholera in the various localities would leave many alternative explanations of any observed differences in cholera incidence. Highly cognizant that science advances by eliminating possible explanations (recall our discussion of falsifiability in Chapter 2), Snow looked for and found a comparison that would eliminate a large class of explanations based on health-related correlates of socioeconomic status.

Snow was fortunate to find a naturally occurring situation that allowed him to eliminate alternative explanations. But it would be absurd for scientists to sit around waiting for circumstances like Snow's to occur. Instead, most scientists try to restructure the world in ways that will differentiate alternative hypotheses. To do this, they must manipulate the variable believed to be the cause (contamination of the water supply, in Snow's case) and observe whether a differential effect (cholera incidence, for Snow) occurs while they keep all other relevant variables constant.

Thus the best experimental design is achieved when the scientist can manipulate the variable of interest and control all the other extraneous variables affecting the situation. Note that Snow did not do this. He was not able to manipulate the degree of water contamination himself but found a situation in which the contamination varied and in which other variables, mainly those having to do with socioeconomic status, were—by lucky chance—controlled. However, this type of naturally occurring situation is not only less common but also less powerful than direct experimental manipulation.

As an example, we need only consider Snow's two groups of subjects: those supplied by the Lambeth Company and those supplied by the Southwark and Vauxhall Company. The mixed nature of the water supply system in that neighborhood probably ensured that the two groups would be of roughly equal social status. However, the drawback of the type of research design used by Snow is that the subjects themselves determined which group they would be in. They did this by signing up with one or the other of the two water companies years before. We must consider why some people signed up with one company and some with another. Did one company offer better rates? Did one advertise the medicinal properties of its water? We do not know. The critical question is: Might people who respond to one or another of the advertised properties of the product differ in other, health-related ways? The answer to this question has to be "It is a possibility."

A design such as Snow's cannot rule out the possibility of spurious correlates more subtle than those that are obviously associated with socioeconomic status. This is precisely the reason that scientists prefer direct manipulation of the variables they are interested in. When manipulation is combined with a procedure known as *random assignment* (in which the subjects themselves do not determine which experimental condition they will be in but, instead, are randomly assigned to one of the experimental groups), scientists can rule out alternative explanations of data patterns that depend on the particular characteristics of the subjects. This is not to say that Snow's approach was meritless. But scientists prefer to manipulate the experimental variables more directly because direct manipulation generates stronger inferences.

Joseph Goldberger did directly manipulate the variables he hypothesized to be the causes of the particular phenomenon he was studying (pellagra). Although Goldberger observed and recorded variables that were correlated with pellagra, he also directly manipulated two other variables in his series of studies. Recall that he induced pellagra in a group of prisoners given a low-protein diet and also failed to induce it in a group of volunteers, including himself and his wife, who ingested the excrement of pellagra victims. Thus Goldberger went beyond observing naturally occurring correlations and created a special set of circumstances designed to yield data that would allow a stronger inference by ruling out a wider set of alternative explanations than Snow's did. Although we could continue to concoct alternative explanations even after observing pellagra being induced by a special diet but not by contaminated excretions, these alternatives would be increasingly far fetched. This is precisely the reason why scientists attempt to manipulate a variable and to hold all other variables constant: in order to eliminate alternative explanations.

The Case of Clever Hans, the Wonder Horse

The necessity of eliminating alternative explanations of a phenomenon by the use of experimental control is well illustrated by a story that is famous in the annals of behavioral science: that of Clever Hans, the mathematical horse. More than 80 years ago, a German schoolteacher presented to the public a horse, Clever Hans, that supposedly knew how to solve mathematical problems. Hans would be presented with addition, subtraction, and multiplication problems by his trainer and would tap out the answer to the problems with his hoof. The horse's responses were astoundingly accurate.

Many people were amazed and puzzled by Clever Hans's performance. Was he really demonstrating an ability thus far unknown in his species? Imagine what the public must have thought. Compelling testimonials to Hans's unique ability frequently appeared in the German press. One Berlin newspaper reporter wrote that "this thinking horse is going to give men of science a great deal to think about for a long time to come" (Fernald, 1984, p. 30), a prediction that turned out to be correct, though not quite in the way the reporter expected. A group of "experts" observed Hans and attested to his abilities. Everyone was baffled. And bafflement was bound to remain as long as the phenomenon was observed merely in isolation and as long as no *controlled* observations were carried out. The mystery was soon dispelled, however, when a psychologist, Oskar Pfungst, undertook systematic studies of the horse's ability.

In the best traditions of experimental design, Pfungst systematically manipulated the conditions under which the animal performed, thus creating "artificial" situations (see Chapter 7) that would allow alternative explanations of the horse's performance to be tested. After much careful testing, Pfungst found that the horse did have a special ability, but it was not a mathematical one. In fact, the horse was closer to being a behavioral scientist than a mathematician. You see, Hans was a very careful observer of human behavior. As it was tapping out its answer, it would watch the head of the trainer or other questioner. As Hans approached the answer, the trainer would involuntarily tilt his head slightly, and Hans would stop. Pfungst found that the horse was extremely sensitive to visual cues. It could detect extremely small head movements. Pfungst tested the horse by having the problems presented in such a way that the presenter did not know the answer to the problem or by having the trainer present the problem away from the horse's view. The animal lost its "mathematical abilities" when the questioner did not know the answer or when the trainer was out of view.

The case of Clever Hans is a good context in which to illustrate the importance of carefully distinguishing between the *occurrence* of a phenomenon and the *explanation* of a phenomenon. That the horse tapped out the correct answers to mathematical problems presented by the trainer is not in dispute. The trainer was not lying. Many observers attested to the fact that the horse actually *did* tap out the correct answers to mathematical problems presented by the trainer. It is in the next step that the problem arises: making the inference that the horse was tapping out the correct answers *because* the horse had mathematical abilities. Inferring that the horse has mathematical abilities is a *hypothesized explanation* for the phenomenon. It does not follow *logically,* from the fact that the horse tapped out the correct answers to mathematical problems, that the horse had mathematical abilities. Positing that the horse had mathematical abilities was only one of many possible explanations of the horse's performance.

Before the intervention of Pfungst, the "experts" who looked at the horse had made this fundamental error: they had not seen that there might be *alternative explanations* for the horse's performance. They thought that, once they had observed that the trainer was not lying and that the horse actually did tap out the correct answers to mathematical problems, it necessarily followed that the horse had mathematical abilities. Pfungst was thinking more scientifically and realized that that was only one of many possible explanations of the horse's performance, and that it was necessary to set up controlled conditions in order to differentiate alternative explanations. By having the horse answer questions posed by the trainer from behind a screen, Pfungst set up conditions in which he would be able to differentiate two possible explanations: that the horse had mathematical abilities or that the horse was responding to visual cues. If the horse actually had such abilities, putting the trainer behind a screen should make no difference in its performance. On the other hand, if the horse was responding to visual cues, then putting the trainer behind a screen should disrupt its performance. When the latter happened, Pfungst was able to rule out the hypothesis that the horse had mathematical abilities.

Clever Hans in the 1990s: An Unfolding Tragedy

The Clever Hans story is often used in methodology classes to teach the important principle of the necessity of experimental control. Unfortunately not only is the *general* import of the Clever Hans case sometimes lost, but even its *direct* lesson has apparently not been learned. Throughout the early 1990s, researchers the world over watched in horrified anticipation—almost as if observing cars crash in slow motion—while a modern Clever Hans case unfolded before their eyes and had tragic consequences.

Autism is a severe developmental disability characterized by impairment in reciprocal social interaction, seriously delayed and often qualitatively abnormal language development, and a restricted repertoire of activities and interests (Frith, 1989, 1993). The extremely noncommunicative nature of many autistic children, who may be normal in physical appearance, makes the disorder a particularly difficult one for parents to accept. It is therefore not hard to imagine the excitement of parents of autistic children when, in the late 1980s and early 1990s, they heard of a technique coming out of Australia that enabled autistic children who had previously been totally nonverbal to communicate. This technique for unlocking communicative capacity in nonverbal autistic individuals is called *facilitated com-*

munication, and it was uncritically trumpeted in such highly visible media outlets as *60 Minutes, Parade* magazine, and the *Washington Post* (see Dillon, 1993; Mulick, Jacobson, & Kobe, 1993; Prior & Cummins, 1992; Shane, 1993). The claim was made that autistic individuals and other children with developmental disabilities who had previously been nonverbal had typed highly literate messages on a keyboard when their hands and arms had been supported over the typewriter by a sympathetic "facilitator." Not surprisingly, these startlingly verbal performances on the part of autistic children who had previously shown very limited linguistic behavior spawned incredible hopes among frustrated parents of autistic children. It was also claimed that the technique worked for severely mentally retarded individuals who were nonverbal.

While the excitement of the parents is easy to understand, the credulousness of many professionals involved is not so easy to accept. Unfortunately, claims for the efficacy of facilitated communication were disseminated to hopeful parents by many media outlets before any controlled studies had been conducted. Had the professionals involved had minimal training in the principles of experimental control, they should have immediately recognized the parallel to the Clever Hans case. The "facilitator," almost always a sympathetic individual who was genuinely concerned that the child succeed, had numerous opportunities to consciously or unconsciously direct the child's hand to the vicinity of keys on the keyboard. That cuing by the facilitator was occurring should also have been suggested by the additional observation that sometimes the children typed out complicated messages while not even looking at the keyboard! Additionally, highly literate English prose was produced by children who had not been exposed to the alphabet.

A number of controlled studies have been reported that have tested the claims of facilitated communication by using appropriate experimental controls. Each study has unequivocally demonstrated the same thing: the autistic child's performance depended on tactile cuing by the facilitator (Cummins & Prior, 1992; Hudson, Melita, & Arnold, 1993; Levine, Shane, & Wharton, 1994; Prior & Cummins, 1992; Shane, 1993; Smith & Belcher, 1993; Wheeler, Jacobson, Paglieri, & Schwartz, 1993). The controls used in several of the studies resembled those of the classic Clever Hans case. A controlled situation was set up in which both the child and the facilitator were presented with a drawing of an object but in which they could not see each other's drawing. When both child and facilitator were looking at the same drawing, the child typed the correct name of the drawing. However, when the child and the facilitator were shown *different* drawings, the child typed the name of the *facilitator's* drawing, not the one at which the child was looking. Thus the responses were determined by the facilitator rather than the child. The conclusion that facilitated communication was a Clever Hans phenomenon and not a breakthrough therapeutic technique brought no joy to the investigators involved in conducting the studies. Psychologists Robert Cummins and Margot Prior (1992) concluded, "It is evident that some assistants through the use either of tactile/visual cues or through the actual imposition of movement, manipulate their clients' responses. This is the unpalatable and unavoidable conclusion drawn from the available empirical data" (p. 240).

But this sad story gets even worse. At some centers where facilitated communication is used, there have been outbreaks of reported sexual abuse by parents during "facilitated" sessions on the keyboard (Dillon, 1993; Seligmann & Chideya, 1992). Children have been removed from their parents' homes, only to be returned when the charges of abuse proved to be groundless: "Several court cases, most notably over criminal charges of abuse, have arisen from facilitated accusations. Court-ordered validations have found that the facilitator was unduly influencing the communications, and charges were subsequently dropped" (Smith & Belcher, 1993, p. 176). Hudson et al. (1993) reported a test of one 29-year-old female who lived at home with her parents and had been considered severely to profoundly mentally retarded. It was alleged that the woman, during a facilitated session, had made allegations of sexual assault by a significant person in her life. In the context of the legal proceedings, Hudson et al. (1993) tested the woman's communicative abilities in a facilitated session by using the logic that Pfungst had used in the Clever Hans case. Questions were read to the subject and to her facilitator through separate earphones. When the same question was read to the subject and to the facilitator, the subject answered correctly each time. When a different question was read to the subject and to the facilitator, the subject never answered correctly and 40 percent of the time gave the answer to the question that the *facilitator* had been asked.

As *Newsweek* (September 21, 1992) reported, "Unsubstantiated claims have cast a wide net of damage. Parents have had children taken away and put in temporary protective custody, faced the scorn of neighbors, borne the expense of hiring lawyers—only to receive belated letters of apology from schools months later. Teachers and aides have had careers ruined simply by the hint of scandal" (Seligmann & Chideya, 1992, p. 75). Competent professional opinion is finally beginning to be heard above the media din as it is increasingly recognized that treatments that lack empirical foundation are not benignly neutral ("Oh, well, it might work, and so what if it doesn't?"). The implementation of unproven treatments has real, concrete, societal costs. Howard Shane (1993), the director of the Communication Enhancement Center at Boston's Children's Hospital, said flatly that, "By all scientifically based indications, facilitated communication does not work. . . . Because of the potential harm inflicted by this method, it is hard to justify its continued use. For example, wrongful allegations of sexual abuse have been made through facilitated communication, inappropriate educational placements have been requested, and considerable training and research dollars have been appropriated to implement a technique that is ineffective" (p. 11). James Mulick (see Mulick, Jacobson, & Kobe, 1993), professor of pediatrics and psychology at Ohio State University, was even more specific in detailing the costs of this educational fad:

> The promotion of FC [facilitated communication] diverts effort and funding from more plausible long-term strategies that have empirical support. The theoretical confusion gratuitously injected into the research and professional literature by FC proponents is damaging to accumulation of knowledge about handicapping conditions and their causes and detracts from the credibility of sincere efforts to integrate findings about abnormal development. The popular confusion

of FC with other nonspeech communication systems that have been used successfully with disabled people will discourage public support. . . . The professional and scientific communities, as well as government human service and regulatory agencies, should not allow people with handicaps and their families to be used by a few professors and therapists who stoke their hopes with empty promises, regardless of their sincerity. . . . Such practices should always be called into question. In our experience, people with handicaps can be valued members of their families and communities without resorting to appeals to miracle cures. There is effective help available, help that makes scientific sense. The genuine efforts of scientifically trained and compassionate professionals surpass all fad treatments, and always will. Advances in treatment and understanding come at the price of rigorous training, dedication to accuracy and scientific standards, and objective verification of all treatment claims. (pp. 278–279)

Here we have another example of the harm done by reliance on testimonial evidence and the fallacy of the idea that therapeutic fads and pseudoscience do no harm (see Chapter 4). We can also see that there is simply no substitute for the control and manipulation of the experimental method when we want to explain behavior.

Prying Variables Apart: Special Conditions

The Goldberger example illustrates a very important lesson that can greatly aid in dispelling some misconceptions about the scientific process, particularly as it is applied in psychology. The occurrence of any event in the world is often correlated with many other factors. In order to separate, to pry apart, the causal influence of many simultaneously occurring events, we must create situations that will never occur in the ordinary world. Scientific experimentation breaks apart the natural correlations in the world to isolate the influence of a single variable.

Psychologists operate in exactly the same manner: by isolating variables via manipulation and control. For example, cognitive psychologists interested in the reading process have studied the factors that make word perception easier or more difficult. Not surprisingly, they have found that longer words are more difficult to recognize than short words. At first glance, we might think that the effect of word length would be easy to measure: simply create two sets of words, one long and one short, and measure the difference in reader recognition speed between the two. Unfortunately it is not that easy. Long words also tend to be less frequent in language, and frequency also affects perception. Thus any difference between long and short words may be due to length, frequency, or a combination of effects. In order to see whether word length affects perception independently of frequency, researchers must construct special word sets in which length and frequency do not vary together.

Similarly Goldberger was able to make a strong inference about causation because he set up a special set of conditions that does not occur naturally. (Considering that one manipulation involved the ingestion of bodily discharges, this is putting it mildly.) Recall that Oskar Pfungst had to set up some special conditions for testing Clever Hans, including trials in which the questioner did not know the answer. Dozens of people who merely observed the horse answer questions under normal conditions (in which the questioner knew the answer) never detected how the horse was accomplishing its feat. Instead, they came to the erroneous conclusion that the horse had true mathematical knowledge.

In short, it is often necessary for scientists to create special conditions that will test a particular theory about a phenomenon. Merely observing the event in its natural state is rarely sufficient. People observed falling and moving objects for centuries without arriving at accurate principles and laws about motion and gravity. Truly explanatory laws of motion were not derived until Galileo and other scientists set up some rather artificial conditions for the observation of the behavior of moving objects. Smooth bronze balls were rarely seen rolling down smooth inclined planes. Lots of motion occurred in the world, but it was rarely of this type. However, it was just such an unnatural situation, and others like it, that led to our first truly explanatory laws of motion and gravity. Speaking of laws of motion, didn't you take a little quiz earlier in this chapter?

Intuitive Physics

Actually the three questions posed at the beginning of this chapter were derived from the work of Michael McCloskey, a psychologist at Johns Hopkins University. McCloskey (1983) has studied what he calls "intuitive physics," that is, people's beliefs about the motion of objects. Interestingly, these beliefs are often at striking variance from how moving objects actually behave.

For example, in the first problem, once the string on the circling ball is cut, the ball will fly in a straight line at a 90-degree angle to the string (tangent to the circle). McCloskey found that one third of the college students who were given this problem thought, incorrectly, that the ball would fly in a curved trajectory. About half of McCloskey's subjects, when given problems similar to the bomber pilot example, thought that the bomb should be dropped directly over the target, thus displaying a lack of understanding of the role of an object's initial motion in determining its trajectory. The bomb should actually be dropped five miles before the plane reaches the target. The subjects' errors were not caused by the imaginary nature of the problem. When asked to walk across a room and, while moving, drop a golf ball on a target on the floor, the performance of more than half the subjects indicated they did not know that the ball would move forward as it fell. Finally, many people are not aware that the bullet fired from the rifle will hit the ground at the same time as a bullet dropped from the same height.

You can assess your own performance on this little quiz. Chances are that you missed at least one if you have not had a physics course recently. "Physics course!" you might protest. "Of course I haven't had a physics class recently. This quiz is unfair!" But hold on a second. Why should you need a physics course? You have seen literally hundreds of falling objects in your lifetime. You have seen them fall under *naturally* occurring conditions. Moving objects surround you every day, and you are seeing them in their "real-life" state. You certainly cannot claim that you have not experienced moving and falling objects. Granted, you have never seen anything quite like the bullet example. But most of us have seen children let go of whirling objects, and many of us have seen objects fall out of planes. And besides, it seems a little lame to protest that you have not seen these exact situations. Given your years of experience with moving and falling objects, why can't you accurately predict what will happen in a situation only slightly out of the ordinary?

McCloskey's work demonstrates something of fundamental importance to understanding why scientists behave as they do. Despite extensive experience with moving and falling objects, people's intuitive theories of motion are remarkably inaccurate. In one of their papers, McCloskey and his colleagues (Caramazza, McCloskey, & Green, 1981) concluded flatly, "The results we have reported lead to the conclusion that simple real-world experience with moving objects does not lead naturally to the abstraction of principles that are consistent with the formal laws of motion" (p. 121).

It is critical to understand that the layperson's beliefs are inaccurate precisely because his or her observations are "natural," rather than controlled in the manner of the scientist's. Thus, if you missed a question on the little quiz, don't feel ignorant or inadequate. Simply remember that some of the world's greatest minds observed falling objects for centuries without formulating a physics of motion any more accurate than that of the average high-school sophomore. In an article in *Scientific American*, McCloskey (1983) observed that many of his subjects had held an incorrect theory about motion that was very similar to one held to be true some three centuries before Newton. McCloskey's modern subjects and medieval philosophers had something in common: both groups had had much exposure to the motion of objects in the ordinary world, but none under the artificially created conditions of scientific manipulation, control, and comparison.

Even large amounts of "personal experience" are insufficient to prevent misconceptions about the nature of physical motion. Writing about the history of the development of knowledge about banked turns in aircraft, pilot William Langewiesche (1993) noted that pilots in the early part of the twentieth century resisted the use of instrumentation such as gyroscopes because they believed in "instinctive balance." However, these "instincts" failed to uncover the existence of unfelt banks in clouds. Enough crashes and near crashes finally taught pilots a sobering lesson: No amount of "instinct" would substitute for knowledge of the actual physics of flight (Langewiesche, 1993).

Intuitive Psychology

Philosopher Paul Churchland (1984) argued that, if our intuitive (or "folk") theories about objects in motion are inaccurate, it is hard to believe that our folk theories in the more complex domain of human behavior could be correct:

> Our early folk theories of motion were profoundly confused, and were eventually displaced entirely by more sophisticated theories. Our early folk theories of the structure and activity of the heavens were wildly off the mark, and survive only as historical lessons in how wrong we can be. Our folk theories of the nature of fire, and the nature of life, were similarly cockeyed. And one could go on, since the vast majority of our past folk conceptions have been similarly exploded.

. . . But the phenomenon of conscious intelligence is surely a more complex and difficult phenomenon than any of those just listed. So far as accurate understanding is concerned, it would be a miracle if we had got that one right the very first time, when we fell down so badly on all the others. (p. 46)

When we look at the actual literature on people's theories of behavior, we find that Churchland's speculation turns out to be right. In Chapter 1 we illustrated that a number of "commonsense" (or "folk") beliefs about human behavior are wrong. Many more examples are contained in Alfie Kohn's book *You Know What They Say . . . : The Truth About Popular Beliefs* (1990). Although written for the general public, Kohn's book does rely on evidence in the peer-reviewed scientific literature for its conclusions. Many of the "popular beliefs" discussed in the book concern human behavior. For example, it turns out that there is no evidence that highly religious people are more altruistic than less religious people (Paloutzian, 1983; Smith, Wheeler, & Diener, 1975). Many studies have indicated that there is no simple relationship between degree of religiosity and the tendency to engage in charitable acts, to aid other people in distress, and to abstain from cheating other people (Paloutzian, 1983). Indeed, within a large research literature, there is no indication at all that people high in religiosity are any more likely to be charitable or to help their fellows than are people who identify themselves as atheists (Paloutzian, 1983).

The list of popular beliefs that are incorrect is long. For example, many people believe that a full moon affects human behavior. It doesn't (see Byrnes & Kelly, 1992; Coates, Jehle, & Cottington, 1989; Culver, Rotton, & Kelly, 1988; Rotton & Kelly, 1985). Some people believe that "opposites attract." They don't (see Buss, 1985; Buss & Barnes, 1986; Murstein, 1980). Some people believe that "familiarity breeds contempt." It doesn't (see Bornstein, 1989). Some people believe that blind people are blessed with supersensitive hearing. They're not (see Niemeyer & Starlinger, 1981; Stankov & Spilsbury, 1978). And the list goes on and on and on. Consult Kohn's (1990) book for a readable account of a couple of dozen popular beliefs about behavior that are not supported by empirical evidence.

The many inadequacies in people's intuitive theories of behavior illustrate why we need the controlled experimentation of psychology: so that we can progress beyond our flat-earth conceptions of human behavior to a more accurate scientific conceptualization.

Chapter 7

"BUT IT'S NOT REAL LIFE!"
The "Artificiality" Criticism and Psychology

Having covered the basics of experimental logic in the previous two chapters, we are now in a position to consider some often-heard criticisms of the field of psychology. In the course of discussing these criticisms we shall further develop our understanding of the scientific method. In particular, we shall discuss at length the criticism that scientific experiments are useless because they are "artificial" and not like "real life." Understanding why this is not a valid criticism will aid in thinking straight about psychology because the criticism is often aimed at psychological experimentation.

From our discussion in Chapter 6, we should already have a good idea of why this criticism is invalid. As was illustrated in that chapter, the artificiality of scientific experimentation is not a weakness but is actually the very thing that gives the scientific method its unique power to yield explanations about the nature of the world. Contrary to common belief, the artificiality of scientific experiments is not an accidental oversight. It is intentionally sought. Scientists *deliberately* set up conditions that are unlike those that occur naturally because this is the only way to separate the many inherently correlated variables that determine events in the world.

Sometimes the necessary conditions already exist naturally, as in the example of Snow and cholera. More often, this is not the case. The scientist must manipulate events in new and sometimes strange ways, as in the example of Goldberger and pellagra. In many instances these manipulations cannot be accomplished in natural environments, and the scientist finds it necessary to bring the phenomenon into the laboratory, where more precise control is possible. Early studies of gravity and motion used specially constructed objects that were designed for no other reason than to create a set of special conditions for the observation of moving objects. It is often necessary to create increasingly "unreal" and extreme conditions in order to analyze a phenomenon.

Indeed, some phenomena would be completely impossible to discover if scientists were restricted totally to observing "natural" conditions. Physicists probing the most fundamental characteristics of matter build gigantic mile-long accelera-

91

tors that induce collisions between elementary particles. Some of the by-products of these collisions are new particles that exist for less than a billionth of a second. The properties of these new particles, however, have implications for theories of atomic structure. Many of these new particles would not ordinarily exist on earth, and even if they did, there certainly would be no chance of observing them "naturally." Yet few people doubt that this is how physicists should conduct their research, that probing nature in unusual and sometimes bizarre ways is a legitimate means of coming to a deeper understanding of the universe. Somehow, though, practices that seem reasonable for physicists are often viewed as invalid when used by psychologists.

Although the actions of all scientists are misunderstood when the public fails to realize the importance of creating special conditions in the laboratory, the work of psychologists is probably most subject to this type of misunderstanding. Many psychologists who have presented experimental evidence on behavior to an audience of laypersons have heard the lament, "But it's not real life!" Further discussion of this criticism usually exposes the audience's belief that knowledge cannot be obtained unless "natural conditions" are studied and that the laboratory studies of psychology are "strange" and probably indicate that it is an inadequate science.

It is not commonly recognized that many of the techniques used by the psychologist that are viewed as strange by the public are in no way unique to psychology; instead, they are manifestations of the scientific method as applied to behavior (Banaji & Crowder, 1989). Similar bizarre ways of acquiring knowledge about the world can be observed in the investigations conducted by every science. Psychology receives the worst of both worlds. The same ignorance of the scientific method that supports the belief that psychology just can't be a science leads to the denigration of psychologists when they, like all other scientists, create the special conditions necessary to uncover more powerful and precise explanations of their phenomena.

Restriction to "real-life" situations would prevent us from discovering many things. For example, biofeedback techniques are now used in a variety of areas such as migraine and tension headache control, hypertension treatment, and relaxation training (Miller, 1985a). These techniques developed out of research indicating that humans could learn to partially control their internal physiological processes if they could monitor the ongoing processes via visual or auditory feedback. Of course, since humans are not equipped to monitor their physiological functions via external feedback, the ability to control such processes does not become apparent except under special laboratory conditions. Observations under "natural conditions" would never uncover it (Henshel, 1980).

The "Random-Sample" Confusion

Sometimes, however, the "It's not real life" complaint arises from a different type of confusion about the purposes of psychological experimentation, one that is actually quite understandable. Through media exposure many people are familiar with survey research, particularly in the form of election and public opinion polling. There is now a growing awareness of some of the important characteristics of election polling. In particular, the media have given more attention to the importance of a random, or representative, sample to the accuracy of election polls. This attention has led many people to believe, mistakenly, that random samples and representative conditions are an essential requirement of all psychological investigations. Since psychological research seldom uses random samples of subjects, the application of the random-sample criterion by the layperson seems to undermine most psychological investigations and to reinforce the criticism that the research is invalid because it doesn't reflect real life.

Again, a moment's thought about the nature of other sciences should go a long way toward exposing the fallaciousness of this belief. Chemists make no attempt to draw random samples of compounds. Biologists do not experiment on random samples of cells or organisms. The rats and monkeys in a medical research facility are hardly representative of their species. The organisms in such laboratories are often studied under conditions that are vastly different from their natural environments. Indeed, these conditions are often utterly unique. Yet they yield insights that help shed great light on human biology. The same is true of most psychological investigations.

Theory-Driven Research Versus Direct Applications

Why is a random sample of subjects important in survey research on voter preferences but of less importance in most research in psychology? The answer to this question can be found in the characteristics that distinguish certain varieties of applied research from most basic research. Douglas Mook (1983, 1989), a psychologist at the University of Virginia, discussed this issue in terms of the different types of prediction that characterize different types of investigation. In many kinds of applied research the goal is to relate the results of the study directly to a particular situation. In applied research the prediction is what Mook termed "analogue"—from the study to the field—and the findings are applied directly. Election polling is an example of applied research that makes use of analogue prediction. The goal is to predict a specific behavior in a very specific setting, in this case, voting on election day. Here, where the nature of the prediction is direct, questions of the randomness of the sample and the representativeness of the conditions are important because the findings of the study are going to be applied directly.

While a growing amount of research in psychology is applied, it would be a mistake to view this class of research as typical. The vast majority of research studies in psychology (or any other science, for that matter) are conducted with a very different purpose in mind. The nature of prediction in most research is from general to specific (or "analytic" in Mook's terms), from a theory to a research situation. The findings of most research are applied only analytically, that is, indirectly through modifications in a theory that, in conjunction with other scientific laws, is then applied to some practical problem. In short, most theory-driven research seeks to test theories of psychological processes rather than to generalize the findings to a particular real-world situation.

In fact, not all theories have applied implications, and for this reason, research that focuses primarily on theory testing is often termed *basic research*. Whereas in applied research the purpose of the investigation is to go from data directly to a real-world application, basic research focuses on theory testing. However, it is probably a mistake to view the basic-versus-applied distinction solely in terms of whether a study has practical applications, because this difference often simply boils down to a matter of time. Applied findings are of use immediately. However, there is nothing so practical as a general and accurate theory. The history of science is filled with examples of theories or findings that eventually solved a host of real-world problems even though the scientists who developed the theories and/or findings did not intend to solve a specific practical problem.

Several examples of basic research which had practical implications are described in an article by Robert Crease and Nicholas Samios (1991), who work at the Brookhaven National Laboratory, a leading physics research center. They cited the case of Wilhelm Roentgen, who "explored the curious fact that a fluorescent screen near his apparatus was glowing, contrary to all expectations; he ended up discovering a whole new phenomenon of nature, which he called X rays. Within three months they had been used to examine bone fractures" (p. 82). Or consider Howard Florey, who, with a colleague, began a survey of antibacterial mechanisms: "On their list of microbes to study was penicillin, which had been discovered accidentally only a few years before but whose antibacterial properties had been neglected. Much of modern medicine is based on substances whose discovery and development were matters of . . . disinterested academic research" (p. 82).

Seymour Kety (1974) described the seemingly unrelated set of scientific findings that led up to the discovery of chlorpromazine, a drug of immense usefulness in treating schizophrenia. Kety made the point that, had a "war on schizophrenia" been launched many years ago which directed scientists to go and find a "cure" for schizophrenia, it could never have directed researchers to look at the right things:

> If scientists had decided in the middle of the last century to target research toward the treatment of schizophrenia, if they had been able to organize such a program, and if they had engaged the greatest minds, which of those crucial discoveries and pathways would they have supported as relevant to their goal? Certainly not the synthesis of phenothiazine by a chemist interested in methylene blue; nor the study of anaphylaxis in guinea pigs (which is more clearly related to asthma); nor the identification of histamine and its pharmacology (a substance that was not known to occur in the brain until many years later and whose role there is still obscure); nor the study of the role of histamine in allergy and anaphylaxis, and the search for antihistaminic drugs; nor the observations and speculations about histamines as a causative factor in surgical shock; nor the studies on the physiology of the peripheral sympathetics, or of epinephrine and its possible role in surgical shock; nor the studies on operant conditioning in animals; and not the search by an anesthesiologist for an antihistaminic-sympatholytic drug that might be useful in mitigating surgical shock. In fact, it was not until 1949, after the synthesis of phenothiazine amines in the search for better antihistaminic drugs and the use of one of them, promethazine, in the management

of surgical shock, that our hypothetical committee to Plan and Direct Research toward the Chemotherapy of Mental Illness would have found an observation that it might have recognized as relevant to its goal. (pp. xii–xiii)

In short, virtually *none* of the precursor discoveries of this treatment for schizophrenia would have been recognized as having anything to *do* with schizophrenia! Again, the most practical thing turned out to be to pursue basic research on problems that were yielding answers—regardless of the content area of the problems. Time and time again, attempts to *control* the direction of science (by trying to tell scientists to "solve" a particular practical problem) turn out to impede rather than facilitate progress. Ironically the urge to have scientists solve only "practical" problems and not bother with the "other stuff" (basic research) turns out to be wildly *im*practical and shortsighted.

A final example comes from the career of biologist Michael Ghiselin (1989). For his doctoral dissertation, Ghiselin studied a group of organisms known as *sea slugs.* He wrote, "The choice of a research problem was dictated by purely intellectual considerations" (p. 196). Ghiselin wanted to find out how these animals had evolved by studying the anatomy of their reproductive system. He wrote that, when he was a graduate student, his research was supported by the National Institutes of Health. One might imagine an "irate taxpayer" complaining that Ghiselin's research had nothing *direct* to do with health. The taxpayer would be right; Ghiselin's research had nothing direct to do with health. However, if the irate taxpayer were to draw the conclusion that medical science does not need Ghiselin's research, the taxpayer would be dead wrong. Fortunately the officials at the National Institutes of Health are not as shortsighted. Years after Ghiselin completed his dissertation, neurophysiologists found out that the perfect organism to use to study how nervous systems are "wired" (including human nervous systems) turns out to be an organism called *Aplysia*, which just turns out to be—a sea slug. Ghiselin's knowledge of these organisms helped neurophysiologists use them better, and thus, as Ghiselin noted, "There is a direct link between my pure research, and something of far more obvious applicability to practical matters. There is no way that either I or the National Institutes of Health could have planned it that way" (p. 197). And neither could have the irate taxpayer, who might have decided that Ghiselin's research was "not practical" and therefore shouldn't be funded. This shortsighted misunderstanding of the importance of basic research is, unfortunately, widespread in our society.

In short, we must recognize that, while some research is designed to predict events directly in a specific environmental situation, much scientific research is basic research designed to test theory. Researchers who conduct these two distinct types of investigation have completely different answers to the question: How do these findings apply to real life? The former answers, "Directly, provided that there is a reasonably close relationship between the experimental situation and the one to which the findings are to be applied." Thus questions of the random sampling of subjects and the representativeness of the experimental situation are relevant to the applicability of the results. However, the investigator in a theory-testing study answers that his or her findings do not apply directly to real life, and that the reason for conducting the study is not to produce findings that would be applicable to some specific environmental situation. Therefore this scientist is not concerned with questions of how similar the subjects of the study are to some other group or whether the experimental situation mirrors some real-life environment. Does this mean, then, that these findings have no implications in the real world? No. These findings apply directly, not to a particular situation, but to a theory. The theory may, at some later date, in conjunction with other scientific laws, be applied to a particular problem.

This type of indirect application through theory has become quite common in some areas of psychology, as Harvard psychologist William Estes (1979) made clear in his discussion of engineering psychology:

> At least within some restricted domains, the experimental psychologists have indeed been able to demonstrate that the gap between the laboratory and the world of everyday affairs can be bridged with some success. Further, the bridging has been done—not as some would have it by modifying laboratory situations in the direction of "ecological validity" (that is, to constitute simple-minded analogies of everyday life situations), but rather by showing that laws and models developed in the laboratory can be applied elsewhere once new boundary conditions are taken into account. This procedure is so closely analogous to the time-tested relationship between physical science and engineering that one of the resulting subdisciplines has come to be known as engineering psychology. (p. 629)

Two Examples: Night Vision and Language Development

Douglas Mook (1983) discussed two examples that illustrate the ideas of theory-testing experimentation and the nature of indirect application in psychology. In the 1930s Selig Hecht published a series of studies of visual sensitivity in the *Handbook of General Experimental Psychology* (Murchison, 1934). These studies concerned the phenomenon of dark adaptation. You have probably experienced the temporary blindness that occurred when you walked into a darkened movie theater. As you waited in your seat, however, you probably noticed that chairs, people, and other objects began to become visible. If you kept concentrating on this phenomenon, you may have been able to observe the visibility of objects in the theater continue to increase for several minutes.

This phenomenon is called *dark adaptation,* and it occurs in two phases. The two phases are composed of a rather quick but fairly small increase in visual sensitivity on entering a darkened room, followed by a delayed but much larger increase in sensitivity. Hecht linked this two-part adaptation curve to the two different types of receptor cells in the retina of the eye. The cones are receptor cells that are densely packed in the center of the fovea (the part of the retina where incoming light is focused) and are very sensitive to red light. The rods are located outside the foveal area, are much less densely packed, and are not very sensitive to red light. Hecht used these facts to establish that the initial phase of dark adaptation (a small, rapid increase in visual sensitivity) is due to the adaptation of the cones and that the second phase (a larger increase in sensitivity taking place over a longer period of time) is due to rod adaptation.

Mook (1983) urged us to consider the complete "unnaturalness" of Hecht's experimental situation. Subjects (who were not randomly chosen) were in a dark room responding, "Yes, I see it" or "No, I don't," depending on whether or not they detected a tiny red light that was flashed at them. We normally do not respond to little red lights in this way in everyday life. Hecht, however, was not concerned about generalizing his findings to individuals in dark rooms responding "yes" or "no" to tiny red lights, so whether such a situation ever actually occurs is irrelevant. Hecht was interested in establishing facts and testing theories about the basic processes that characterize the visual system, such as dark adaptation. He was not concerned about whether his experimental situation was realistic but with whether it adequately isolated the specific visual process he was interested in studying.

Hecht's findings gain generalizability not through the nature of the setting in which they occur, but by their ability to establish a theory of basic visual processes that are implicated in many tasks. His research uncovered the basic functional relationships that characterize the human visual system, precisely because his situation was controlled and "artificial." If the theoretical model for the relationships is correct, then it should have wide applicability and should account for performance in a variety of situations much different from the one within which it was derived. In other words, Hecht's findings have indirect applications through their influence on theory. For example, the basic understanding of the visual system promoted by Hecht's findings has helped in the treatment of night blindness and in the problem of reading X rays. And more dramatically, while awaiting the night raids of Hitler's bombers during the blitz in World War II, the British fighter pilots who were to engage the German planes wore red goggles (this way, the rods—not being sensitive to red light—would stay dark-adapted; see Mook, 1982). The leap from subjects judging little red dots to the dangerous sky over London was made through theory, not through a redesign of Hecht's lab to resemble a Spitfire airplane.

A second example discussed by Mook (1983) will illustrate some other aspects of theory-testing experimentation. For several decades some influential psychological theories posited that children learned the grammatical patterns of speech through direct and indirect adult guidance. That is, people believed that parents corrected ungrammatical utterances and reinforced grammatical ones. This is how most people think children learn grammatical speech. However, when psychologists began investigating the question, they found that the theory's predictions were not confirmed. They found that correct grammatical form has very little relation to the nature of the reinforcement children receive in response to their speech. Instead, the reward contingencies seem to revolve almost entirely around accuracy of content. This is a case of a disconfirmed theoretical prediction. The approval elicited by the children's utterances was not strongly related to their grammar. Therefore, the mechanism of parental approval cannot be entirely responsible for the developmental increase in this language capability.

Now, we could ask questions about the representativeness of the group of children on which this conclusion was based. But it is important to realize the implications of the answer to this question. There is no doubt that the subjects in these language studies were not a random sample of American children. They were a small group of children from a few highly educated families in Boston. It is not unreasonable to wonder whether the same results would be obtained from children in different socioeconomic environments, in different geographic regions, or in different language groups. However, asking these questions in no way invalidates the results obtained in Boston. Further work with different types of samples will most certainly refine the conclusions of the Boston studies, but one basic theoretical implication will remain regardless of the outcome of subsequent studies. The Boston work demonstrated that the universal theory that children's speech becomes increasingly grammatical because of parental approval is false.

It is true that, in the absence of further work with other samples, there remain two possibilities between which we cannot choose. The idea of grammatical development via parental conditioning may be universally invalid. On the other hand, further work may disclose that some degree of parental shaping is involved in some languages or for children in certain types of environments. If the latter is the case, we may retain a parental approval theory in which shaping takes place only in certain types of environments. This theory will undoubtedly require further empirical work that will accurately specify the environmental factors that make the approval mechanism effective, and it is important to note that comparisons with the Boston data will be critical in determining these specific environmental factors. Even if the Boston data patterns are not obtained in tests of other groups of children, we would never have been aware of the importance of environmental variables without the Boston study.

People sometimes incorrectly attempt to undermine data with an observation such as, "Yes, but maybe this result only holds in Boston." They often fail to realize that the researcher's proper response to this statement is not "My God! Maybe it only holds in Boston!" but is, instead, "If the findings don't hold up outside Boston, it will be interesting to track down the reasons why, and perhaps in tracking them down, we will be led to a better theory of language development."

The point is that the question being raised concerns the generality of a theory and therefore is manifestly an empirical question. It calls for more data, not for the abandonment of data that have already been collected. The Boston findings were not collected to be specifically applied to a nursery in Topeka, Kansas, but to test a general theory of language learning. Contrary findings in Topeka would not render the Boston results useless; rather, they would help to elaborate a theory tested in both settings. The failure of a theory in a particular experimental environment often leads to important modifications in the theory that, in the long run, make it more powerful. While cases of premature overgeneralization do occur in psychology, they are tempered by the fact that when an overgeneralization is uncovered, it often leads to fruitful theoretical adjustments.

Applications of Psychological Theory

Once we understand that the purpose of most research is to develop theory rather than to predict events in a specific environment and that the findings of most research are applied indirectly, through theory, rather than directly in a specific environmental situation, we can legitimately ask how much application through theory has been accomplished in psychology. That is, have psychology's theories been put to the test of generality? Have they been shown to apply across a variety of domains, or alternatively, have they been elaborated through contrasting findings in different domains, as in our Boston–Topeka example. How much of this tracking down of interesting differences in study results goes on in psychology?

On this point, we must admit that the record is extremely spotty. But it is wise to keep psychology's diversity in mind here. It is true that some areas of research have made very little progress along these lines. However, other areas have quite impressive records of experimentally derived principles of considerable explanatory and predictive power (see Farley & Null, 1987; Kolb & Whishaw, 1990; Posner, 1989). For example, even applied areas like counseling psychology and psychotherapy have benefited from theory-driven basic research (Stone, 1984; Strupp, 1989).

Consider also the basic behavioral principles of classical and operant conditioning. These principles and their elaborating laws were developed almost entirely from experimentation on nonhuman subjects, such as pigeons and rats in highly artificial laboratory settings. Yet these principles have been successfully applied to a wide variety of human problems, including the treatment of autistic children, the teaching of large amounts of factual material, the treatment of alcoholism and obesity, the management of residents in state mental hospitals, and the treatment of phobias, to name just a few.

The principles from which these applications were derived were identified precisely because the laboratory experimentation allowed researchers to specify the relationships between environmental stimuli and behavior with an accuracy not possible in a natural situation, in which many behavioral relationships may be operating simultaneously. This is not to say that we do not intend to understand situations with many simultaneously occurring relationships, only that, in order to do so, we must begin by isolating individual relationships. As for the use of nonhuman subjects, in many cases theories and laws derived from their performance have provided good first approximations to human behavior. When humans were examined, their behavior often followed laws that were very similar to those derived from other animals. Findings such as these should hardly surprise anyone today, when just about every medical advance in the treatment of human illness has involved data from animal studies. The understanding of human biology and behavior has been remarkably illuminated through the study of other animals. For example, research with animals has contributed to developments in behavioral medicine, stress reduction, psychotherapy, the rehabilitation of injured and handicapped individuals, and the treatment of chronic pain (Feeney, 1987; Miller, 1985b).

Psychologists studying perceptual processes have made impressive theoretical progress, and the laws and theories they have derived have been applied to problems as diverse as radar monitoring, street lighting, and airplane cockpit design (Nickerson, 1992; Wickens, 1992). Similarly, cognitive psychologists have produced a wealth of replicable findings about how people process and remember information. Theories in this newer area of psychology have been put to fewer practical applications than those in some older research areas, but their general applicability is beginning to be tested in some industrial and educational settings

(Wickens, 1992). Much is now known about the cognitive effects of aging (Rabbitt, 1993; Salthouse, 1991, 1993, 1994), and this new knowledge has direct implications for efforts to design systems that help people to compensate for cognitive loss (Backman & Dixon, 1992; Poon, Rubin, & Wilson, 1989). Psychological studies of judgment and decision making have had implications for medical decision making (Dowie & Elstein, 1988; Eddy, 1982). An exciting new development is the increasing involvement of cognitive psychologists in the legal system, where problems of memory in information collection, evidence evaluation, and decision making present opportunities to test the applicability of cognitive theories (Diamond, 1993; Fong, Lurigio, & Stalans, 1990; Loftus, 1993; Loftus & Ketcham, 1991; Neisser, 1982). Also, since the mid-1980s, theory and practice in the teaching of reading have begun to be affected by research in cognitive psychology (Adams, 1990; Adams & Bruck, 1993; Gough et al., 1992; Joshi & Leong, 1993; Lyon, 1994; Stanovich, 1991, 1993). Finally, psychologists have played an important role in providing scientific evidence to inform the public debate about the status of children's testimony in legal proceedings (Ceci & Bruck, 1993a, 1993b) and about the validity of "recovered" memories of child abuse (Loftus, 1994).

As previously mentioned, findings in cognitive psychology have met the basic test of replicability. Many of the fundamental laws of information processing have been observed in dozens of laboratories all over the world. It is not often realized that replication goes a long way toward answering the "What if it only holds in Boston?" complaint. If a psychologist at the University of Michigan obtains a finding of true importance, similar experiments will soon be attempted at Stanford, Minnesota, Ohio State, Cambridge, Yale, Toronto, and elsewhere. Through this testing we will soon know whether the finding is due to the peculiarities of the Michigan subjects or the study's experimental setting.

Of course, not all psychological findings replicate (see Carroll & Nelson, 1993). On the contrary, replication failures do happen, and they are often more instructive than confirmations. However, in cognitive psychology, replication failures are rarely due to the peculiarities of the subjects. Instead, most are due to subtle differences in experimental stimuli and methods. By closely examining exactly what experimental conditions are necessary for the demonstration of a phenomenon, scientists come to a more precise understanding of the phenomenon and lay the foundation for a more precise theory about its occurrence.

But how can any psychological findings be applied if replication failures sometimes occur? How can applications be made if knowledge and theories are not established with certainty, when there is not complete agreement among scientists on all the details? This particular worry about the application of psychological findings is common because people do not realize that findings and theories in other sciences are regularly applied before they are firmly established. Of course, Chapter 2 should have made it clear that all scientific theories are subject to revision. If we must have absolutely certain knowledge before we can apply the results of scientific investigations, then no applications will ever take place. Applied scientists do their best to use the most accurate information available, realizing at the same time that the information is fallible.

Jacobo Varela, author of the article "Social Technology" (1977), specializes in using psychological findings to solve social problems. In the following passage, he explained that all applied scientists must work with information that is less than certain:

> We do use findings that have not been thoroughly validated and are still held to be dubious by some serious researchers. But this is not unique to social technology. Were those scientists who formulate this objection to delve deeply into other technologies and see their bases, they would be amazed to discover that the products they so confidently use are based on findings that researchers in the particular area deem to be more controversial. For example, consider the use of presumably noncombining "noble" gases in technological applications. It was shown in 1960 that such gases unexpectedly and quite easily enter into combination with other elements. However, this finding did not detract from the fact that humanity had benefited from equipment designed on a principle now known to be false. I am not making a case for the use of false findings, but merely stating that problem solving often involves taking risks if any kind of progress is to be attained. If we wait for everything to be proved, we will not solve social problems until we know everything—an unlikely occurrence. (p. 20)

Varela's point relates to an analysis published in the *American Psychologist* by University of Chicago researcher Larry Hedges (1987). The paper was titled "How Hard Is Hard Science, How Soft Is Soft Science?" Hedges's research investigated whether people might be overestimating the degree of consistency of research in the physical sciences and underestimating the degree of consistency in psychology. He developed statistical measures of the consistency of replicated results in some typical problem areas in physics and in some typical problems in psychology. Surprisingly he did not find that research results in psychology were markedly more inconsistent than those in physics:

> What is surprising is that the research results in the physical sciences are not markedly more consistent than those in the social sciences. The notion that experiments in physics produce strikingly consistent (empirically cumulative) results is not supported by the data. Similarly, the notion that experiments in the social sciences produce relatively inconsistent (empirically noncumulative) results is not supported by these data either. (p. 450)

Similarly, Harvard psychologist Robert Rosenthal (1990) demonstrated that the results of psychology research are often as reliable as results in medical science.

The "College Sophomore" Problem

The concerns of many people who question the "representativeness" of psychological findings focus on the subjects of the research rather than on the intricacies of the experimental design. However, in many areas of psychology such as the study of basic perceptual and cognitive processes, conflicting results are more often due to the latter than to the former. The basic information-processing operations, the functional organization of the brain, and the nature of the visual systems of people in Montana tend to be very similar to those of people in Florida (or Argentina, for that matter). In addition, these characteristics of humans also depend very little on whether one's parents are tinkers, tailors, or professors.

All sciences assume that certain factors are so tangential that they will make no difference in the final results. Biologists do not generally worry that the slightly different thickness of petri dishes will significantly affect the bacteria in them. These differences, of course, may have an effect—every assumption in science is tentative—but biologists must expend their effort investigating possibilities with a higher probability. Similarly, Hecht assumed that dark adaptation did not depend on a person's religious affiliation, so he did not ask his subjects whether they were Lutherans or Roman Catholics.

We are confronting here what is sometimes called the *college sophomore problem,* that is, the worry that, because college sophomores are the subjects in an extremely large number of psychological investigations, the generality of the results are in question. Psychologists are concerned about the college sophomore issue because it is a real problem in certain areas of research. Nevertheless, it is important to consider the problem in perspective and to understand that psychologists have several legitimate responses to this criticism. We have already discussed three of them. To recapitulate:

1. The college sophomore criticism does not invalidate results but is simply a call for more findings that will allow assessment of the theory's generality. Adjustments in theory necessitated by contrary data from other groups can be made accurately only because we have the college sophomore data. In the worst case of a failure to replicate, it will mean that theories developed on the basis of college sophomore data are not necessarily wrong, but merely incomplete.
2. In many areas of psychology, the college sophomore issue is simply not a problem because the processes investigated are so basic (the visual system, for example) that virtually no one would believe that their fundamental organization depends on the demographics of the subject sample.
3. Replication of findings ensures a large degree of geographic generality and, to a lesser extent, generality across socioeconomic factors, family variables, and early educational experience. As opposed to studies conducted 50 years ago, when the sample of college subjects participating would have represented an extremely elite group, research now goes on in universities that serve populations from a great variety of backgrounds.

It would be remiss, however, not to admit that the college sophomore issue is a real problem in certain areas of research in psychology. Nevertheless, psychologists are now making greater efforts to correct the problem. For example, developmental psychologists are almost inherently concerned about this issue. Each year hundreds of researchers in this area test dozens of findings and theories that were developed from studies of college subjects against data provided by subjects of different ages.

The results from subject groups of different ages do not always replicate those from college students. Developmental psychology would be starkly boring if they did. But this sizable group of psychologists is busy building an age component into psychological theories, demonstrating the importance of this factor, and ensuring that the discipline will not end up with a large theoretical superstructure founded on a thin database derived from college students.

Developmental psychologists also conduct cross-cultural research in order to assess the generality of the developmental processes uncovered by researchers working only with North American children. For example, Stevenson et al. (1985) gave a large battery of cognitive tasks to Chinese, Japanese, and American children and concluded, "The organization of cognitive abilities tapped in these tasks was very similar among the children in the three cultures" (p. 727). Other comparisons across racial and cultural groups have shown the same thing (Rowe, Vazsonyi, & Flannery, 1994).

Educational psychologists have also addressed the college sophomore problem. For example, educational psychologists, in conjunction with developmental psychologists and other educational researchers, have constructed measures of basic cognitive skills that predict future educational achievements, such as the rate of reading acquisition, with a moderate degree of accuracy. The predictive accuracy of these measures has been shown to be very similar for children of different socioeconomic status and race, and from different geographic regions and school districts.

The college sophomore problem and criticisms of representativeness are most often aimed at social psychology, which makes frequent use of college subjects in laboratory paradigms in an attempt to develop theories of social interaction, group behavior, and information processing in social situations. Here the criticism is most well taken. However, even in this area of psychology, where the criticisms would seem most applicable, evidence has indicated that the laboratory-derived relationships and theories do in fact predict behavior in a variety of other situations involving different types of individuals.

For example, several years ago, Leonard Berkowitz, a psychologist at the University of Wisconsin, demonstrated the so-called weapons effect, that is, the fact that the mere presence of a weapon in a person's environment increases the probability of an aggressive response. This finding originated in the laboratory and is a perfect example of an "unrepresentative" situation. The results were strongly criticized as misleading because they were products of a contrived situation. Yet the fact remains that the finding has been replicated in experiments using different measures of aggression, has been obtained in Europe as well as the United States, has been found to hold for children as well as adults, and has been found outside the laboratory in field studies in which the subjects did not know they were part of an experiment (Berkowitz & Donnerstein, 1982; Turner, Simons, Berkowitz, & Frodi, 1977).

Another example is the question of whether the amount of television viewing is negatively correlated with academic achievement in children. This issue has been debated in the media as concern about national educational standards has risen. It is a difficult problem to study, but researchers have uncovered a small negative relationship (Neuman, 1988; Williams, Haertel, Haertel, & Walberg, 1982). Significantly, this correlation has been observed in studies conducted in every region of the United States, as well as in Canada, England, and Japan.

Cognitive, social, and clinical psychologists have also studied various human decision-making strategies. Most of the original studies in this research area were done in laboratories, used college students as subjects, and employed extremely artificial tasks. However, the principles of decision-making behavior derived from these studies have been observed in a variety of nonlaboratory situations, including the prediction of closing stock prices by bankers, actual casino betting, the prediction of patient behavior by psychiatrists, economic markets, military intelligence analysis, the estimation of repair time by engineers, business decision making, and diagnoses by physicians (Braun & Yaniv, 1992; Davis & Holt, 1993; Dowie & Elstein, 1988; Saks & Kidd, 1980–1981; Wagenaar, 1988). These principles are also now being applied in the very practical domain of personal financial counseling (Fridson, 1993; Thaler, 1992; Willis, 1990).

These few examples illustrate that the degree of consistency and generality of the findings of psychological research is often underestimated (see Hedges, 1987; Lipsey & Wilson, 1993; Rosenthal, 1990; Schmidt, 1992; Simon, 1992).

The Real-Life and College Sophomore Problems in Perspective

Several issues have been raised in this chapter, and it is important to be clear about what has, and what has not, been said. We have illustrated that the frequent complaint about the artificiality of psychological research arises from a basic misunderstanding not only of psychology, but of basic principles that govern all sciences. We have seen why people are understandably concerned that psychologists do not use random samples in all their research, and also why this worry is often unfounded. Finally, we have seen that a legitimate concern, the college sophomore problem, is sometimes overstated, particularly by those who are unfamiliar with the full range of activities and the diverse types of research that go on in psychology (see Chapter 1).

Nevertheless, psychologists should always be concerned that their experimental conclusions not rely too heavily on any one method or particular subject population. The next chapter deals with this very point. Indeed, some areas of psychology *are* plagued by a college sophomore problem, particularly certain areas of social psychology. Cross-cultural psychology, an antidote to the college sophomore problem (Buss, 1992), is a very underdeveloped field. However, there is reason for optimism because self-criticism is valued highly among research psychologists (see Chapter 11; Anderson & Gunderson, 1991; Bevan, 1986; Cicchetti & Grove, 1991; Dawes, 1994; Kimble, 1994; Kruglanski, 1975, 1976; Schneider, 1990). In fact, there are many psychologists who are well known because they have made a career of criticizing the field. Not a year goes by without many articles in scientific journals warning psychologists of flaws in their methods and pointing out the college sophomore problem. The latter has been an issue of great concern within psychology for decades, and no psychologist is unaware of it. So, while we should not ignore the issue, we must also keep it in perspective.

Chapter 8

AVOIDING THE
EINSTEIN SYNDROME

The Importance of Converging Evidence

"**B**iological Experiment Reveals the Key to Life," "New Breakthrough in Mind Control," "California Scientist Discovers How to Postpone Death"—as you can see, it is not difficult to parody the "breakthrough" headlines of the tabloid press. Since such headlines regularly come from the most irresponsible quarters of the media, it should not be surprising that most scientists recommend that they be approached with skepticism. The purpose of this chapter, though, is not only to warn against the spread of misinformation via exaggeration or to caution that the source must be considered when one evaluates reports of scientific advances. In this chapter we also want to develop a more complex view of the scientific process than was presented in earlier chapters. We shall do this by elaborating the ideas of systematic empiricism and public knowledge that were introduced in Chapter 1.

The "breakthrough" headlines in the media obscure an understanding of psychology and other sciences in many ways. One particular misunderstanding that arises from breakthrough headlines is the implication that all problems in science are solved when a single, crucial experiment completely decides the issue, or that theoretical advance is the result of a single critical insight that overturns all previous knowledge.

Such a view of scientific progress fits in nicely with the operation of the news media, in which history is tracked by presenting separate, disconnected "events" in bite-sized units. It is also a convenient format for the entertainment industry, where events must have beginnings and satisfying endings that resolve ambiguity. However, this is a gross caricature of scientific progress and, if taken too seriously, leads to misconceptions about scientific advance and impairs the ability to evaluate the extent of scientific knowledge concerning a given issue. In this chapter, we will discuss two principles of science—the connectivity principle and the principle of converging evidence—that describe scientific progress much more accurately than the breakthrough model.

THE CONNECTIVITY PRINCIPLE

In denying the validity of the "great-leap" or "crucial-experiment" model of all scientific progress, we do not wish to argue that such critical experiments and theoretical advances never occur. On the contrary, some of the most famous examples in the history of science represent just such occurrences. The development of the theory of relativity by Albert Einstein is by far the most well known. Here, a reconceptualization of such fundamental concepts as space, time, and matter was achieved by a series of remarkable theoretical insights.

The monumental nature of Einstein's achievement has made it the dominant model of scientific progress in the public's mind. This dominance is perpetuated because it fits in nicely with the implicit "script" that the media use to report most news events. More nonsense has been written about, and more unwarranted conclusions drawn from, relativity theory than perhaps any other idea in all of history. Take, for instance, the fallacious statement, "After all, Einstein said that everything is relative." Of course, our purpose is not to deal with all of these fallacies here. There is one, however, that will throw light on our later discussions of theory evaluation in psychology.

The reconceptualization of ideas about the physical universe contained in Einstein's theories is so fundamental that popular writing often treats it as if it were similar to conceptual changes in the arts (a minor poet is reevaluated and emerges with the status of a genius; an artistic school is declared dead). Such presentations ignore a basic difference between conceptual change in the arts and in the sciences. Conceptual change in science obeys a principle of connectivity that is absent or, at least, severely limited in the arts (see Bronowski, 1956, 1977; Popper, 1972).

A new theory in science must make contact with previously established empirical facts. To be considered an advancement, it must not only explain new facts but account for old ones. The theory may explain old facts in quite a different way from a previous theory, but explain them it must. This requirement ensures the cumulative progress of science. Genuine progress does not occur unless the realm of our explanatory power has been widened. If a new theory accounts for some new facts but fails to account for a host of old ones, it will not be considered a complete advance over the old theories and thus will not immediately replace them. Instead, the old and new theories will contend simultaneously in the marketplace of ideas until a new synthesis renders them all obsolete.

Despite the startling reconceptualizations in Einstein's theories (clocks in motion running slower, mass increasing with velocity, and so on), they did maintain the principle of connectivity. In rendering Newtonian mechanics obsolete, Einstein's theories did not negate or render meaningless the facts about motion on which Newton's ideas were based. On the contrary, at low velocities the two theories make essentially the same predictions. Einstein's conceptualization is superior because it accounts for a wide variety of new, sometimes surprising, phenomena that Newtonian mechanics cannot accommodate. Thus even Einstein's theories, some of the most startlingly new and fundamental reconceptualizations in the history of science, maintain the principle of connectivity.

A Consumer's Rule: Beware of Violations of Connectivity

The breakthrough model of scientific progress—what we might call the Einstein syndrome—leads us astray by implying that new discoveries violate the principle of connectivity. This implication is dangerous because, when the principle of connectivity is abandoned, the main beneficiaries are the purveyors of bogus theories. These theories derive part of their appeal and much of their publicity from the fact that they are said to be startlingly new. "After all, wasn't relativity new in its day?" is usually the tactic used to justify novelty as a virtue. Of course, the data previously accumulated in the field that the pseudoscientists wish to enter would seem to be a major obstacle. Actually, however, it presents only a minor inconvenience because two powerful strategies are available to dispose of it. One strategy that we have already discussed (see Chapter 2) is to explain the previous data by making the theory unfalsifiable. Of course, this strategy renders the theory useless, but the intended audience—the general public—rarely notices.

The second stratagem is to dismiss previous data by declaring them irrelevant. This dismissal is usually accomplished by emphasizing what a radical departure the new theory represents. The phrases "new conception of reality" and "radical new departure" are frequently used. The real sleight of hand, though, occurs in the next step of the process. The new theory is deemed so radical that experimental evidence derived from the testing of other theories is declared irrelevant. Only data that can be conceptualized within the framework of the new theory are to be considered; that is, the principle of connectivity is explicitly broken. Obviously, since the theory is so new, such data are said not yet to exist. And there you have it: a rich environment for the growth of pseudoscience. The old, "irrelevant" data are gone, and the new, relevant data do not exist. The scam is easily perpetrated because the Einstein syndrome obscures the principles of connectivity, the importance of which is ironically illustrated by Einstein's theories themselves.

Philosopher Mario Bunge (1983), writing in the journal *New Ideas in Psychology,* discussed the importance of the principle of connectivity in a way that is useful for psychologists. He titled his essay "Speculation: Wild and Sound," to illustrate that speculation is very much a part of science, but that there is a right way and a wrong way to speculate. Speculation that dispenses with the connectivity principle is always unsound. Bunge dealt with the mistaken view that the connectivity principle precludes scientific revolutions:

> This apprehension comes from [the] mistaken conception of a scientific revolution. A genuine scientific revolution, unlike a scientific counterrevolution, does not wipe out all past achievements but corrects and enriches them. Moreover, scientific revolution is always partial, never total: i.e., far from negating the entire scientific heritage, it questions only a few components of it. If this were not so it would be impossible to evaluate the proposed changes. Thus relativity and quantum mechanics were accepted not only because they solved new problems but also because they yielded some of the true classical results. Likewise a cognitive psychology that were to deny that there is classical and operant conditioning, and that learning is partly a conditioning process, would stand no chance. . . . In all scientific revolutions there is discontinuity in some respects and continuity in others. (p. 5)

The "Great-Leap" Model and the Gradual-Synthesis Model

The tendency to view the Einsteinian revolution as typical of what science is like tempts us to think that all scientific advances occur in giant leaps. This aspect of the Einstein syndrome is not caused by blatant inaccuracy, for many advances in science did involve such sharp and sudden increases in conceptual understanding. The problem is that people tend to generalize such examples into a view of the way all scientific progress *should* take place. In fact, many areas in science have advanced not by single, sudden breakthroughs but by a series of fits and starts that are less easy to characterize.

There is a degree of "fuzziness" in the scientific endeavor that most of the public is unaware of. Experiments rarely completely decide a given issue, supporting one theory and ruling out all others. New theories are rarely clearly superior to all previously existing competing conceptualizations. Issues are most often decided not by a critical experiment, as movies about science imply, but when the community of scientists gradually begins to agree that the preponderance of evidence is supporting one alternative theory rather than another (Forsyth, 1976). Indeed, philosopher of science Imre Lakatos (1970) discussed how many so-called critical experiments are recognized as such only with historical hindsight. The evidence that scientists evaluate is not the data from a single experiment that has finally been designed in the perfect way. Instead, scientists most often must evaluate data from literally dozens of experiments, each containing some flaws but providing part of the answer. This alternative model of scientific progress has been obscured because the Einstein syndrome creates in the public a tendency to think of all science by reference to physics, to which the great-leap model of scientific progress is perhaps most applicable.

A consideration of other sciences would suggest caution in applying the great-leap model universally. For example, in his book *The Eighth Day of Creation* (1979), Horace Judson provided a marvelous chronicle of the rapid advances in genetics and molecular biology that have occurred in this century. These advances have occurred not because one giant Einstein came onto the scene at the key moment to set everything straight. Instead, dozens of different insights based on hundreds of flawed experiments have contributed to the modern synthesis in biology. These advances occurred not by the instantaneous recognition of a major conceptual innovation, but by long, drawn-out haggling over alternative explanations that each had partial support. It took over ten years of inconclusive experimentation, along with much theoretical speculation, argument, and criticism, for scientists to change their view about whether genes were made of protein or nucleic acid. The consensus of opinion changed, but not in one great leap.

Judson himself argued the very point that is the focus of this chapter:

> Historians of science, in trying to account for revolutionary change, have relied upon the history of physics almost exclusively, and in physics have appealed to certain great set-piece battles. The important and fascinating cases, since the beginning of the history of science, have been those associated with the eras of Copernicus, Newton, Einstein, and the quantum. In each of these, it can be asserted that one cluster of ideas, closely interrelated and fully worked out, was overturned and replaced by another cluster of ideas, closely interrelated and fully

worked out. . . . The rise of molecular biology asks for a different model [because] biology has no such towering, overarching theory save the theory of evolution by mutation and natural selection. . . . Biology has proceeded not by great set-piece battles but by multiple small-scale encounters—guerrilla actions—across the landscape. In biology, no large scale, closely interlocking, fully worked out, ruling set of ideas has ever been overthrown. . . . Revolution in biology, from the beginnings of biochemistry and the study of cells, and surely in the rise of molecular biology and on to the present day, has taken place not by overturnings but by openings-up. Is it not so, further, that physics too, even at classical periods, has sometimes gone like that? (p. 612)

Indeed, Ernest Rutherford, discoverer of the atom's nucleus, agreed that even physics has "sometimes gone like that" in a statement that also stressed the importance of the principle of connectivity:

> It is not in the nature of things for any one man to make a sudden violent discovery; science goes step by step and everyone depends on the work of predecessors. . . . Scientists are not dependent on the ideas of a single man, but on the combined wisdom of thousands. (Holton & Roller, 1958, p. 166)

Rutherford's point emphasizes another consumer rule for separating scientific from pseudoscientific claims. Science—a cumulative endeavor that respects the principle of connectivity—is characterized by the participation of many individuals, whose contributions are judged by the extent to which they further our understanding of nature. No single individual can dominate discourse simply by virtue of his or her status. Science rejects claims of "special knowledge" available to only a few select individuals. This, of course, follows from our discussion of the public nature of science in Chapter 1.

In contrast, pseudosciences often claim that certain authorities or investigators have a "special" access to the truth. As psychologist Donald McBurney (1983) put it:

> Although there are leaders in every field of endeavor, pseudosciences are characterized by the dominance of one person or a few persons whose work is taken as revolutionary and fundamental to further progress in the field. A science that is the province of one or a few persons is almost certain to be a pseudoscience. Most sciences have a historical continuity with science as a whole and have enough people working in the field to prevent domination by one person. (pp. 34–35)

Psychology Is a Gradual-Synthesis Science

We have presented two ideas here that provide a useful context for understanding the discipline of psychology. First, no experiment in science is perfectly designed. There is a degree of ambiguity in the interpretation of the data from any one experiment. Scientists often evaluate theories not by waiting for the ideal or crucial experiment to appear, but by assessing the overall trends in a large number of partially flawed experiments. Second, many sciences have progressed even though they are without an Einstein. Their progress has occurred by fits and starts, rather than by discrete stages of grand Einsteinian syntheses.

Psychology is similar to biology and geology (see Laudan, 1980) in that it does not have large-scale unifying theories of the Einsteinian type. In Chapter 1, we said that most psychologists view the possibility of a theory that would unify the entire discipline as highly unlikely. It is a mistake, though, to assume that the absence of such a unification indicates lack of scientific status. Like psychology, many other sciences are characterized instead by growing mosaics of knowledge that lack a single integrating theme. Similarly the presence or absence of an Einstein figure is entirely irrelevant to projections of future progress in a science.

Psychologist Ray Hyman (1964) warned us that even psychologists themselves have been subtly affected by the Einstein syndrome and that its influence on young researchers in particular has hindered the cumulative growth of knowledge in the field:

> Encouraging "originality" or "being different" for its own sake seems often to result in an unwillingness to tackle currently accepted or standard problems. The young and ambitious psychologist does not want to cover old ground. . . . Unfortunately, the consequences of such ambition all too frequently are a spate of isolated reports leading nowhere and making contact with neither the past nor the present. Such efforts fly in the face of the fact that the scientific enterprise is a cumulative affair; each new addition to the edifice grows out of, and builds upon, what has already been done. Emphasis on novelty and rejection of the accepted viewpoint distorts one of the major functions of scientific inquiry. For the value of a scientific investigation does not lie in its novelty. Rather it lies in its additions to our understanding and mastery of the domain under scrutiny. Sometimes such an addition to our knowledge does require new ideas or rejection of the old. But this kind of novelty or revolution is a consequence of the search for a more adequate picture, not the object of the search. . . . Changes in our thinking and our image of man will not result from our flitting about from idea to idea. Rather they will come about by our selecting important problems, formulating ideas within these problem areas, and then carefully and thoroughly exploiting these ideas by means of empirical observation. (pp. 28, 31)

CONVERGING EVIDENCE

The previous discussion has led to a principle of evidence evaluation of much importance in psychology. This idea is sometimes called the principle of *converging evidence* (or *converging operations*). Scientists and those who apply scientific knowledge must often make a judgment about where the "preponderance of evidence" points. When this is the case, the principle of converging evidence is an important tool, both for evaluating the state of the research evidence and for deciding how future experiments should be designed.

The principle of converging evidence is also a very useful tool for the lay consumer of scientific information and is particularly useful in evaluating psychological claims. Although a full technical discussion of the idea of converging evidence would soon take us far afield, the aspects most useful in the practical application of the concept are actually easy to understand. We will explore two ways of expressing the principle, one in terms of the logic of flawed experiments and the other in terms of theory testing.

Progress Despite Flaws

In the abstract there is an infinite number of ways in which an experiment can go wrong (or become *confounded,* to use the technical term). In most cases, however, there is usually not a large number of critical contaminating factors. A scientist with much experience in working on a particular problem usually has a good idea of what most of the critical factors are. Thus, when surveying the research evidence, scientists are usually aware of the critical flaws in each experiment. The idea of converging evidence, then, tells us to examine the pattern of flaws running through the research literature because the nature of this pattern can either support or undermine the conclusions that we wish to draw.

For example, suppose that the findings from a number of different experiments were largely consistent in supporting a particular conclusion. Given the imperfect nature of experiments, we would go on to evaluate the extent and nature of the flaws in these studies. If all the experiments were flawed in a similar way, this would undermine confidence in the conclusions drawn from them because the consistency of the outcome may simply result from a particular flaw that all the experiments shared. On the other hand, if all the experiments were flawed in *different* ways, our confidence in the conclusions would be increased because it is less likely that the consistency in the results was due to a contaminating factor that confounded all the experiments.

Each experiment helps to correct errors in the design of other experiments and is itself bolstered by other studies that examine *its* flaws. When evidence from a wide range of experiments, each flawed in a somewhat different way or carried out with techniques of differing strengths and weaknesses, points in a similar direction, then the evidence has converged. A reasonably strong conclusion is justified even though no one experiment was perfectly designed. Thus the principle of converging evidence urges us to base conclusions on data that arise from a number of slightly different experimental sources. The principle allows us to draw stronger conclusions because consistency that has been demonstrated in such a context is less likely to have arisen from the peculiarities of a single type of experimental procedure.

Theory Evaluation

The principle of converging evidence can also be stated in terms of theory testing. Most areas of science contain competing theories. The extent to which one particular theory can be viewed as uniquely supported depends on the extent to which other competing explanations have been ruled out. A particular experimental result is never equally relevant to all competing theoretical explanations. A given experiment may be a very strong test of one or two alternative theories but a weak test of others.

For example, suppose that five different theoretical accounts (call them A, B, C, D, and E) of a given set of phenomena exist at one time and are investigated in a series of experiments. Suppose that one set of experiments represents a strong test of theories A, B, and C, and that the data largely refute theories A and B and support C. Imagine also that another set of experiments is a particularly strong test of theories C, D, and E, and that the data largely refute theories D and E and support C. In such a situation, we would have strong converging evidence for theory C. Not only do we have data supportive of theory C, but we have data that contradict its major competitors. Note that no one experiment tests all the theories, but taken together, the entire set of experiments allows a strong inference.

In contrast, if all the available research represents strong tests of B, C, and E, and the data strongly support C and refute B and E, the overall support for theory C would be less strong than in our previous example. The reason is that, although data supporting theory C have been generated, there is no strong evidence ruling out two viable alternative theories (A and D). Thus research is highly convergent when a series of experiments consistently supports a given theory while collectively eliminating the most important competing explanations. Although no single experiment can rule out all alternative explanations, taken collectively a series of partially diagnostic experiments can lead to a strong conclusion if the data converge in the manner of our first example.

The introduction of the idea of converging evidence allows us to dispel a misconception that may have been fostered by our oversimplified discussion of falsifiability in Chapter 2. That discussion may have seemed to imply that a theory is falsified when the first piece of evidence that disconfirms it comes along. This is not the case, however. Just as theories are confirmed by converging evidence, they are also disconfirmed by converging results. The point was clearly stated by psychologist Mark Leary (1979): "Although single tests can provide only very tenuous disconfirmatory evidence, a long series of interrelated studies that all appear to disconfirm experimental hypotheses can, when considered as a whole, certainly call the theory into question" (p. 152). Thus no theory that has some degree of support will be abandoned at the first appearance of a piece of contradictory information. Instead, a series of converging falsifying outcomes must occur, and an alternative theory must be available.

Converging Evidence in Psychology

The reason for stressing the importance of convergence is that conclusions in psychology are often based on the principle of converging evidence. There is certainly nothing unique or unusual about this fact. Conclusions in many other sciences rest not on single, definitive experimental "proofs," but on the confluence of dozens of "fuzzy" experiments. There are reasons that this might be especially true of psychology. Experiments in psychology are usually of fairly low diagnosticity. That is, the data that support a given theory usually rule out only a small set of alternative explanations, leaving many additional theories as viable candidates. As a result, strong conclusions are usually possible only after data from a very large number of studies have been collected and compared. Criteria of convergence are very important in this amalgamation process.

It should not be surprising that experiments in psychology have a high "fuzzy factor," given the enormous complexity of the problems concerning behavior. Better public understanding will come about if psychologists openly acknowledge this fact and then take pains to explain to the layperson just what follows from it. Psychologists should admit that, while a science of psychology exists and is progressing, progress is slow, and our conclusions come only after a sometimes excruciatingly long period of research amalgamation and debate. Media claims of breakthroughs should always engender skepticism, but this is especially true of psychological claims.

In psychology we have to walk a very fine line. For example, we must resist the temptation to regard a particular psychological hypothesis as "proven" when the evidence surrounding it is still ambiguous. This skeptical attitude has been reinforced in several chapters of this book. The cautions against inferring causation from correlation and against accepting testimonial evidence have served as examples. At the same time, we should not overreact to the incompleteness of knowledge and the tentativeness of conclusions by doubting whether firm conclusions in psychology will ever be reached. Nor should we be tempted by the irrational claim that psychology cannot be a science. From this standpoint the principle of converging evidence can be viewed as a counterweight to the warnings against overinterpreting tentative knowledge. Convergence allows us to reach many reasonably strong conclusions *despite* the flaws in all psychological research.

The best way to see the power of the principle of converging evidence is to examine some problem areas in psychology where conclusions have been reached by an application of the principle. In doing so, we will recognize an important corollary of the principle of convergence: Many different methodologies and experimental techniques exist in psychology, and this should be viewed as a strength of the field rather than a weakness.

Dyslexia: An Example of Convergence

Learning to read is the single most important skill that a child must gain on entering school. Children who fail to acquire this skill rapidly have always drawn the attention of educators. With the advent of the postindustrial information-oriented society, the low level of literacy attained by many children has escalated into a major national problem. In response, a large research literature has developed concerning the problem of delayed reading acquisition. This literature has spanned many different disciplines, including education, sociology, neurology, and many areas of psychology (for instance, educational psychology, developmental psychology, and cognitive psychology).

Many factors contribute to the "national reading problem," including inadequate educational resources, home environments that inhibit literacy, poor instruction, the low priority of education at the federal level during the 1980s, motivational problems, and a host of variables associated with poverty. Psychological research has focused on several aspects of this problem.

Many psychologists have attempted to discover which cognitive processes are specifically linked to reading difficulties in children who do not suffer from poor instruction and/or poor home backgrounds. An adequate model of how various cognitive processes are associated with individual differences in reading ability would make it easier to investigate which processes are *causally* linked to reading failure. This knowledge would provide a foundation for the design and evaluation of remedial techniques. The task has not been easy. For decades research in this area was a mass of confusion. Examining how the confusion came about, as well as how it has been partially resolved, will help us to understand the principle of converging evidence, as well as many other concepts we have discussed in previous chapters.

Research on the psychology of reading failure was greatly hampered by the fact that medicine got to the problem first. The problem of early and persisting reading failure first entered the scientific literature at the turn of the century in the form of case reports made by a few physicians. The first unfortunate consequence was that an unclearly defined behavioral phenomenon was given a specific name: *dyslexia* (Benton & Pearl, 1978; Ellis, 1985). This prematurely applied label had many negative effects. Sometimes the name was not recognized for what it was: a totally meaningless label that explained nothing:

> Question: What shall we call unexpected early reading failure?
> *Answer: Dyslexia.*
> Question: How do we know that a child has dyslexia?
> *Answer: He or she experiences unexpected reading failure.*

The term functions here as merely a label for an unexplained disorder. But this label often misled the public into thinking that a clearly defined medical syndrome had been identified. Nothing could have been further from the truth. The physicians who popularized the label hadn't the foggiest idea of what the physiological underpinnings of the disability were, and they were not competent to fully investigate its behavioral manifestations. This task is more properly the work of the psychologist.

Unfortunately, from this unpromising beginning things got worse. Teachers and parents accepted inferences from the case study reports as definitive evidence of the psychological mechanisms underlying the disability. Unsupported neurological speculation entered medical and psychology textbooks. The label was generalized from a name for a small group of highly unusual clinical cases to cover all children who were delayed in acquiring reading skills. Inconsistencies in the application of the label were invariably ignored. While certain professional and parent groups argued that more than 25 percent of all children suffered from this disability, reports in the medical literature were suggesting the discovery of a highly specific neurological syndrome. Rarely did commentators point out the absurdity of a specific medical "syndrome" that applied to 25 percent of the population (see Coles, 1987).

In the 1920s and 1930s, Samuel Orton promoted what was to become one of the most influential theories of early reading failure. He hypothesized that certain children were delayed in developing the brain asymmetry characteristic of adults, in which one side of the brain dominates processing in some situations. This lack of asymmetry, according to Orton, resulted in "strephosymbolia," in which the mirror image of the letter or word in one hemisphere of the brain was not "suppressed" by the other, normally dominant, hemisphere. (Please note that Orton's account of brain functioning has not been supported by modern evidence.)

According to Orton, strephosymbolia resulted in perceptual confusion such as mistaking *b* for *d* and *was* for *saw*. These were the so-called reversal errors that were destined to loom so large in the dyslexia and learning-disabilities literature.

Thus the stage was set for dyslexia to be characterized as a visual problem. And indeed, evidence did accumulate to support this hypothesis. This evidence was basically of two types. One was case reports that dyslexic children frequently confused reversible letters and words. The other was laboratory studies indicating that dyslexic children performed worse on visual perception tasks than nondyslexic children. In describing how this evidence was later discredited, we shall see the principle of converging evidence in action and also demonstrate the relevance of several of the principles discussed in earlier chapters.

That case reports supporting Orton's hypotheses appeared in the literature should surprise no one who has read Chapter 4. Had Orton predicted that dyslexic children would have warts on their left thumb, within weeks someone would have reported a case that startlingly confirmed Orton's prediction. Of course, what such case reports lacked was the necessary baseline information from control groups. Unfortunately information of this type was not collected for years. In fact, most of this work has appeared only since the early 1970s, after decades during which the mythology surrounding "reversal" errors was widely disseminated to teachers and the general public.

What do more carefully controlled studies show? Dyslexic subjects do make reversal errors, but so do nondyslexic subjects. Ah, but don't dyslexic children make more reversal errors? Yes, they do. The problem is that they also make more *non*reversal errors, too. In short, they make more errors of all types. Thus, for reversal errors to have any unique diagnosticity, they must be higher in dyslexic children as a *proportion* of all errors. This is not the case. The proportion of errors of different types is the same for dyslexic and nondyslexic children. The number of reversal errors shown by dyslexic subjects does not indicate a syndrome unique to them but is simply a performance characteristic of all readers when they are at that particular stage of reading acquisition (Fischer, Liberman, & Shankweiler, 1978; Holmes & Peper, 1977; Taylor, Satz, & Friel, 1979). Again, we have another example of the pitfalls inherent in relying on case study evidence, pitfalls that can be avoided only by the use of control groups.

What about the experimental evidence indicating that poor readers did not perform as well on visual perception tasks as skilled readers? Here the principle of converging evidence comes into play. Simply because a test is labeled a test of visual perception does not necessarily mean it measures only that particular psychological process. In fact, for many years, educational test publishers had the disturbing tendency to label tests intuitively ("Oh, here the child must discriminate between lines. We'll call this a perceptual test") rather than on the basis of an extensive performance-based analysis of the processes involved in the test. In fact, many tasks that were labeled "perceptual" actually required the operation of many other processes in order to be successfully completed (for instance, memory of the problem components, verbal labeling, attention to the stimuli, response choice, and an adequate understanding of task instructions). Thus a performance difference between good readers and poor readers on a task labeled "perceptual" does not *prove* that the cause of reading failure lies in visual perception. Instead, such a finding should provide only the impetus for a long series of converging investigations designed to rule out alternative explanations of the performance difference.

For a long while this kind of converging evidence was not generated. Instead, investigators continued to generate evidence that, while consistent with a perceptual deficit hypothesis, did not rule out any alternative hypotheses. By analogy with our previous discussion, investigators kept obtaining evidence consistent with hypotheses A, B, C, and D, but instead of designing experiments that would differentiate the alternatives, they simply declared that B was correct. Again, this situation has been remedied only in the past 10 to 20 years. When the proper converging experiments were finally conducted, the results obtained did not support the visual deficit hypothesis.

Frank Vellutino, a psychologist at the State University of New York at Albany, published the most influential review of this evidence in his book *Dyslexia: Theory and Research* (1979). He concluded that the evidence has indeed converged but that the convergence falsifies the visual deficit hypothesis and supports an alternative. A review of the research literature indicates that, when stimuli with commonly applied names such as letters of the alphabet and common objects were used in copying and discrimination tasks, there was a large discrepancy between groups differing in reading ability. However, when the same tasks used stimuli that neither group had seen before or stimuli that did not have a name (such as random squiggles), the difference between the reader groups disappeared.

Apparently difficulty in perceiving visual stimuli was not the cause of the original difference; instead, the cause is other processes that come into play when verbal stimuli are used. For example, verbal labeling can help maintain traces of stimuli in memory. So, if one group is superior at verbal labeling, it will display superior performance on a supposedly "visual" task for reasons that have nothing to do with visual perception. Similarly, many tasks carrying the visual perception label contain a memory component that may affect performance. Research has found that, when verbal memory components are eliminated from these tasks, the performance discrepancies between groups differing in reading ability tend to disappear.

During the past two decades, there have been hundreds of studies that trace links between psychological processes and reading ability. Given the fuzziness inherent in any one study conducted in this area, such a large number of studies was probably necessary for patterns to emerge. Most researchers now agree that convergence is apparent in the reading disability literature. Orton's theory and related visual-deficit hypotheses appear to be incorrect. The vast majority of reading problems do not originate from visual dysfunction. The cause of reading disability is a language problem in the phonological domain (Adams & Bruck, 1993; Bruck, 1992; Fletcher et al., 1994; Olson, Wise, Conners, Rack, & Fulker, 1989; Snowling, 1991; Stanovich, 1986a, 1986b; Stanovich & Siegel, 1994; Torgesen, Wagner, & Rashotte, 1994). Most educational psychologists feel confident about this conclusion, which derives almost entirely from converging evidence rather than from a single critical investigation. For example, Vellutino's book, which is several years old and which did not include all of the existing literature even when published, cites more than six hundred papers in the research literature.

The history of research in the psychology of reading disability also illustrates the danger of inferring causation from correlational evidence. The initial correlational investigations that linked (incorrectly, as we have seen) visual perception to reading disability were immediately interpreted as indicating the causal connection running from the former to the latter. Various programs of "visual perceptual training" were developed as remedial techniques for problem readers. A large body of converging evidence indicating the ineffectiveness of such programs has now accumulated (Kavale & Mattson, 1983). Once again, the moral of the story is that this educational debacle was exacerbated by the tendency to jump too quickly to causal conclusions. Visual training programs were under way well before the hypothesis of a causal connection had been adequately tested. A similar unfortunate series of events characterized the research on eye movement training and reading mentioned in Chapter 5.

Finally, research on reading disabilities has uncovered another "folk belief" that has turned out to be inaccurate—another example like those described in Chapter 1. It was accepted for many years in both the popular media and in clinical practice that, among all poor readers, the underlying cognitive problems of children with high intelligence were different from the underlying cognitive problems of children with low intelligence. This assumption turns out not to be true. The underlying cognitive problem in phonological processing that causes reading difficulty is very similar in poor readers with and poor readers without high intelligence (Fletcher et al., 1994; Siegel, 1988, 1989; Stanovich, 1994; Stanovich & Siegel, 1994).

Television Violence and Aggression: Convergence Again

Another research problem that illustrates the importance of the principle of converging evidence is the question of whether exposure to violent television programming increases children's tendencies toward aggressive behavior. There is now a scientific consensus on this issue: The viewing of violent television programming does appear to increase the probability that children will engage in aggressive behavior. The effect is not extremely large, but it is real. Again, the confidence that scientists have in this conclusion derives not from a single definitive study, but from the convergence of the results of dozens of different investigations (Berkowitz, 1984; Eron, 1982; Friedrich-Cofer & Huston, 1986; Huesmann & Eron, 1986; Huesmann, Lagerspetz, & Eron, 1984; Josephson, 1987; Liebert & Sprafkin, 1988; Pearl, Bouthilet, & Lazar, 1982; Williams, 1986: Wood, Wong, & Chachere, 1991). The general research designs, subject populations, and specific techniques used in these investigations differed widely, and as should now be clear, this difference is a strength of the research in this area, not a weakness.

Television network executives, naturally resistant to hard evidence of the negative effects of their industry on children, have carried on a campaign of misinformation that capitalizes on the public's failure to realize that research conclusions are based on the convergence of many studies rather than on a single critical demonstration that decides the issue (that is, the public is victimized by the Einstein syndrome). The television networks continually single out individual studies for criticism and imply that the general conclusion is undermined by the fact that each study has demonstrated flaws. While social science researchers may contest particular criticisms of a specific study, it is not commonly recognized that many times researchers candidly *admit* the flaws in a given study. The critical difference is that researchers reject the implication that admitting a flaw in a given study undermines the general scientific consensus on the effects of televised violence on aggressive behavior. The reason is that the general conclusion derives from a convergence. Research without the specific flaws of the study in question has produced results pointing in the same direction. This research may itself have problems, but other studies correct for these and also produce similar results.

For example, very early in the investigation of this issue, evidence of the correlation between the amount of violent programming viewed and aggressive behavior in children was uncovered. It was correctly pointed out that this correlational evidence did not justify a causal conclusion. Perhaps a third variable was responsible for the association, or perhaps more aggressive children chose to watch more violent programming.

But the conclusion of the scientific community is not based on this correlational evidence alone. There are more complex correlational techniques than the simple measurement of the association between two variables, and these correlational techniques allow some tentative conclusions about causality (one, that of partial correlation, was mentioned in Chapter 5). One of these techniques involves the use of a longitudinal design in which measurements of the same two variables—here, television violence and aggression—are taken at two different points in time. Certain correlational patterns suggest causal connections. Studies of this type have been conducted, and the pattern of results suggested that viewing televised violence did tend to increase the probability of engaging in aggressive behavior later in life.

Again, it is not unreasonable to counter that these longitudinal correlational techniques are controversial, because they are. The important point is that the conclusion of a causal connection between televised violence and aggressive behavior does not depend entirely on correlational evidence, either simple or complex, because numerous laboratory studies have been conducted in which the amount of televised violence was *manipulated* rather than merely assessed. In Chapter 6, we discussed how the manipulation of a variable, used in conjunction with other experimental controls, prevents the interpretation problems that surround most correlational studies. If two groups of children, experimentally equated on all other variables, show different levels of aggressive behavior, and if the only difference between the two is that one group viewed violent programming and one did not, then we are correct in inferring that the manipulated variable (televised violence) caused the changes in the outcome variable (aggressive behavior). This result has occurred in the vast majority of studies.

These studies have prompted some to raise the "It's not real life!" argument discussed in the previous chapter and to use the argument in the fallacious way discussed in that chapter. In any case, the results on the effects of television violence are not peculiar to a certain group of children because these results have been replicated in different regions of the United States and in several countries around the world. The specific laboratory setup and the specific programs used as stimuli have varied from investigation to investigation, yet the results have held up.

Importantly, the same conclusions have been drawn from studies conducted in the field rather than in the laboratory. A design known as the *field experiment* has been used to investigate the televised-violence–aggressive-behavior issue. The existence of this type of design reminds us to avoid assuming a necessary link between experimental design and experimental setting. People sometimes think that studies that manipulate variables are conducted only in laboratories and that correlational studies are conducted only in the field. This assumption is incorrect. Correlational studies are often conducted in laboratories, and variables are often manipulated in nonlaboratory settings. Although they sometimes require considerable ingenuity to design, field experiments, in which variables are manipulated in nonlaboratory settings, are becoming more common in psychology.

Of course, field experiments themselves have weaknesses, but many of these weaknesses are the strengths of other types of investigations. In summary, the evidence linking the viewing of televised violence to increased probabilities of aggressive behavior in children does not rest only on the outcome of one particular study or even one generic *type* of study. In summarizing the results of the assessment of the evidence undertaken by the National Institute of Mental Health (NIMH), Eli Rubenstein (1983) pointed to the importance of converging evidence:

> Granted that the data are complex and that no single study unequivocally documents the connection between televised violence and later aggressive behavior, the convergence of evidence from many studies is overwhelming and was so interpreted by the NIMH report. . . . What is self-evident in this situation, as with other complicated scientific questions, is that the research is almost never unequivocal in its interpretation. Nevertheless, this major finding of the NIMH report regarding the linkage of televised violence to later aggressive behavior clearly represents the position of the great majority of scientists working in this field. (p. 821)

The situation is analogous to the relationship between smoking and lung cancer. Cigarette company executives often attempt to mislead the public by implying that the conclusion that smoking causes lung cancer rests on some specific study, which they then go on to criticize. Instead, the conclusion is strongly supported by a wealth of converging evidence (Brandt, 1990). The convergence of data from several different types of research is quite strong and will not be substantially changed by the criticism of one study.

Actually it is quite appropriate here to discuss a medical problem like the causes of lung cancer. Most issues in medical diagnosis and treatment are decided by an amalgamation of converging evidence from many different types of investigations. For example, medical science is quite confident of a conclusion when the results of epidemiological studies (field studies of humans in which disease incidence is correlated with many environmental and demographic factors), highly controlled laboratory studies using animals, and clinical trials with human patients all converge. When the results of all these types of investigation point to a similar conclusion, medical science feels quite assured of the conclusion, and physicians feel confident in basing treatment on the evidence.

However, each of the three different types of investigation has its drawbacks. Epidemiological studies are always correlational, and the possibility of spurious links between variables is high. Laboratory studies can be highly controlled, but the subjects are often animals rather than humans. Clinical trials in a hospital setting use human subjects in a real treatment context, but there are many problems of control because of placebo effects and the expectations of the medical treatment team that deals with the patients. Despite the problems in each type of investigation, medical researchers are justified in drawing strong conclusions when the data from all the different methods converge strongly, as in the case of smoking and lung cancer. Just such a convergence also justifies the conclusions that psychologists draw from the study of a behavioral problem like the effect of televised violence on aggressive behavior.

SCIENTIFIC CONSENSUS

The problem of assessing the impact of televised violence is quite typical of how data finally accumulate to answer questions in psychology. Particularly in areas of pressing social concern, it is wise to remember that the answers to these problems emerge only slowly, after the amalgamation of the results from many different experiments. They are unlikely to be solved by a single breakthrough study. To put things in the form of a simple rule: When evaluating the empirical evidence in the field of psychology, think in terms of *scientific consensus* rather than *breakthrough*, in terms of *gradual synthesis* rather than *great leap*.

It will very often take longer than we should like to arrive at the answers to the difficult social problems we should like to solve. Psychologist David Pillemer (1991) warned that in social science, where statistical power is typically low, effect sizes are modest, and effects are interactive, broad variation in outcomes, including both positive and negative results, will be the rule rather than the exception. Isolated hypothesis tests rarely settle issues, but taken together they can contribute to the overall, meta-analytic pattern of results on which practical decisions will ultimately be based (p. 16).

Although we often must act on whatever information is available, however imperfect, action based on an inadequate empirical foundation sometimes causes more harm than no action at all, as the example of the visual-perception-training programs in reading education demonstrates quite well.

The usefulness of applying the "consensus-rather-than-breakthrough" rule is illustrated by the controversy surrounding the effects of early-childhood compensatory-education programs. In the late 1960s and early 1970s, when debate over the efficacy of President Lyndon B. Johnson's Great Society programs was raging, the public was treated to headlines such as "Early Intervention Raises IQs by Thirty Points" and "Head Start a Failure." What was the concerned layperson to make of such contradictory information? In this case, the consensus-breakthrough rule would clearly have provided some assistance, because it would suggest that *both* headlines were probably premature. In fact, it took another decade of research to arrive at a scientific consensus on this important social issue.

The consensus arose not from the results of a single critical study, but when a group of Cornell University researchers (Lazar, Darlington, Murray, Royce, & Sniper, 1982) combined the data from hundreds of subjects in 11 different early-education projects conducted in the 1960s and early 1970s. Although the results of individual programs were sometimes hard to interpret, the overall results were reasonably clear-cut when they were pooled together. Brief programs of early educational intervention did not routinely lead to IQ gains of 30 points. On the other hand, Head Start and programs like it were definitely not failures. Programs of early education intervention did have concrete and replicable effects on the later educational histories of the children who had participated in them. Such children were less likely to be held back a grade, were less likely to be assigned to special-education classes, had more positive attitudes toward school and school achievement, and showed lasting academic achievement gains (see also, Lee, Brooks-Gunn, Schnur, & Liaw, 1990).

Similarly, during the early 1980s, public attention focused on the question of whether school achievement was negatively associated with the amount of television a child watched. Again, this is a very difficult problem to study. The trends in the data that existed were difficult to discern, in part because the relationship appeared to be weak (Neuman, 1988). Nevertheless, when researchers analyzed 274 different correlations that had been observed in 23 separate studies (Williams et al., 1982), a pattern emerged (see also, Comstock & Paik, 1991; Neuman, 1988). Television viewing and school achievement showed little relationship when the amount of viewing was low (less than ten hours per week) but were negatively associated when the amount of viewing was above ten hours per week. By *negatively associated* we mean that more viewing was associated with poorer school achievement. However, because the data were correlational, it was difficult to draw causal conclusions from them (see Chapter 5).

Methods and the Convergence Principle

The convergence principle also implies that we should expect many different methods to be used in all psychological research areas. A relative balance among the methodologies used to arrive at a given conclusion is desirable because the various classes of research techniques have different strengths and weaknesses.

Psychology has long been criticized for relying too heavily on laboratory-based experimental techniques. This criticism is a subject of controversy among psychologists. Its validity depends on the specific research area that is the focus of discussion. Nevertheless, an unmistakable trend in recent years has been to expand the variety of methods used in all areas of psychology. For example, social psychologists, who have perhaps received the most criticism for overreliance on laboratory techniques, have turned to increasingly imaginative field designs in search of converging evidence to support their theories.

The work of psychologists Bibb Latané and John Darley provides a good example. These investigators are well known for their work on what has been termed the *unresponsive bystander phenomenon,* that is, the failure of some people to respond with help when observing another individual in an emergency situation. Latané and Darley (1970) documented the fact that in many emergency situations the probability that a given bystander will respond with help is lower when other bystanders are present.

However, the investigators were well aware that their conclusions would be tenuous if they were based only on the responses of individuals who witnessed emergencies after reporting to a laboratory to participate in an experiment. In an interesting experiment, Latané and Darley attempted to observe the phenomenon in another setting. They found a cooperative liquor store that agreed to have fake robberies occur in the store 96 different times. While the cashier was in the back of the store getting some beer for a "customer," who was actually an accomplice of the experimenter, the "customer" walked out the front door with a case of beer. This was done in the view of either one or two real customers who were at the checkout counter. The cashier then came back and asked the customers, "Hey, what happened to that man who was in here? Did you see him leave?" thus giving the customers a chance to report the theft. Consistent with the laboratory results, the presence of another individual inhibited the tendency to report the theft.

Similarly a study by psychologist Lawrence Wrightsman (1969) addressed the issue of whether the behavior of supporters of a political candidate coincides with the major social themes that the candidate articulates. In 1968, presidential candidate George Wallace ran on a strong platform of "law and order." Wrightsman investigated whether, in one specific aspect of behavior, supporters of George Wallace were actually more law-abiding than supporters of the other two candidates, Richard Nixon and Hubert Humphrey.

At that time Nashville-Davidson County in Tennessee had just instituted a new automobile tax of $15. A sticker indicating that the tax had been paid had to be displayed on all vehicles by November 1, 1968. From November 1 until Election Day, November 5, Wrightsman and his colleagues sampled and recorded information from 843 cars that bore Nashville-Davidson County tags and that displayed a bumper sticker supporting one of the presidential candidates. Specifically they recorded the name of the presidential candidate on the bumper sticker and whether or not the car displayed the sticker indicating that the county auto tax had been paid. They found that the Wallace supporters were significantly *less* likely to have complied with the new auto-tax law. Wrightsman eliminated one alternative explanation of the results, that Wallace supporters were less economically advantaged, by recording the make and year of the cars. To the extent that a car reflects economic status, this variable could not have accounted for the law compliance difference among the groups. At least in this specific law-abiding behavior, the actions of the individuals supporting a candidate did not reflect the major philosophy of the candidate, although they may have reflected other minor themes (such as resisting taxes). Irrespective of the reasons behind the finding, Wrightsman demonstrated a behavioral-attitudinal correlation of considerable psychological and perhaps political significance.

It is important to note that Wrightsman's results are interesting even though they are entirely correlational (and are subject to selection biases). This example is an important antidote to a misconception that some readers may have mistakenly derived from Chapter 5, that is, that correlational studies are not useful in science. It is true that when a causal hypothesis is at issue and correlational and manipulative studies can both be used, the study in which manipulation is possible is preferred. However, this does not mean that correlational studies cannot contribute to knowledge. First, many scientific hypotheses are stated in terms of correlation or lack of correlation, so that such studies are directly relevant to these hypotheses. Second, while correlation does not imply causation, causation *does* imply correlation. That is, while a correlational study cannot definitively prove a causal hypothesis, it may *rule one out.* Third, correlational studies are more useful than they may seem, because some of the recently developed complex correlational designs allow for some very limited causal inferences.

Perhaps most important, however, some variables simply cannot be manipulated for ethical reasons (for instance, human malnutrition or physical disabilities). Other variables, such as birth order, sex, and age, are inherently correlational because they cannot be manipulated, and therefore the scientific knowledge concerning them must be based on correlational evidence. This circumstance, again, is not unique to psychology. Astronomers obviously cannot manipulate all the variables affecting the objects they study, yet they are able to arrive at conclusions.

Social psychologists are not the only ones who have attempted to replicate their findings in a variety of settings. Cognitive psychologists have also begun to explore the generality of many of their laboratory results. For example, psychologist Murray Singer (1982) tested memory of prose reading in natural and laboratory situations. His stimulus material was a story that appeared in a university newspaper. Singer tested the recall and recognition of a group of students who had read the story. He compared the performance of this group of subjects to that of a group of students who had not read the story in the newspaper but had read it on a computer display screen in the laboratory. On several measures of recall and recognition, the memory performance of the laboratory readers was similar to that of those who had read the story outside the laboratory.

Similarly, Gigerenzer (1984) examined the generality of the frequency-validity effect. In this effect the mere repetition of a plausible but unfamiliar assertion increases people's belief in the assertion, whether it is true or false. This effect had been replicated, but only with college subjects (mostly in the United States) and only in a laboratory setting. Gigerenzer examined whether the relationship obtained for noncollege subjects responding outside the laboratory. He tested noncollege adults in Munich, Germany, in their own homes and found that the fequency-validity effect was present and that its magnitude was almost identical to that in college subjects in the United States responding in the laboratory.

Many of the principles of probabilistic decision making to be discussed in Chapter 10 originated in the laboratory but have also been tested in the field. For example, researchers have examined the way that physicians, stockbrokers, jurors, economists, and gamblers reason probabilistically in their environments (Arkes & Hammond, 1986; Braun & Yaniv, 1992; DeBondt & Thaler, 1985; Dowie & Elstein, 1988; Schwartz & Griffin, 1986; Wagenaar, 1988). Principles of behavioral decision theory have been used in such applied situations as deciding the optimal type of bullet to be used by the Denver Police Department (Hammond, Harvey, & Hastie, 1992) and deciding whether to build a dam in central Arizona (Hammond et al., 1992).

Convergence of laboratory and nonlaboratory results has also characterized several areas of educational psychology. For example, both laboratory studies and field studies of different curricula have indicated that early phonics instruction facilitates the acquisition of reading skill (Adams, 1990; Adams & Bruck, 1993; Chall, 1983, 1989; Stanovich, 1993).

In summary, current research in psychology uses a wide variety of experimental techniques and settings. The convergence of results from laboratory and nonlaboratory settings has characterized most areas of psychology that have shown steady progress. Experiments in which variables are manipulated, correlational studies, and investigations using naturalistic observations are frequently seen in the same research area. Although research on many problems has sometimes been overly focused on the use of certain techniques, the distribution of research methods in psychology is now much more balanced than it was just a few years ago.

The Progression to More Powerful Methods

Research on a particular problem often proceeds from weaker methods to ones that allow more powerful conclusions to be drawn. For example, interest in a particular hypothesis may originally stem from a particular case study of unusual interest. As we discussed in Chapter 4, this is the proper role of case studies: to suggest hypotheses for further study with more powerful techniques and to motivate scientists to apply more rigorous methods to a research problem. Thus, following the case studies, researchers undertake correlational investigations to verify whether the link between variables is real rather than the result of the peculiarities of a few case studies. If the correlational studies support the relationship between relevant variables, researchers will attempt experiments in which variables are manipulated in order to isolate a causal relationship between the variables. The progression, then, is from case studies, to correlational studies, to experiments with manipulated variables. While this gradual progression toward more powerful research methods is not always followed in every research area (sometimes different types of investigations go on in parallel), the progression quite commonly occurs.

An example of this evolution of research methods is provided by the work concerning the link between the type A behavior pattern and coronary heart disease (Friedman & Booth-Kewley, 1987; Friedman & Ulmer, 1984; Glass, 1977; Jenkins, Zyzanski, & Rosenman, 1976; Matthews, 1982; Miller et al., 1991; Wright, 1988). The original observations that led to the development of the concept of the type A behavior pattern occurred when two cardiologists thought they noticed a pattern in the behavior of some of their coronary patients that included a sense of time urgency, free-floating hostility, and extremely competitive striving for achievement. Thus the idea of the type A personality originated in a few case studies made by some observant physicians. These case studies suggested the concept, but they were not taken as definitive proof of the hypothesis that a particular type of behavior pattern is a partial cause of coronary heart disease.

Proving the idea required more than just the existence of a few case studies. It involved decades of work by teams of cardiologists, biochemists, and psychologists.

The research quickly moved from merely accumulating case studies, which could never establish the truth of the hypothesis, to more powerful methods of investigation. Researchers developed and tested operational definitions of the type A concept. Large-scale epidemiological studies established a correlation between the presence of type A behavior and the incidence of coronary heart disease. The correlational work then became more sophisticated. Researchers used complex correlational techniques to track down potential third variables. The relation between type A behavior and heart attacks could have been spurious because the behavior pattern was also correlated with one of the other traditional risk factors (such as smoking, obesity, or serum cholesterol level). However, results showed that type A behavior was a significant independent predictor of heart attacks. When other variables were statistically partialed out, there was still a link between the type A behavior pattern and coronary heart disease.

Finally, researchers undertook experimental studies with manipulated variables to establish whether a causal relationship could be demonstrated. Some of the studies attempted to test models of the physiological mechanisms that affected the relationship and used animals as subjects—what some might call "not real life." Another experimental study used subjects who had had a heart attack. These subjects were randomly assigned to one of two groups. One group received counseling designed to help them avoid traditional risky behavior such as smoking and eating fatty foods. The other group received this counseling and were also given a program designed to help them reduce their type A behavior. Three years later there had been significantly fewer recurrent heart attacks among the patients given the type A behavior counseling. In short, the evidence has converged to support the hypothesis of the type A behavior pattern as a significant causal factor in coronary heart disease. The investigation of this problem provides a good example of how research gradually moves from interesting case studies, to correlational techniques, to more complex correlational techniques, and finally to studies in which variables are manipulated.

A final lesson we can draw from this example is that scientific concepts evolve, an issue first raised in Chapter 3 when we discussed operational definitions. Recent research seems to indicate that it is oversimplifying to talk about the connection between heart attacks and the type A behavior pattern *as a whole*. The reason is that only certain components of the pattern (particularly "antagonistic hostility") appear to be linked to coronary heart disease (Dembroski & Costa, 1988). Thus we have an example of how science uncovers increasingly specific relationships as it progresses and how theoretical concepts become elaborated.

A Counsel Against Despair

One final implication of the convergence principle is that we should not despair when the initial results of studies on a problem appear to be contradictory. The process of evidence amalgamation in science is like a projector slowly bringing an unknown slide into focus. At first, the blur on the screen could represent just about anything. Then, as the slide is focused a bit more, many alternative hypotheses may be ruled out even though the image cannot be unambiguously identified. Finally, an identification can be made with great confidence. The early stages of the evidence amalgamation process are like the beginning of the focusing process. The ambiguous blur of the slide corresponds to contradictory data or to data that support many alternative hypotheses.

Thus contradictory data obtained at the beginning of an investigation should not drive us to despair of ever finding the truth. Nor is such a situation unique to psychology. It also occurs in more mature sciences. Indeed, the public is usually unaware that contradictory data are obtained quite often in science. Such contradictory data are simply the result of our current inadequate understanding of the problem. The contradictions may be simply chance occurrences (something we will discuss at length in Chapter 10), or they may be due to subtle methodological differences between experiments.

For example, shortly after most scientists had begun to accept the notion that the speed of light was invariant (based on the ether drift experiments of Michelson and Morley and the theoretical arguments of Einstein), several experiments by Dayton Miller produced evidence contradicting this conclusion. However, physicists did not stop their research, throw up their hands, and despair of ever finding the truth because of this new evidence. Instead, they persevered in their work, confident that the natural progress of science would eventually yield an explanation of Miller's results, which it did.

As discussed in Chapter 7, tracking down the reasons for apparent contradictions between the results of experiments often leads to great advances in our understanding of a phenomenon. In psychology, where most of the "slides" are quite fuzzy, such perseverance is doubly necessary, but it is also doubly rewarded when the complex and fascinating questions about behavior that have puzzled us for centuries prove solvable. Those who are uncomfortable working in an atmosphere of ambiguity generally stay away from science, because science is filled with uncertainties. Its blurry slides violate the aesthetic sense of some people. The scientist's attitude, however, is one of intense curiosity about what the blur will turn out to be when it is finally brought into focus. This attitude is captured in Jacob Bronowski's (1973) statement, "Science is a tribute to what we can know *although* we are fallible" (p. 374).

In this chapter, we have seen how the breakthrough model of scientific advance is a bad model for psychology and why the gradual-synthesis model provides a better framework for understanding how conclusions are reached in psychology. The principle of converging operations describes how research results are synthesized in psychology: each experiment is somewhat flawed in its conceptualization and execution but nevertheless helps us to rule out at least some alternative explanations and thus aids in the process of homing in on the truth. The use of a variety of different methods makes psychologists more confident that their conclusions rest on a solid empirical foundation. Finally, when conceptual change occurs, it adheres to the principle of connectivity: new theories not only must account for new scientific data but must also provide an explanation of the previously existing database.

Chapter 9

THE MISGUIDED SEARCH FOR THE "MAGIC BULLET"

Multiple Causation

In Chapter 8 we focused on the importance of converging operations and the need to progress to more powerful research methods in order to establish a single connection between variables. In this chapter, we go beyond a simple connection between two variables to highlight an important point: behavior is multiply determined. Any particular behavior is caused not by one variable but by a large number of different variables. To conclude that there is a significant causal connection between variable A and behavior B does not mean that variable A is the *only* cause of behavior B.

Multiple causation characterizes virtually all the situations we have discussed in this book. For example, researchers have found a relationship between television viewing and academic achievement, but they do not claim that the amount of television viewed is the *only* thing that determines academic achievement. That, of course, would be silly, because academic achievement is partially determined by a host of other variables (home environment, quality of schooling, and the like). In fact, television viewing is only a minor determinant of academic achievement when compared with these other factors. Similarly the amount of television violence viewed by children is not the only reason that they may display aggressive behavior. It is one of many contributing factors.

Like so many of the principles in this book, it is important to put the idea of multiple causes in perspective. On the one hand, it warns us not to overinterpret a single causal connection. The world is complicated, and the determinants of behavior are many and complex. Just because we have demonstrated a cause of behavior does not mean that we have uncovered *the only* cause or even the most important cause. To provide a thorough explanation of *a* particular behavior, researchers must study the influence of many different variables and amalgamate the results of these studies to give a complete picture of all the causal connections.

On the other hand, to say that a variable is only one of many determinants and that it explains only a small portion of the variability in a given behavior is not to say that the variable is unimportant. First, the relationship may have far-reaching theoretical implications. Second, the relationship may be practically useful, particularly if the variable can be controlled, as is the case with television violence, for example. Few would argue that a variable that could reduce the number of acts of physical violence by as much as 1 percent annually is not of enormous importance. In short, if the behavior in question is of great importance, then knowing how to control only a small proportion of it can be extremely useful.

The idea of multiple causation leads to an important concept that is often discussed at length in methodology texts, although we can only mention it here: A factor that influences behavior may have different effects when operating in conjunction with another factor and when acting alone. This is called the concept of *interaction:* The effect that one variable has may depend on the presence or absence of another variable. Research conducted by Simmons, Burgeson, Carlton-Ford, and Blyth (1987) provides an example. These investigators examined the self-esteem and academic grade-point averages of a group of adolescents as a function of life changes (school transition, pubertal development, early dating behavior, residential mobility, and family disruption). They found that the *combination* of life changes was the critical factor in cases of negative outcome. Another example occurs in Michael Rutter's (1979) review of the factors related to psychiatric disorders in children, in which he stated:

> The first very striking finding is that single isolated chronic stresses carry no appreciable psychiatric risk. . . . None of these risk factors, when they occurred in isolation, was associated with disorder in the children; the risk was no higher than that for children without any family stresses. However, when any two stresses occurred together, the risk went up no less than fourfold. With three and four concurrent stresses, the risk went up several times further still. It is clear that the combination of chronic stresses provided very much more than an additive effect. There was an interactive effect such that the risk which attended several concurrent stresses was much more than the sum of the effects of the stresses considered individually. (p. 295)

Developmental psychology contains many examples like this one. Researchers Bonnie Breitmeyer and Craig Ramey (1986) studied two groups of infants, one that had a nonoptimal perinatal status and the other of normal status. One half of the members of each group were randomly assigned at birth either to a day care program designed to prevent mild mental retardation or to a control group that did not receive special treatment. Measures of cognitive maturity taken when the children reached 4 years of age indicated that there was no difference between those children who were at risk perinatally and the normal children when *both* had been given the educational program. However, the children with nonoptimal perinatal scores showed slower cognitive development when neither they nor the control group received the special educational program. Thus biology interacted with environment in this situation to illustrate that a complex outcome (cognitive development) is determined by a multitude of factors. The researchers concluded, "The results provide support for a framework stressing initial biological vulnerability and subsequent environmental insufficiency as cumulative risk factors in the development of children from low SES [socioeconomic status] families" (p. 1151).

Another example comes from a study of prosocial behavior on the part of 6- to 9-year-old children. Knight, Johnson, Carlo, and Eisenberg (1994) studied the psychological factors that were associated with children's tendency to help other children (which was operationalized as donating money to children in need). They found that certain variables, such as levels of sympathy, affective reasoning, and knowledge about money (when taken alone), were only weakly related to prosocial behavior (donating more money to help others). However, in combination these variables were much more potent predictors of prosocial behavior. For example, children high in sympathy, affective reasoning, and knowledge about money donated four times as much as the children low on all of these variables.

Thus the concept of multiple causes involves even more complexities than you might have thought at first. Not only is it necessary to track down the many factors that may influence the behavior in question, but it is also necessary to investigate how these factors operate together.

It seems, though, that the basic idea that complex events in the world are multiply determined should be an easy one to grasp. In fact, the concept *is* easy to grasp and to apply *when* the issues are not controversial. However, when our old nemesis, preexisting bias, rears its head, people have a tendency to ignore the principle of multiple causation. How many times do we hear people arguing about such emotionally charged issues as the causes of crime, the distribution of wealth, the treatment of women and minorities, the causes of poverty, capital punishment, the level of taxation, and censorship in a way that implies that these issues are simple and unidimensional and that outcomes in these areas have a single cause?

These examples make it clear that, as Nisbett and Ross (1980) argued:

> Although people sometimes acknowledge the existence of multiple causes, it is clear that they frequently act in ways far more consistent with beliefs in unitary causation. In a sense, they behave as if causation were "hydraulic" or as if causal candidates competed with one another in a zero-sum game. (p. 128)

A zero-sum game—where one candidate's gain is another's loss—often characterizes our discussions of emotionally charged issues. We tend to forget, under emotional influence, the principle of multiple causation.

Nisbett and Ross (1980) used as an example the heated debate over President Richard Nixon's trip to China in 1972. Some commentators argued that Nixon went only for purposes of domestic political gain; others argued that Nixon went as the result of a deep conviction about America's foreign policy needs. The argument about the purposes of Nixon's visit continued without an acknowledgment of the more complex possibility that Nixon's decision was based on a delicate balancing of his assessment of America's foreign policy needs *and* his own political interests.

But the complex possibility of multiple causation is often left out when the issues involve preexisting biases. For example, consider discussions of crime by people on opposite ends of the political spectrum. Liberals may argue that people of low socioeconomic status who commit crimes may themselves be victims of their circumstances (e.g., joblessness, poor housing, poor education, and lack of hope about the future). Conservatives may reply that a lot of poor people do not commit crimes; therefore economic conditions are not the cause. Instead, the conservative may argue, it is personal values and personal character that determine criminal behavior. Neither side in the debate ever seems to acknowledge that *both* individual factors and environmental factors may contribute to criminal behavior.

Political writer Richard Cohen (1985) also noted how we often turn our "single-cause" explanations around through 180 degrees, depending on the direction of our preexisting biases. He cited the case of a 63-year-old farmer who was deep in debt and losing his farm because of the severe 1985 farm recession in Iowa. The man shot the banker to whom he was hopelessly in debt and then shot himself and his wife. The conventional wisdom of neighbors and of the media regarding this event was that the man simply "snapped" because of his immense financial difficulties. Media coverage was highly favorable. As Cohen described it, the farmer was presented as a "hard-working entrepreneur, up against nature, the bank, and the vagaries of traders in places such as Chicago. He is honest, thrifty and the embodiment of almost every American virtue—self-employed, self-reliant and God-fearing" (p. 11).

But, Cohen wondered, if this man could simply "snap" because of economic difficulties, why do we not invoke this same (single-cause) theory when explaining the behavior of the ghetto resident who shoots someone? "If this is the case when it comes to farmers on besieged farms, why is it not also the case with the ghetto resident? Why is it that even to suggest that poverty, lack of opportunity, lousy schools and brutality contribute to crime, brings nothing but scorn?" (p. 11). The ghetto resident is seen as "individually responsible" and thus deserving of severe punishment, whereas the Iowa farmer was seen as a "victim of circumstances," and public opinion displayed sympathy in his case. Cohen was, of course, pointing out a further absurdity in our tendency toward single-cause explanations: we use them in ways that conveniently fit in with our biases. He argued that we might be less prone to do this if, from the beginning, we recognized that both of these cases were probably multiply determined. The actions of the Iowa farmer who killed someone and the ghetto resident who kills someone are both influenced by their individual psychological-biological characteristics *and* environmental pressures. There is no one explanation of crime. Criminal behavior is determined by a multitude of factors, some of which are environmental and some of which are characteristics of the individual.

An example is provided by discussions of the causes of complex economic outcomes. These also often fall into the single-cause trap, a point made by economist Lester Thurow (1987) in an article on economic productivity and why U.S. productivity lagged behind that of some other countries. Thurow argued, "Wisdom starts with recognizing that there is no 'silver bullet' solution. No one action—no matter how major—is going to cure the problem. The solutions essentially involve changing many of the organizational details of the US economy, the US educational system, and the US firm" (p. 1663). Thurow's discussion emphasizes that our economic problems, vis-à-vis those of our competitors, are multiply determined, but that "correcting each of many small causes is not part of the American style" (p. 1661). Instead, we keep searching for the "magic bullet" that will cure the (note the word *the,* implying a single cause) problem. In contrast, Thurow made the case that our lack of economic productivity was due to a variety of problems that involved a number of domains of our national life. For example, he argued that our economic productivity was held back because (1) our top managers were trained in business rather than engineering and technology, as was the case of our competitors; (2) our work force lacked math skills, which are critical to production in a high-tech economy; (3) our nation's low rate of savings had driven up our interest rates, hurting the economy; (4) our workers had less job security than workers in other nations and thus tended to resist technology more than workers in Japan, who did not have to worry that they would be displaced by technological advance; and (5) our expenditure on industrial research and development was low because our military expenditure was so high. These were just a few of the reasons that Thurow cited for our low productivity. There were many more. In short, there was no "magic bullet" to remedy our economy. As is the case today, if we want to progress, we must make a lot of different changes because the problem is multiply determined.

Like economic problems, virtually all of the complex problems that psychologists investigate are multiply determined. Take the problem of learning disabilities, for example, which educational psychologists, cognitive psychologists, and developmental psychologists have investigated extensively. Research has revealed that there are brain anomalies associated with learning disabilities (Galaburda, 1994; Hynd, Marshall, & Gonzalez, 1991). Studies have also indicated that there is a genetic component in learning disabilities (Olson, Rack, Conners, DeFries, & Fulker, 1991; Pennington, 1990; Stevenson, 1992; Stevenson, Graham, Fredman, & McLoughlin, 1987). These two findings may seem to suggest the conclusion that learning disabilities are solely biological-brain problems. This conclusion would be wrong. The reason it would be wrong is that research has *also* revealed that learning disabilities are in part caused by the lack of certain instructional experiences in early schooling (Ehri, 1989) *and* by poor home environments (Coles, 1987). There is no *single* cause of learning disabilities; instead, there is a confluence of biological predispositions and environmental causes. This problem is typical of psychological issues and illustrates quite well the single lesson of this chapter: When thinking about the causes of behavior, think in terms of *multiple* causes.

Chapter 10

THE ACHILLES' HEEL
OF HUMAN COGNITION
Probabilistic Reasoning

Question: "Men are taller than women, right?"
Answer: "Right."
Question: "All men are taller than all women, right?"
Answer: "Wrong."

Correct. Believe it or not, we are going to devote part of this chapter to something that you just demonstrated you knew by answering the previous two questions. But don't skip this chapter just yet, because there are some surprises waiting in the explanation of what seems like a very simple principle.

You answered affirmatively to the first question because you did not interpret "Men are taller than women" to mean what the second statement said: "All men are taller than all women." You correctly took the first statement to mean "*There is a tendency for* men to be taller than women," since everyone knows that not all men are taller than all women. You correctly interpreted the statement as reflecting a probabilistic trend rather than a fact that holds in every single instance. By *probabilistic trend,* we simply mean that it is more likely than not but does not hold true in all cases. That is, the relationship between sex and height is stated in terms of likelihoods and probabilities rather than certainties. Many other relationships in nature are probabilistic: It tends to be warmer near the equator. Families tend to have fewer than eight children. Most parts of the earth tend to have more insects than humans. These are all statistically demonstrable trends, yet there are exceptions to every one of them. They are probabilistic trends and laws, not relationships that hold true in every single case.

Virtually all the facts and relationships that have been uncovered by the science of psychology are stated in terms of probabilities. There is nothing unique about this. Many of the laws and relationships in other sciences are stated in probabilities rather than certainties. The entire subdiscipline of population genetics, for example, is based on probabilistic relationships. Physicists tell us that the distribution of the electron's charge in an atom is described by a probabilistic function. It is true that most of the probabilistic trends uncovered in psychology are weaker than those in other sciences. However, the fact that behavioral relationships are stated in probabilistic form does not distinguish them from those in many other sciences. Jacob Bronowski (1978a) discussed the difficulties that many people have in accepting the idea that, as science progresses into new areas, more and more of its laws are stated in probabilistic terms:

> If I say that after a fine week, it always rains on Sunday, then this is recognized and respected as a law. But if I say that after a fine week, it rains on Sunday more often than not, then this somehow is felt to be an unsatisfactory statement; and it is taken for granted that I have not really got down to some underlying law which would chime with our habit of wanting science to say decisively either "always" or "never." Even if I say that after a fine week, it rains on seven Sundays out of ten, you may accept this as a statistic, but it does not satisfy you as a law. Somehow it seems to lack the force of a law. Yet this is a mere prejudice. . . . The idea of chance as I have explained it here is not difficult. But it is new and unfamiliar. We are not used to handling it. . . . We seem to be in a land of sometimes and perhaps, and we had hoped to go on living with always and with certainty. . . . Yet I believe that the difficulty is only one of habit. We shall become accustomed to the new ideas just as soon as we are willing and as we have to. And we are having to. (pp. 81–82, 94–95)

In this chapter, we will try to make you more comfortable in the "land of sometimes and perhaps," because to understand psychology one must be comfortable with the subject of this chapter: probabilistic reasoning.

"Person-Who" Statistics

Most of the public is aware that many of the conclusions of medical science are statements of probabilistic trends and are not predictions of absolute certainty. Smoking causes lung cancer and a host of other health problems. Voluminous medical evidence documents this fact (Brandt, 1990; Jeffrey, 1989). Yet will everyone who smokes get lung cancer, and will everyone who refrains from smoking be free of lung cancer? Most people know that these implications do not follow. The relationship is probabilistic. Smoking vastly increases the *probability* of contracting lung cancer but does not make it a certainty. Medical science can tell us with great confidence that more people in a group of smokers will die of lung cancer than in an equivalent group of nonsmokers. It cannot tell us *which* ones will die, though. The relationship is probabilistic; it does not hold in every case. We are all aware of this—or are we? How often have we seen a nonsmoker trying to convince a smoker to stop by citing the smoking–lung-cancer statistics, only to have the smoker come back with, "Oh, get outta here! Look at old Joe Ferguson down at the store. Three packs of Camels a day since he was sixteen! Eighty-one years old and he looks great!" The obvious inference that one is supposed to draw is that this single case somehow invalidates the relationship. It is surprising and distressing how often this ploy works. Too frequently, a crowd of people begin to nod their heads in assent when a single case is cited to invalidate a probabilistic trend. This agreement reflects a failure to understand the nature of statistical laws. If people think a single example can invalidate a law, they must feel the law should hold in every case. In short, they have failed to understand the law's probabilistic nature. There will always be a few "people who" go against even the strongest of trends. Consider our smoking example. Only 5 percent of men who live to the age of 85 are smokers (University of California, Berkeley, 1991). Or to put it another way, 95 percent of men who live to age 85 are either nonsmokers or have smoked for a period and then quit. Continuous smoking without quitting markedly shortens lives (University of California, Berkeley, 1991). Yet a few smokers do make it to 85.

Adapting the terminology of psychologists Richard Nisbett and Lee Ross (1980), we will call instances like the "Joe Ferguson" story examples of the use of "person-who" statistics: situations in which well-established statistical trends are not believed because someone knows a "person who" went against the trend, for example, "You say job opportunities are expanding in service industries and con-tracting in heavy industry? No way, I know a man who got a job in a steel mill just last Thursday"; "You say families are having fewer children than they did 30 years ago? You're crazy! The young couple next door already has three and they're both under 30"; "You say children tend to adopt the religious beliefs of their par-ents? Well, I know a man at work whose son converted to another religion just the other day"; "You say the average food-stamp recipient receives a subsidy av-eraging 49 cents per meal? Yeah, but what about a woman I saw at a store who purchased lots of expensive meat with her stamps."

The ubiquitous person-who is usually trotted out on stage when we are con-fronted with hard statistical evidence that contradicts a previously held belief. Thus it could be argued that people actually know better and simply use the per-son-who as a technique to invalidate facts that go against their opinions. However, the work of psychologists who have studied human decision making and reasoning suggests that the tendency to use the person-who comes not sim-ply from its usefulness as a debating strategy. Instead, it appears that this fallacious argument is used so frequently because people experience great difficulty in deal-ing with probabilistic information. New work in the psychology of decision making has indicated that probabilistic reasoning may well be the Achilles' heel of human cognition.

PROBABILISTIC REASONING AND THE MISUNDERSTANDING OF PSYCHOLOGY

Probabilistic thinking is involved in many areas of science, technology, and hu-man affairs. Thus there is no necessary reason why this type of thinking is more important to an understanding of psychology. However, the findings of psychol-ogy are quite often misunderstood because of the problems people have in deal-ing with probabilistic information. We all understand "Men are taller than women" as a statement of probabilistic tendency. We realize that it is not invalidated by a single exception (a single man who is shorter than a woman). Most people understand the statement "Smoking causes lung cancer" in the same way, although old "Joe Ferguson" can be convincing to some smokers who do not want to believe that their habit may be killing them. However, very similar probabilistic statements about behavioral trends cause widespread disbelief and are often dismissed by many people with the first appearance of a single person-who. Most psychology instructors have witnessed a very common reaction when they discuss the evidence on certain behavioral relationships. For example, the instructor may present the fact that children's scholastic achievement is related to the socioeconomic status of their households and to the educational level of their parents. This statement often prompts at least one student to object that he has a "friend who" is a National Merit Scholar and whose father only finished eighth grade. Even those who understood the smoking–lung-cancer example tend to waver at this point.

Presentations of psychological findings in the general media often reflect the failure to understand the probabilistic nature of most scientific findings. Too often they also further this misunderstanding. The following sequence is very common in newspapers. A science writer or a wire service story about a scientific conference reports a behavioral relationship. The paper then prints in the letters-to-the-editor section responses by readers describing their person-who went against the reported trend. The letters often ridicule psychology and question the expertise of psychologists because, after all, how could they say such a thing when everyone can name a neighbor who doesn't fit the pattern.

People who would never think of using person-who arguments to refute the findings of medicine and physics routinely use them to refute psychological research. Most people understand that many treatments, theories, and facts developed by medical science are probabilistic. They understand that, for example, a majority of patients, but not all of them, will respond to a certain drug. Medical science, however, often cannot tell in advance *which* patients will respond. Often all that can be said is that if 100 patients take treatment A and 100 patients do not, after a certain period the 100 patients who took treatment A will *collectively* be better off. No one would doubt the worth of this medical knowledge just because it was probabilistic and did not apply in every case. Yet this is exactly what happens in the case of many psychological findings and treatments. The fact that a finding or treatment does not apply in every case often engenders profound disappointment and denigration of psychology's progress. When the issues are psychological, people tend to forget the fundamental principle that knowledge does not have to be certain to be useful—that even though individual cases cannot be predicted, the ability to accurately forecast *group* trends is often very informative. The prediction of outcomes based on group characteristics is often called *aggregate* or *actuarial prediction* (we will discuss actuarial prediction in more detail later in this chapter).

For these reasons a thorough understanding of probabilistic reasoning is critical to an understanding of psychology. There is a profound irony here. Psychology probably suffers the most from the general public's inability to think statistically. Yet psychologists have done the most research into the nature of probabilistic reasoning abilities.

PSYCHOLOGICAL RESEARCH ON PROBABILISTIC REASONING

In the past two decades, the research of psychologists such as Daniel Kahneman of the University of California at Berkeley, Amos Tversky and Lee Ross at Stanford, and Richard Nisbett at the University of Michigan has revolutionized the way we think about people's reasoning abilities. In the course of their studies these investigators have uncovered some fundamental principles of probabilistic reasoning that are absent or, more commonly, insufficiently developed in many people. As has often been pointed out, this actually should not be surprising. As a branch of mathematics, statistics is a very recent development. Games of chance existed centuries before the fundamental laws of probability were discovered. Here is another example of how personal experience does not seem to be sufficient to lead to a fundamental understanding of the world (see Chapter 7). It took formal study of the laws of probability to reveal how games of chance work: thousands of gamblers and their "personal experiences" were insufficient to uncover the underlying nature of games of chance.

The problem is that, as society becomes more complex, the need for probabilistic thinking becomes greater for everyone. If ordinary citizens are to have a basic understanding of the society in which they live, they must possess at least a rudimentary ability to think statistically.

"Why did they raise my insurance rate," you might wonder, "and why is John's rate higher than Bill's? Is social security going broke? Is our state lottery crooked? Is crime increasing or decreasing? Why do doctors order all those tests? Why can people be treated with certain rare drugs in Europe and not in the United States? Do women really make less than men in comparable jobs? What can be done about the federal budget deficit? Is educational achievement in Japan really higher than here? Is Canadian health care better than that in the United States and cheaper as well? Does giving tax breaks to industry to move to our state pay off in the long run?" These are all good questions—concrete, practical questions about our society and how it works. To understand the answers to each of them, one must think statistically.

Clearly, though, a complete discussion of statistical thinking is beyond the scope of this book. We will, however, briefly discuss some of the more common pitfalls of probabilistic reasoning. A good way to start developing the skill of probabilistic thinking is to become aware of some of its most common fallacies. Many of these fallacies were brought to light by psychological research. In addition, many are particularly relevant to psychological findings and theories.

Insufficient Use of Probabilistic Information

Consider the following problem, developed by Tversky and Kahneman (1982): A cab was involved in a hit-and-run accident at night. Two cab companies, the Green and the Blue, operate in the city in which the accident occurred. You are given the following data:

1. Eighty-five percent of the cabs in the city are Green and 15 percent are Blue.

2. A witness identified the cab as Blue. The court tested the reliability of the witness under the same circumstances that existed on the night of the accident and concluded that the witness had correctly identified each of the two colors 80 percent of the time.

What is the probability that the cab involved in the accident was Blue rather than Green?

The answer to this question is not merely a matter of opinion. There is a specific rule of probability, Bayes's theorem, that dictates how the probability assessment in such a question is to be calculated. The theorem provides the optimal way of combining the two pieces of information that have been given: overall, 15 percent of the cabs are Blue, and a witness whose identification accuracy is 80 percent identified the cab in question as Blue. Most people do not naturally combine the two pieces of information in the optimal manner. In fact, many people are surprised to learn that the probability that the cab is Blue is .41, and that, despite the witness's identification, it is still more likely that the cab involved in the accident was Green rather than Blue. The reason is that the general or prior probability that the cab is Green (85 percent) is higher than the credibility of the witness's identification of Blue (80 percent). Many people have been given this problem, and most estimates cluster in the range of .60–.80. That is, most people greatly overestimate the probability that the cab is Blue. They overweight the witness's identification and underweight the base rate, or prior probability, that the cab is Blue. This is another example of the tendency for concrete single-case information to overwhelm more abstract statistical information. Of course, in this case people seem to forget or ignore the fact that the identification by the witness is *just* as probabilistic as the base rate information.

Another example from the work of Kahneman and Tversky (1973) illustrates the tendency to underweight prior probabilities. Subjects were given the following problem: A panel of psychologists has interviewed and administered personality tests to 30 engineers and 70 lawyers, all successful in their respective fields. On the basis of this information, thumbnail descriptions of the 30 engineers and 70 lawyers have been written. You will now be given forms on which five descriptions chosen at random from the 100 available descriptions have been printed. For each description, please indicate, on a scale from 0 to 100, what you think the probability is that the person described is an engineer.

One of the descriptions was as follows: Jack is a 45-year-old man. He is married and has four children. He is generally conservative, careful, and ambitious. He shows no interest in political and social issues and spends most of his free time on his many hobbies, which include home carpentry, sailing, and mathematical puzzles. The probability that Jack is one of the 30 engineers in the sample of 100 is what percentage?

One group of subjects is given the problem as just described, while the other is given the same problem with the baseline probabilities reversed. That is, they are told that there are 70 engineers and 30 lawyers. The description given above is biased toward most people's stereotype of an engineer. However, it is not necessary to know how strongly characteristic of an engineer the description is in actuality to demonstrate the point of this example. No matter how diagnostic it is, the descriptive information should be combined with the prior probability, again via Bayes's theorem, to form the probability assessment. This means that, even if we accept each person's individualized assessment of the description, there are still rules that put constraints on probabilistic judgments in such a situation. [The probability that the description represents an engineer should be higher for the subjects for which the prior probability of an engineer was 70 percent than for the subjects in which the prior probability was 30 percent.] However, in several experiments it has been found that the subjects presented with this problem do not take prior probability into account (Lyon & Slovic, 1976). The probability assessments by the two subject groups are frequently very similar, an indication that they ignored the prior probabilities and relied entirely on the diagnosticity of the descriptive information (Dawes, Mirels, Gold, & Donahue, 1993), which, by the way, other research on personality indicates is often lower in validity than most people think.

What is more surprising, this particular error in probabilistic reasoning is not limited to the scientifically unsophisticated layperson. Casscells, Schoenberger, and Graboys (1978) gave a variant of the following problem to 20 house officers, 20 medical students, and 20 attending physicians at four Harvard Medical School teaching hospitals: Imagine that the virus (HIV) that causes AIDS occurs in 1 in every 1,000 people. Imagine also that there is a test to diagnose the disease that always indicates correctly that a person who has HIV actually has it. Finally, imagine that the test has a false-positive rate of 5 percent. This means that the test wrongly indicates that HIV is present in 5 percent of the cases where the person does not have the virus. Imagine that we choose a person randomly and administer the test, and that it yields a positive result (indicates that the person is HIV-positive). What is the probability that the individual actually has the HIV virus, assuming that we know nothing else about the individual's personal or medical history?

The average of all responses to the question was 55.9 percent, and the most common answer was 95 percent. The correct answer is approximately 2 percent. The physicians vastly overestimated the probability that a positive result truly indicated the disease because of the same tendency to overweight the case information and underweight the base rate information that we discussed previously. Although the correct answer to this problem can be calculated by means of Bayes's rule, a little logical reasoning can help to illustrate the profound effect that base rates have on probabilities. Of 1,000 people, 1 will actually be HIV-positive. If the other 999 (who do not have the disease) are tested, the test would indicate incorrectly that approximately 50 of them had the virus (.05 multiplied by 999) because of the 5 percent false-positive rate. Thus, of the 51 patients testing positive, only 1 (approximately 2 percent) would actually be HIV-positive. In short, the base rate is such that the vast majority of people do not have the virus. This fact, combined with a substantial false-positive rate, ensures that, in absolute numbers, the vast majority of positive tests will be of people who do not have the virus.

Although all the physicians in the Casscells et al. study would have immediately recognized the correctness of this logic, their initial tendency was to discount the base rates and overweight the clinical evidence. In short, the physicians actually knew better but were initially drawn to an incorrect conclusion. Psychologists have termed problems like these *cognitive illusions.* In cognitive illusions, even when people know the correct answer, they may be drawn to an incorrect conclusion by the structure of the problem.

All the examples given here are cognitive illusions because they capitalize on a fallacy of human reasoning: the tendency to overweight individual case evidence and underweight statistical information. The case evidence (the witness's identification, the description of the individual, and the laboratory test result) seems "tangible" and "concrete" to most people, whereas the probabilistic evidence seems—well—probabilistic. This reasoning, of course, is fallacious because case evidence itself is always probabilistic. A witness can make correct identifications with only a certain *degree* of accuracy, a description has only a *probability* of characterizing an engineer, and a clinical test misidentifies the presence of the disease with a certain *probability.* The situation is one in which *two* probabilities, the probable diagnosticity of the case evidence and the prior probability, must be combined if one is to arrive at a correct decision. There are right and wrong ways of combining these probabilities, and more often than not—particularly when the case evidence gives the illusion of concreteness (recall our discussion of the vividness problem in Chapter 4)—people combine the information in the wrong way. This particular failure of probabilistic reasoning may very well hinder the use of psychological knowledge, which is often stated in the form of probabilistic relationships between behaviors.

Finally, the AIDS example above is a good illustration of the importance of statistical-probabilistic thinking in our society. This was not a made-up problem. Mandatory AIDS testing in various employment and government settings has been a hotly debated issue for almost ten years, and sadly it will probably continue to be an issue in our society. As mathematics professor Lynn Steen (1990) argued:

> The continuing debate over mandatory AIDS testing provides a good example of quantitative issues hidden just beneath the surface of many public debates. . . . There will always be a small number (perhaps 2 percent) of errors. . . . The public infers from this that testing is 98 percent accurate. But since the actual incidence of AIDS in the general population is less than the error in the test, any widespread test administered to a random sample of citizens will produce more results indicative of AIDS because of errors in the test than the actual AIDS in the population. The personal consequences of these erroneous messages in psychological, economic, and emotional grief are rarely recognized by a public which naively assumes that any accurate test will produce accurate results when put into widespread use. (p. 218)

Inverting Conditional Probabilities

All dogs are mammals. Correct. All mammals are dogs. Incorrect. We realize the simple rule that if all A are B it does not necessarily follow that all B are A. Even with so simple a rule, though, things can sometimes get confusing. Consider the following two premises: All flowers have petals; roses have petals. Does it follow logically from these two premises that roses are flowers? At first glance you might think yes. But look more closely. The statement "Roses are flowers" does *not* follow logically from the previous two premises, although even many college-educated subjects think it does (Markovits & Nantel, 1989). The error that even many educated subjects fall into is that they invert the first premise. They read all flowers have petals as implying that all things with petals are flowers. This inversion is what invites the inference that roses are flowers when one is given the premise that roses have petals. In fact, however, because some things with petals may not be flowers, the statement that roses have petals does not guarantee that roses are flowers.

Inverting premises is a common error of logical thinking. The mistaken inversion of statements happens even more frequently in the domain of probabilistic reasoning, particularly in reasoning about conditional probabilities. By *conditional probability*, we mean the probability of a particular event, A, given that another, B, has happened. The inversion error in probabilistic reasoning is thinking that the probability of A, given B, is the same as the probability of B, given A. The two are not the same, yet they are frequently treated as if they are. Sometimes the difference between these two probabilities is easy to see because of the content of the problem. For example, it is obvious that the probability of pregnancy, given that intercourse has occurred, is different from the probability of intercourse, given that pregnancy has occurred!

However, sometimes the content of the problem leads us astray. For example, Dawes (1988) described an article in a California newspaper that ran a headline implying that most student users of marijuana were using hard drugs. However, the first couple of lines of the article reported a survey indicating that most students who were using hard drugs had once smoked marijuana. The newspaper article had clearly inverted the probabilities. To put it in probabilistic terms, the headline implied that the survey was about the probability of using hard drugs, given that marijuana had been smoked, but actually the article was about the inverse probability: the probability of having smoked marijuana, given that the student was using hard drugs. The problem is that the two probabilities are vastly different. The probability that students use hard drugs, given that they have smoked marijuana, is much, much smaller than the probability of having smoked marijuana given that students are using hard drugs. The reason is that most people who smoke marijuana do not use hard drugs, but most people who use hard drugs have tried marijuana.

Dawes (1988) cited the humorous example of a magazine article titled "This Quiz Could Save Your Life Next Weekend." The author of the article made the somewhat startling statement that "the farther one drives from home the safer one might be" (Dawes, 1988, p. 72). The basis of this statement was the statistic that most automobile deaths occur within 25 miles of home. In implying that if one drives farther from home one will decrease the probability of death, the author had inverted probabilities: the probability of death, given long distance, is not the same as the probability of long distance, given death!

Not so humorous, however, is a domain in which the inversion of conditional probabilities happens quite often: medical diagnosis (Eddy, 1982; Schwartz & Griffin, 1986). It has been found that physicians (and sometimes their textbooks) tend to invert probabilities, thinking, mistakenly, that the probability of disease, given a particular symptom, is the same as the probability of the symptom, given the disease.

What if I told you that you had been given a cancer test and that the results were positive? Furthermore, what if I told you that this particular test had a diagnostic accuracy of 90 percent—that is, that 90 percent of the time, when cancer was present this test gave a positive result? You might well be extremely upset. However, you might be much less upset if I told that you that the chances that you had cancer were less than 20 percent. How can this be if the test has a diagnostic accuracy of 90 percent? Imagine that a study of this test was done in which 1,000 patients were tested, and that 100 of them actually had cancer. Imagine that the results were as follows:

	Cancer present	Cancer absent
Test positive	90	500
Test negative	10	400

In this table, we can see the test's diagnostic accuracy of 90 percent. Of the 100 people with cancer, the test gave a positive result for 90. But you can immediately see that this is not the probability that is relevant to you. The 90 percent figure is the probability that the test result will be positive for someone who *has* cancer. But what you are interested in is the inverse: the probability that you have cancer, *given* that the test result is positive. That probability is only 15.3 percent (90 divided by 590).

Unfortunately, this example is not just imaginary. Dawes (1988, p. 73) discussed a physician who was recommending a type of preventive treatment because he confused the probability of cancer, given the diagnostic indicator, with the probability of the diagnostic indicator, given that the patient had cancer. Since the preventive treatment was a type of mastectomy, we can readily understand how serious this error in probabilistic reasoning can be.

Failure to Use Sample Size Information

Consider these two problems, developed by Tversky and Kahneman (1974):

1. A certain town is served by two hospitals. In the larger hospital about 45 babies are born each day, and in the smaller hospital about 15 babies are born each day. As you know, about 50 percent of all babies are boys. However, the exact percentage varies from day to day. Sometimes it is higher than 50 percent, sometimes lower. For a period of one year, each hospital recorded the days on which more than 60 percent of the babies born were boys. Which hospital do you think recorded more such days?

    a. The larger hospital
    b. The smaller hospital
    c. About the same

2. Imagine an urn filled with balls, two thirds of which are of one color and one third of which are of another. One individual has drawn 5 balls from the urn and found that 4 are red and 1 is white. Another individual has drawn 20 balls and found that 12 are red and 8 are white. Which of the two individuals should feel more confident that the urn contains two-thirds red balls and one-third white balls, rather than vice versa? What odds should each individual give?

In problem 1, the majority of people answer "about the same." People not choosing this alternative pick the larger and the smaller hospital with about equal frequency. Since the correct answer is the smaller hospital, approximately 75 percent of subjects given this problem answer incorrectly. These incorrect answers result from an inability to recognize the importance of sample size in the problem. Other things being equal, a larger sample size always more accurately estimates a population value. Thus, on any given day, the larger hospital, with its larger sample size, will tend to have a proportion of births closer to 50 percent. Conversely, a small sample size is always more likely to deviate from the population value. Thus the smaller hospital will have more days on which the proportion of births displays a large discrepancy from the population value (60 percent boys, 40 percent boys, 80 percent boys).

In problem 2, most people feel that the sample of 5 balls provides more convincing evidence that the urn is predominantly red. Actually, the probabilities are in the opposite direction. The odds are 8 to 1 that the urn is predominantly red for the 5-ball sample, but they are 16 to 1 that the urn is predominantly red for the 20-ball sample. Even though the proportion of red balls is higher in the 5-ball sample (80 percent versus 60 percent), this is more than compensated for by the fact that the other sample is four times as large and thus is more likely to be an accurate estimate of the proportions in the urn. The judgment of most subjects, however, is dominated by the higher proportion of red in the 5-ball sample and does not take adequate account of the greater reliability of the 20-ball sample.

An appreciation of the influence of sample size on the reliability of information is a basic principle of evidence evaluation that applies in many different areas but, again, is particularly relevant to understanding research in the behavioral sciences. Whether we realize it or not, we all hold generalized beliefs about large populations. What we often do not realize is how tenuous the database is on which our most steadfast beliefs rest. Throw together some observations about a few neighbors and a few people at work, add some random anecdotes from the TV news, and we are all-too-ready to make statements about "human nature" or "the American people." This is to say nothing of the lack of representativeness of the sample, which is another issue entirely.

The Tendency to Try to Explain Chance Events

Our brains have evolved in such a way that they engage in a relentless search for patterns in the world. We seek relationships, explanations, and meaning in the things that happen around us. This is obviously a very adaptive characteristic that allows us to predict what will happen in the world and perhaps eventually to develop more powerful explanations of why certain patterns exist. This search for patterns is, of course, what the scientist does. But the tendency to seek meaning and patterns in the world is certainly not limited to scientists. It is something we all do every day of our lives. This strong tendency to search for structure has been studied by psychologists. It is characteristic of human intelligence, and it accounts for many of the most astounding feats of information processing and knowledge acquisition that humans can perform.

Nevertheless, this extremely adaptive aspect of human cognition sometimes backfires on us. The quest for conceptual understanding is maladaptive when it takes place in an environment in which there is nothing to conceptualize. What plays havoc with one of the most distinguishing features of human cognition? What confounds our quest for structure and obscures understanding? You guessed it: probability. Or more specifically: chance and randomness.

Chance and randomness are integral parts of our environment. The mechanisms of biological evolution and genetic recombination are governed by laws of chance and randomness. Physics has taught us to explain the fundamental structure of matter by invoking statistical laws of chance. Many things that happen in nature are a complex result of systematic, explainable factors and chance. Again, recall a previous example: smoking causes lung cancer. A systematic, explainable aspect of biology links smoking to this particular disease. But not all smokers contract lung cancer. The trend is probabilistic. Perhaps we will eventually be able to explain why some smokers do not contract cancer. However, for the time being, this variability must be ascribed to the multitude of chance factors that determine whether a person will contract a particular disease.

As this example illustrates, when we say that something is due to chance, we do not necessarily mean that it is *indeterminate,* only that it is currently *indeterminable.* A coin toss is a chance event, but not because it is in principle impossible to determine the outcome by measuring the angle of the toss, the precise composition of the coin, and many other variables. In fact, the outcome of a toss is determined by all these variables. Instead, a coin toss is called a chance event because there is no easy way to measure all the variables in the event. The outcome of a toss is not in principle indeterminate, just currently indeterminable. As Alcock (1981) stated, "When we say that the outcome of a coin toss is due to chance, we mean that it is governed by variables that we are not able to measure" (p. 155).

Many events in the world are not entirely explainable in terms of systematic factors, at least not currently. We must invoke the multitude of chance factors that are operating. However, most people do not find this a satisfying answer. This kind of hesitance is fine when it serves to spur us on to the further investigation of a phenomenon, but it is a hindrance when it lures us into prematurely accepting an explanation that falsely promises full understanding in the absence of empirical support.

Although sometimes no systematic explanation of a particular phenomenon is currently available, our conceptualizing apparatus still grinds away, imposing meaningless theories on data that are inherently random. Psychologists have conducted experiments on this phenomenon. In one experimental situation, subjects view a series of stimuli that vary in many different dimensions. The subjects are told that some stimuli belong to one class and other stimuli belong to another. Their task is to guess which class each of a succession of stimuli belongs to. However, the researcher actually assigns the stimuli to classes randomly. Thus there is no rule except randomness. The subjects, however, rarely venture randomness as a guess. Instead, they often concoct extremely elaborate and complicated theories to explain how the stimuli are being assigned. Even when informed that the assignment was random, the subjects often express displeasure and insist that the experimenter was actually using the elaborate theory that they had derived.

Similarly, "conspiracy theories" of various types usually require layers and layers of complicated schemes to explain the sequence of random events that their adherents are desperately seeking to understand. This phenomenon is characteristic even of various authorities working in their area of expertise. For example, the thinking of many financial analysts illustrates this fallacy. They routinely concoct elaborate explanations for every little fluctuation in stock market prices. In fact, much of this variability is simply random fluctuation (Fama, 1965; Malkiel, 1990; Shefrin & Statman, 1986; Shiller, 1987). Nevertheless, stock market "analysts" continue to imply to their customers (and perhaps themselves believe) that they can "beat the market" when there is voluminous evidence that the vast majority of them can do no such thing. If you had bought all of the 500 stocks in the Standard and Poor's Index and simply held them throughout the 1970s, you would have had higher returns than 80 percent of the money managers on Wall Street (Malkiel, 1990). If you had done the same thing in the 1980s, you would have beaten two thirds of the money managers on Wall Street (Malkiel, 1990). You would also have beaten 80 percent of the financial newsletters which subscribers buy at rates of up to $500 per year (Kim, 1994). Even in the 1990s—which have been termed a "stock picker's market"—the same "no-brain" strategy would have beaten roughly half of the money managers on Wall Street.

But what about the 50 percent of the managers that beat the no-brain strategy? You might be wondering whether this means that this 50 percent has some special skill. We can answer that question by considering the following thought experiment. One hundred monkeys have each been given ten darts, and they are each going to throw them at a wall containing the names of each of the Standard and Poor's 500 stocks. Where the darts land will define that monkey's stock picks for the year. How will they do a year later? How many will beat the Standard and Poor's 500 Index? You guessed it. Roughly half of the monkeys (the S & P 500 Index beat *more* than 50 percent of the managers during the two decades of the 1970s and 1980s because it incurred no trading costs and because it was fully invested in a time of rising markets). Would you be interested in paying the 50 percent of the monkeys who beat the index a commission charge to make your picks for you next year?

The logic by which purely random sequences seem to be the result of predictable factors is illustrated by a continuation of this example of financial predictions. The following example is taken from Paulos (1988) and Fridson (1993). Imagine that a letter comes in the mail informing you of the existence of a stock-market-prediction newsletter. The newsletter does not ask for money but simply tells you to test it out. It tells you that IBM stock is going to go up during the next month. You put the letter away, but you do notice that, next month, IBM stock does go up. Having read a book like this one, however, you know better than to make anything of this result. You chalk it up to a lucky guess. You then receive another newsletter from the same investment-advice company telling you that IBM stock will go down next month. When the stock does go down, you again chalk the prediction up to a lucky guess, but you do get a bit curious. When the third letter from the same company comes and predicts that IBM will go down again the following month, you do find yourself watching the financial pages a little more closely, and you confirm for the third time that the newsletter's prediction was correct. IBM went down that month. When the fourth newsletter arrives from the same company and tells you that the stock will rise the next month, and it actually does move in the predicted direction for the fourth time, it becomes difficult to escape the feeling that this is for real, difficult to escape the feeling that maybe you should send in the $29.95 for a year's worth of this newsletter that you have finally been offered in the fourth letter. Difficult to escape the feeling, that is, unless you can imagine the cheap basement office in which someone is preparing next week's batch of 1,600 newsletters to be sent to 1,600 phone book addresses: 800 of the newsletters predict that IBM will go up during the next month, and 800 of the newsletters predict that IBM will go down during the next month. When IBM does go up, that office sends out letters to *only* the 800 addressees who got the correct prediction the month before (400 predicting that the stock will go up in the next month and 400 predicting that it will go down, of course). Then you can imagine the "boiler room"—probably with telemarketing scams purring on the phones in the background—sending the third month's predictions to only the 400 who got the correct prediction the second week. And, yes, you were one of the lucky 100 who received four correct random predictions in a row! One of the lucky 100 (very impressed) individuals asked to pay $29.95 to keep the newsletters coming.

Now this seems like a horrible scam to play on people. And indeed it is. But it is no less a scam than when "respectable" financial magazines and TV shows present to you the "money manager who has beaten more than half his peers four years in a row!" Again, think back to our monkeys throwing the darts. Imagine that they were money managers making stock picks year after year. By definition, 50 percent of them will beat their "peers" during the first year. Half of these will again—by chance—beat their peers in the second year, making a total of 25 percent who beat their peers two years in a row. Half of these will again—by chance—beat their peers in the third year, making a total of 12.5 percent who beat their peers *three* years in a row. And finally, half of these 12.5 percent (i.e., 6.25 percent) will again beat their peers in the fourth year. Thus about 6 of the 100 monkeys will have, as the financial shows and newspapers say, "consistently beaten other money managers for four years in a row." These 6 monkeys who beat their dartboard peers (and, as we saw above, would beat most *actual* Wall Street money managers; see Malkiel, 1990) should certainly deserve spots on the *Wall Street Week* television program, don't you think?

Commenting on the logic of the "beating-their-peers-X-years-in-a-row" fallacy, Martin Fridson (1993) noted that

> the analysis you've just read exposes a fallacy that is repeated every day in the financial markets. Investment advisers regularly win new clients on the strength of performance records that are not demonstrably better than chance results. Market forecasters routinely persuade investors of their excellence by stringing together just a few correct predictions. If these representations of superior skill can be discredited so easily, why do people persist in relying on them? . . . Investors simply do not understand the basic principles of probability. (p. 67)

Explaining Chance: Illusory Correlation and the Illusion of Control

The tendency to explain chance events is illustrated in a phenomenon that psychologists have studied that is called *illusory correlations*. When people believe that two types of events should commonly occur together, they tend to think that they are seeing co-occurrences with great frequency, even when the two critical events are occurring randomly and thus do not co-occur more frequently than any other combination of events. In short, people tend to see their expected "correlation" even in random events (Nisbett & Ross, 1980). They see structure where there is none.

Controlled studies (e.g., Broniarczyk & Alba, 1994; Chapman & Chapman, 1969; Nisbett & Ross, 1980) have demonstrated that, when people have a prior belief that two variables are connected, they tend to see that connection even in data in which the two variables are totally unconnected. Unfortunately this finding generalizes to some real-world situations that adversely affect people's lives. For example, many psychological practitioners continue to believe in the efficacy of the Rorschach test. This is the famous inkblot test, in which the subject responds to blotches on a white paper. Because the inkblots lack structure, the theory is that people will respond to them in the same style that they typically respond to ambiguity and thus reveal "hidden" psychological traits. The test is called *projective* because the subject presumably "projects" unconscious psychological thoughts and feelings in their responses to the inkblots. The problem with all of this is that there is no evidence that the Rorschach test has any diagnostic utility when used as "projective" test (Dawes, 1994; Shontz & Green, 1992; Widiger & Schilling, 1980). Belief in the Rorschach test arises from the phenomenon of illusory correlation. Clinicians see relationships in response patterns because they believe they are there, not because they are actually present in the pattern of responses being observed (Broniarczyk & Alba, 1994; Chapman & Chapman, 1967, 1969).

Psychologist Ray Hyman (1981) discussed the tendency to see patterns when there are none:

> We have to bring our knowledge and expectations to bear in order to comprehend anything in our world. In most ordinary situations this use of context and memory enables us to correctly interpret statements and supply the necessary in-

ferences to do this. But this powerful mechanism can go astray in situations where there is no actual message being conveyed. Instead of picking up random noise we still manage to find meaning in the situation. (p. 96)

Many of the interpersonal encounters in our lives have a large amount of chance in them (Bandura, 1982): the blind date that leads to marriage, the canceled appointment that loses a job, the missed bus that leads to a meeting with an old high-school friend. It is a mistake to think that each chance event of our lives requires an elaborate explanation. But when essentially chance events lead to important consequences, it is difficult to avoid constructing complicated theories to explain them.

The tendency to try to explain chance probably derives from a deep desire to believe that we can control such events. Psychologist Ellen Langer (1975) studied what has been termed the *illusion of control,* that is, the tendency to believe that personal skill can affect outcomes determined by chance. In one study two employees of two different companies sold lottery tickets to their co-workers. Some people were simply handed a ticket, while others were allowed to choose their ticket. Of course, in a random drawing it makes no difference whether a person chooses a ticket or is assigned one. The next day the two employees who had sold the tickets approached each individual and attempted to buy the tickets back. The subjects who had chosen their own tickets demanded four times as much money as the subjects who had been handed their tickets! In several other experiments Langer confirmed the hypothesis that this outcome resulted from an inability to accept the fact that factors of skill cannot affect chance events. Evidence of the widespread nature of this fallacy comes from the experience of states in which lotteries have been instituted. These states are descended on by purveyors of bogus books advising people how to "beat" the lottery (Clotfelter & Cook, 1989), books that sell because people do not understand the implications of randomness. In fact, the explosion in the popularity of state lotteries in the United States did not occur until the mid-1970s, when New Jersey introduced "participatory" games in which players could scratch cards or pick their own numbers (Clotfelter & Cook, 1989; Thaler, 1992). These participatory games exploit the illusion of control investigated by Langer: people's mistaken belief that their behavior determines random events.

Other psychologists have studied a related phenomenon known as the *just-world hypothesis,* that is, the fact that people tend to believe that they live in a world in which people get what they deserve (Lerner & Miller, 1978). Researchers have found empirical support for one corollary of the belief in a just world: that people tend to derogate the victims of chance misfortune. The tendency to seek explanations for chance events contributes to this phenomenon. People apparently find it very hard to believe that a perfectly innocent or virtuous person can suffer misfortune purely because of chance. We long to believe that good things happen to good people and bad things happen to the bad. Chance, though, is completely unbiased. It operates on a completely different principle, one in which the frequency of good and bad chance events is equal for all types of people.

The belief in a just world can, when taken to an extreme, result in very harmful and dehumanizing doctrines. Consider its logical end point in the statement of an official in the U.S. Department of Education in the early 1980s, that hand-icapped individuals "falsely assume that the lottery of life has penalized them at random. This is not so. Nothing comes to an individual that he has not, at some point in his development, summoned. . . . As unfair as it may seem, a person's external circumstances do fit his level of inner spiritual development" (Gilovich, 1991, p. 143). As Gilovich noted, "This is not exactly the philosophy that one would want in the upper reaches of the Department of Education, the department that is responsible for overseeing educational opportunities for the handi-capped" (pp. 143–144)—but it is the point that we invariably reach if we refuse to attribute any outcomes to chance.

People's misunderstanding of chance that is reflected in their belief in a just world serves to support many other incorrect folk beliefs. It leads to the tendency to see illusory correlations. We mentioned in Chapter 6, for example, the incor-rect belief (see Niemeyer & Starlinger, 1981; Stankov & Spilsbury, 1978) that blind people are "blessed" with supersensitive hearing, a folk myth probably per-petuated because people desire to see a correlation that "evens things out."

Accepting Error in Order to Reduce Error: Clinical Versus Actuarial Prediction

The reluctance to acknowledge the role of chance when trying to explain out-comes in the world can actually *decrease* our ability to predict real-world events. Acknowledging the role of chance in determining outcomes in a domain means that we must accept the fact that our predictions will never be 100 percent accu-rate, that we will always make some errors in our predictions. But interestingly, acknowledging that our predictions will be less than 100 percent accurate can ac-tually help us to *increase* our overall predictive accuracy. It may seem paradoxical, but it is true that we must *accept* error in order to *reduce* error (Dawes, 1991; Einhorn, 1986).

The concept that we must accept error in order to reduce error is illustrated by a very simple experimental task that has been studied in cognitive psychology laboratories for decades (Tversky & Edwards, 1966). The subject sits in front of two lights (one red and one blue) and is told that she or he is to predict which of the lights will be flashed on each trial and that there will be several dozen such trials (subjects are often paid money for correct predictions). The experimenter has actually programmed the lights to flash randomly, with the provision that the red light will flash 70 percent of the time and the blue light 30 percent of the time. Subjects do quickly pick up the fact that the red light is flashing more, and they predict that it will flash on more trials than they predict that the blue light will flash. In fact, they predict that the red light will flash approximately 70 per-cent of the time. However, as discussed earlier in this chapter, subjects come to believe that there is a pattern in the light flashes and almost never think that the sequence is random. Instead, they attempt to get every prediction correct, switch-ing back and forth from red to blue, predicting the red light roughly 70 percent of the time and the blue light roughly 30 percent of the time. Subjects rarely re-alize that *if they would give up trying to predict every trial correctly they would actually do better!* How can this be?

Let's consider the logic of the situation. How many predictions will subjects get correct if they predict the red light roughly 70 percent of the time and the blue light roughly 30 percent of the time and the lights are really coming on randomly in a ratio of 70 to 30? We will do the calculation on 100 trials in the middle of the experiment—after the subject has noticed that the red light comes on more often and is thus predicting the red light roughly 70 percent of the time. Let's consider what will happen in a block of 100 trials in the middle of this experiment. In 70 of the 100 trials, the red light will come on and the subject will be correct about 70 percent of those 70 trials (because the subject predicts the red light 70 percent of the time). That is, in 49 of the 70 trials (70 times .70), the subject will correctly predict that the red light will come on. In 30 of the 100 trials, the blue light will come on, and the subject will be correct in 30 percent of those 30 trials (because the subject predicts the blue light 30 percent of the time). That is, in 9 of the 30 trials (30 times .30), the subject will correctly predict that the blue light will come on. Thus, in 100 trials, the subject is correct 58 percent of the time (49 correct predictions in red light trials and 9 correct predictions in blue light trials). But notice that this is a poorer performance than could be achieved if the subject simply noticed which light was coming on more often and then predicted it in every trial—in this case, noticing that the red light came on more often and predicting it in every trial (let's call this the 100 percent red strategy). Of the 100 trials, 70 would be red flashes, and the subject would have predicted 70 of these correctly. Of the 30 blue flashes, the subject would have predicted none correctly, but this still leaves a prediction accuracy of 70 percent—12 percent better than the 58 percent correct that the subject achieved by switching back and forth trying to get every trial correct!

The superior accuracy of the 100 percent red strategy is achieved at a cost, however: the cost of giving up the hope of getting each trial correct (obviously, if the blue light is coming up occasionally and the subject is always predicting red, the subject gives up any chance of getting the blue trials correct). This is what we mean by accepting error in order to make less error. By giving up the hope of predicting every single case, the subject achieves better overall accuracy. Predicting human behavior with some accuracy often involves accepting error in order to reduce error, that is, of getting better prediction by relying on general principles but acknowledging that we cannot be right in every single case.

Accepting error in order to make fewer errors is a difficult thing to do, however, as evidenced by the the forty-year history of research on clinical versus actuarial prediction in psychology. The term *actuarial prediction* refers to predictions of group trends based on probabilities derived from statistical records, the type of group, or aggregate, predictions that we discussed at the beginning of this chapter. A simple actuarial prediction is one that predicts the same outcome for all individuals sharing a certain characteristic. So, for example, predicting a life span of 77.5 years for people who do not smoke and a life span of 64.3 years for individuals who smoke would be an example of an actuarial prediction. More accurate predictions can be made if we take more than one group characteristic into account (using the complex correlational techniques mentioned in Chapter 5—specifically a technique known as *multiple regression*). For example, predicting a life span of 58.2 years for people who smoke, are overweight, and do not exercise would be an example of an actuarial prediction based on a set of variables (smoking behavior, weight, and amount of exercise), and such predictions are almost always more accurate than predictions made from a single variable. Such actuarial predictions are common in economics, human resources, criminology, business and marketing, and the medical sciences.

Knowledge in most subareas of psychology, such as cognitive psychology, developmental psychology, organizational psychology, personality psychology, and social psychology, is stated in terms of actuarial predictions. In contrast, some subgroups of clinical psychological practitioners claim to be able to go beyond group predictions and to make accurate predictions of the outcomes of particular individuals. This is called *clinical,* or *case, prediction.* When engaged in clinical prediction, as opposed to actuarial prediction, "professional psychologists claim to be able to make predictions about individuals that transcend predictions about 'people in general' or about various categories of people. . . . Where professional psychologists differ is in their claim to understand the single individual as unique rather than as part of a group about which statistical generalizations are possible. They claim to be able to analyze 'what caused what' in an *individual's* life rather than to state what is 'in general' true" (Dawes, 1994, pp. 79–80). Clinical prediction would seem to be a very useful addition to actuarial prediction. There is just one problem, however. Clinical prediction doesn't work.

For clinical prediction to be useful, the clinician's experience with the client and her or his use of information about the client would have to result in better predictions than we can get from simply coding information about the client and submitting it to the multiple-regression procedure (a complex correlational technique designed to optimize the process of combining quantitative data in order to derive predictions). In short, the claim is that the experience of psychological practitioners allows them to go beyond the aggregate relationships that have been uncovered by research. The claim that clinical prediction is efficacious is thus easily testable. Unfortunately the claim has been tested, and it has been falsified.

Research on the issue of clinical versus actuarial prediction has been stunningly consistent. Since the publication in 1954 of Paul Meehl's classic book *Clinical Versus Statistical Prediction,* four decades of research consisting of over a hundred research studies has shown that, in just about every clinical prediction domain that has ever been examined (psychotherapy outcome, parole behavior, college graduation rates, response to electroshock therapy, criminal recidivism, length of psychiatric hospitalization, and many more), actuarial prediction has been found to be superior to clinical prediction (e.g., Dawes, 1994; Dawes, Faust, & Meehl, 1989; Faust, Hart, Guilmette, & Arkes, 1988; Goldberg, 1959, 1968, 1991; Leli & Filskov, 1981; Sawyer, 1966). In a variety of clinical domains, when a clinician is given information about a client and asked to predict the client's behavior, and when the same information is quantified and processed by a multiple-regression equation that has been developed based on actuarial relationships that research has uncovered, invariably the equation wins; that is, the actuarial prediction is more accurate than the clinician's prediction (e.g., Dawes, 1994; Dawes, et al., 1989). In fact, even when the clinician has more information available than is used in the actuarial method, the latter is superior. That is, when the clinician has information from personal contact and interviews with the client, in addition to the same information that goes into the actuarial equation, the clinical predictions still do not achieve an accuracy as great as the actuarial method: "Even when given an information edge, the clinical judge still fails to surpass the actuarial method; in fact, access to additional information often does nothing to close the gap between the two methods" (Dawes et al., 1989, p. 1670).

A final type of test in the clinical-actuarial prediction literature involves actually giving the clinician the predictions from the actuarial equation and asking the clinician to adjust the predictions based on his or her personal experience with the clients. When the clinician makes adjustments in the actuarial predictions, the adjustments actually *decrease* the accuracy of the predictions (see Dawes, 1994). Here we have an example of failing to "accept error in order to reduce error" that is directly analogous to the light prediction experiment that was previously described. Rather than relying on the "actuarial" information that the red light came on more often and predicting red each time (and getting 70 percent correct), the subjects tried to be correct on each trial by alternating red and blue predictions and ended up being 12 percent less accurate (they were correct on only 58 percent of the trials). Analogously the clinicians in these studies believed that their experience gave them "clinical insight" and allowed them to make better predictions than those that can be made from quantified information in the client's file. In fact, their "insight" is nonexistent and leads them to make predictions that are worse than those they would make if they relied only on the public, actuarial information.

Regarding the research showing the superiority of actuarial prediction over clinical prediction, Paul Meehl (1986) said, "There is no controversy in social science which shows such a large body of qualitatively diverse studies coming out so uniformly in the same direction as this one" (pp. 373–374). Yet, embarrassingly, the field of psychology does not act on this knowledge. For example, the field continues to use personal interviews in the graduate admissions process and in the mental-health-training admissions process, even though voluminous evidence suggests that these interviews have virtually no validity. Instead, practitioners continue to use specious arguments to justify their reliance on "clinical intuition" rather than aggregate predictions which would work better. For example, Dawes et al. (1989) noted that "a common anti-actuarial argument, or misconception, is that group statistics do not apply to single individuals or events. The argument abuses basic principles of probability. . . . An advocate of this anti-actuarial position would have to maintain, for the sake of logical consistency, that if one is forced to play Russian roulette a single time and is allowed to select a gun with one or five bullets in the chamber, the uniqueness of the event makes the choice arbitrary" (p. 1672).

Dawes et al. were illustrating here how our failure to think probabilistically can lead to some fairly strong illusions. For example, the Russian roulette example jars us into realizing the fallaciousness of the view that probabilities are not relevant to a single event. However, this particular illusion (that probabilities are not relevant to a single event) is so strong that social practices are often built on it. Neuroscientist Robert Sapolsky (1994) described how some states administer the death penalty by lethal injection. The state-of-the-art technology uses two control stations and two sets of syringes. Two different people activate a switch at the same time, and a computer with a binary random-number generator determines which syringe will be injected into the prisoner. Both syringes are destroyed in a collection vial. Thus neither of the switch throwers knows whose switch caused the death. All that the excutioners know is that they had a 50 percent chance of causing the death. Thus each can rest easily at night, correct? Executioner A thinks, "After all, there is only a 50 percent chance that my switch did it. Since I can't be *certain* that I did it, I really shouldn't think that I killed anyone." Of course, executioner B thinks exactly the same thing. Thus no one killed anyone, right?

Sapolsky (1994) discussed how these modern computer randomization procedures are simply the contemporary variant of the nineteenth-century procedure of giving one of the five men in a firing squad a blank. The logic was the same. Each man goes home at night thinking, "Since there is only an 80 percent probability that I killed the man, I can't be certain that I was the executioner, and because I can't be *certain,* I really shouldn't think I killed anyone." Thus *none* of the five members of the firing squad is supposed to feel responsible for the death. That was the theory in an era when it was believed that probabilities were irrelevant to the responsibility for single events. For example, before 1927 it was believed, and codified in the law, that the responsibility for a single event could not be distributed proportionally among parties:

> A different version of that principle is central to the idea of causation as taught in the law schools. Suppose two men start fires simultaneously, at opposite ends of a property. The fires merge and burn down the property. Who is responsible for the damage? The logic adopted by nineteenth-century American courts would have given solace to any participant in a firing squad. Each of the two arsonous defendants can correctly make the same point: If I had not set the fire, the property would still have burned. So how can I be guilty? Both of them would have walked free. (Sapolsky, 1994, p. 11)

But legal logic changed markedly in 1927 with a landmark court decision in the case of *Kingston v. Chicago and NW Railroad*. Two fires (one caused by a locomotive and another of unknown origin) had joined together to burn down a plaintiff's property. The railroad company made the—for that time—standard argument: "We can't be 50 percent responsible for the destruction of the property; if we are only 50 percent responsible, it is not *certain* that we are *totally* responsible, and therefore we are not responsible." The railroad company argued just like the executioner ("A 50 percent chance of responsibility means that I'm not *totally* responsible; therefore I am not responsible"). Contrary to the outcome in previous cases, this time the railroad lost. Conceptualizations of probability and responsibility had changed. The judge this time said, in effect, "A 50 percent chance of responsibility means *some* responsibility, and therefore you *are*—partially—responsible." As Sapolsky (1994) noted, "Before *Kingston,* judges would have ruled that the guilt of the singular burning of a property could not be distributed among multiple parties. But in the *Kingston* case, the courts declared for the first time that guilt for a singular burning, a singular injury, a singular killing could be distributed among contributing parties. . . . Suddenly it was possible for a number of people to be statistically guilty for a singular event" (p. 11–12).

And this has been the trend of modern society ever since. We are realizing that most guilt is probabilistic guilt, that most responsibility is probabilistic responsibility. To think otherwise is to absolve *all* our actions of guilt (because virtually all of our actions have probabilistic effects), and to absolve *every* person of responsibility. Sapolsky (1994) caricatured the attitude that we need not feel responsible for bad outcomes that are measured statistically. He asked us to imagine

> an archetypally villainous industrialist . . . contemplating a new profitable venture for his factory. His minions of advisers, on the basis of their calculations, tell him that the pollution his factory will dump into the drinking water will probably lead to three cancer deaths in his town of 100,000. Naturally he decides to go ahead with his plans. But that night he surely doesn't think in integers: "Today, for profit, I have consigned three innocents to their deaths." Instead, all his cognitive biases lead him to frame the matter in terms of statistical guilt: "All it does is increase the cancer risk .003 percent for each person. Trivial. Charles, you may serve me my dinner." (p. 12)

However, such an attitude is becoming more of a historical curiosity as society comes increasingly to recognize that probabilistic guilt is real. Our new attitude is most forcefully displayed by a comment from the leader of the Citizens' Clearinghouse for Hazardous Wastes, who asked, "Would you let me shoot into a crowd of one hundred thousand people and kill one of them? No? Well, how come Dow Chemical can do it?" (Greider, 1992, p. 56). The point here is that we must come to understand that exposing 100,000 people to a factor that increases the annualized death probability by .003 *is* the equivalent of shooting into a crowd.

Dawes (1994) discussed another objection to actuarial prediction: it is "impersonal." He pointed out that the issue of "personal" versus "impersonal" is not really relevant. Whether we are in the domain of clinical psychology, medical treatment, or financial advice, what we are debating is *what works*. Dawes conjectured that most people would prefer an impersonal treatment that worked to a personal one that didn't:

> What could possibly be of more personal importance to the person infected with HIV than the impersonal development of an HIV treatment? What could be more personally important to graduate school applicants, parolees, and heart attack patients . . . than an improvement in impersonal, statistical prediction techniques? It would mean fewer failures in careers, fewer victims of parolees who return to crime, fewer failed parolees, better medical treatment, and so on. . . . More personal benefit can be obtained by the impersonal development of a vaccine or by an understanding of the importance of sterile medical procedures, than by a great deal of personal caring—however well-motivated—that doesn't do much. (p. 182)

The field has little to lose in prestige by admitting the superiority of actuarial to clinical judgment in a domain such as predicting psychotherapeutic outcome because the same is true of professionals in numerous other domains as varied as medicine, business, criminology, accounting, and livestock judging (see Dawes, 1994; Dawes et al., 1989; Dowie & Elstein, 1988). Although the *field* as a whole would have little to lose, individual practitioners who engage in activities in the role of "experts" (i.e., in courtroom testimony) and imply that they have unique "clinical knowledge" of individual cases would, of course, lose prestige and perhaps income.

In fact, the field, and society, would benefit if we developed the habit of "accepting error in order to reduce error." In attempting to find unique explanations of every single unusual case (unique explanations that simply may not be possible given the present state of our knowledge), we often lose predictive accuracy in the more mundane cases. Recall the red–blue light experiment again. The "100 percent red strategy" makes incorrect predictions of all of the "minority" or "unusual" events (when the blue lights flash). What if we focused more on those "minority" events by adopting the "70-percent-red–30-percent-blue strategy"? We would now be able to predict 9 of those 30 "unusual" events (30 times .30). But the cost is that we lose our ability to predict 21 of the "majority" events. Instead of 70 correct predictions of red, we now only have 49 correct predictions (70 times .70). Predictions of behavior in the clinical domain have the same logic. In concocting complicated explanations for every case, we may indeed catch a few more "unusual cases"—but at the cost of losing predictive accuracy in the majority of cases, where simple actuarial prediction would work better.

Dawes (1991) told a funny story about meeting an inmate from a prison education program run by the university for which Dawes was working. The inmate had been a bartender in a tavern and had also had a side job collecting gambling debts (at gunpoint if necessary). One day, he was sent to another state, Oregon, to collect a sum of money. When he got to Oregon, he cornered the man owing the money and drew out his gun. Just then, the police jumped from hiding and arrested him on the spot. After telling Dawes the story, the inmate declared confidently that he would never go to jail again. When Dawes asked how he knew that he would never go to jail again, the inmate replied, "Because I'll never go to Oregon again!"

Now what was wrong with the inmate's thinking? If we ignore its context and accept it on its own terms, the inmate's deduction isn't bad. As Dawes (1991) wrote, "People laugh when I tell that story, but viewed in non-probabilistic terms, the enforcer's inference isn't that bad. He had collected debts at gunpoint many times without being arrested, and he had been in Oregon only once. To believe that there was something special about Oregon that 'caused' his arrest is compatible with the canons of inductive inference" (p. 245). The problem here is not the inference per se, but the focus on trying to explain a *particular* instance. The inmate was trying to explain why he was arrested in *Oregon*—why he was arrested *that particular time.* And it was this focus on the *instance, this* particular case, that was leading the inmate to an absurd conclusion. Instead, the inmate should have been thinking probabilistically. There was some probability of his being arrested each time he collected debts at gunpoint (perhaps 3 times in 100). The inmate had done it many times. This time he got arrested. It was simply 1 of those 3 times. The odds simply caught up with him. A general trend (such-and-such a probability of being arrested each time he collected a debt at gunpoint) explains why he was arrested. There was probably nothing unique about the fact that it happened to be in Oregon.

In this example we can see, by analogy, the harm done by ignoring more accurate actuarial information and relying on clinical prediction. The inmate was mimicking a clinical predictor by ignoring probabilities and relying on unique case knowledge, in this instance, intimate knowledge of his own particular history. The inmate's real-world experience—his personal insight and his intuition—led him to make the clinical prediction that he would not be arrested again if he collected debts at gunpoint outside Oregon. In contrast, the actuarial prediction is that, if he continued to collect debts—anywhere—he would eventually be arrested (if the odds are 9 to 1 against his getting arrested each time he collected a debt, there is still more than a 50 percent probability that he would be arrested before he had collected debts eight times). There may or may not have been anything special about the situation that occurred in Oregon, but as Dawes (1991) argued, "Certainly, there was a sequence of events preceding that incident that was not present in others, but is it productive to think of this sequence as a 'cause'? In fact, the attempt to discover such causes may contribute to the maintenance of behavior that is self-defeating or socially pernicious, because once we decide 'why' such a behavior led to bad consequences on one occasion but not on others, we may feel safe in repeating it" (p. 245).

The debt-collector example actually has a direct parallel in some real research results. Indeed, the research finding of the superiority of actuarial prediction over clinical prediction extends to the situation in which the clinical or case knowledge is as good as it could possibly be: knowledge about ourselves. Vallone, Griffin, Lin, and Ross (1990) studied college students' ability to predict future events in their own lives during an academic year. The subjects had to predict whether a particular event would occur in their lives and give a confidence judgment in terms of how probable they thought the event was. The events concerned academics (e.g., "I will drop a course this year"), friendships (e.g., "I will have a steady girl/boyfriend"), contact with home (e.g., "I will call my parents more than twice a month"), and activities (e.g., "I will visit San Francisco"; "I will join a fraternity/sorority"). Vallone et al. (1990) found that, in general, the students were overconfident in their predictions: they were more certain that they could predict their future behavior than they should have been. This finding replicates a well-known laboratory relationship involving the prediction of knowledge: people tend to be overconfident (Fischhoff, 1988; Griffin & Tversky, 1992; Lundeberg, Fox, & Puncochar, 1994).

When Vallone et al. (1990) looked at the *type* of errors their subjects had made when predicting their own future behavior, they found an interesting thing: these subjects had made errors in prediction primarily when they went against the base rate probability of that particular event. The base rate probability is simply the overall probability that the event would happen when the sample of subjects was considered as a whole. Some events have high base rates (they happen to most people in a sample), and some events have low base rates (they happen to only a few people in a sample). Almost all of the errors that the students made—and almost all of the mistaken overconfidence that they exhibited—were the result of predictions that went against the base rate, that is, when the subjects responded by saying, "Well, this may happen to most people, but it is *not* going to happen to me," or alternatively, "This may not be true of most people, but it *is* going to happen to me." In fact, the subjects would have been more accurate if they had just predicted the base rate for themselves and had not seen themselves as exceptions. Thinking that they had "special" knowledge about themselves actually made them more *in*accurate.

Here we have the clinical-actuarial situation again, and another example of not "accepting error in order to reduce error." As Vallone et al. (1990) pointed out, "No amount of knowledge about the actor, even knowledge that actors possess about themselves and their own past behavior, could have enhanced predictive accuracy and improved calibration as successfully as the judicious use of accurate baserate knowledge" (p. 590).

Wagenaar and Keren (1986) illustrated how overconfidence in personal knowledge and the discounting of statistical information can undermine safety campaigns advocating seat belt use because people think, "I am different, I drive safely." The problem is that over 85 percent of the population thinks that it is "better than the average driver" (Svenson, 1981)—obviously a patent absurdity.

The same fallacy of believing that "statistics don't apply to the single case" is an important factor in the thinking of individuals with chronic gambling problems. In his study of gambling behavior, Wagenaar (1988) concluded that "from our discussions with gamblers it has become abundantly clear that gamblers are generally aware of the negative long-term result. They know that they have lost more than they have won, and that it will be the same in the future. But they fail to apply these statistical considerations to the next round, the next hour, or the next night. A rich repertoire of heuristics . . . gives them the suggestion that statistics do not apply in the next round, or the next hour. That they can predict the next outcome" (p. 117). Wagenaar found that compulsive gamblers had a strong tendency not to "accept error in order to reduce error." For example, blackjack players had a tendency to reject a strategy called *basic* (see Wagenaar, 1988, Chapter 2) that is guaranteed to decrease the casino's advantage from 6 or 8 percent to less than 1 percent. Basic is a long-term statistical strategy, and the compulsive players tended to reject it because they believed that "an effective strategy ought to be effective in every single instance" (p. 110). The gamblers in Wagenaar's study "invariably said that the general prescriptions of such systems could not work, because they neglect the idiosyncrasies of each specific situation" (p. 110). Instead of using an actuarial strategy that was guaranteed to save them thousands of dollars, these gamblers were on a futile chase to find a way to make a "clinical" prediction based on the "idiosyncrasies of each specific situation."

Of course, this discussion of the literature on clinical versus actuarial prediction is not meant to imply that there is not a role for case study in psychology. Keep in mind that we have been speaking about the specific situation of the prediction of behavior. Recall the discussion of the role of the case study in Chapter 4. Case information is highly useful in drawing attention to variables that are important and that need to be measured. What we have been saying in this section is that, once the relevant variables have been determined and we want to use them to predict behavior, measuring them and using a regression equation to determine the predictions make up the best procedure. First, we get more accurate predictions by using the actuarial approach. Second, the actuarial approach has an advantage over clinical prediction in that an actuarial equation is public knowledge—open for all to use, modify, criticize, or dispute. In contrast, the use of clinical prediction amounts to reliance on an authority whose assessments—precisely *because* these judgments are claimed to be singular and idiosyncratic—are not subject to public criticism. As Dawes (1994) noted, "a professional psychologist who claims in court that a particularly devastating 'clinical judgment' is based on years of experience and cannot be explicitly justified can be challenged only on irrelevant grounds—such as training, years of giving similar testimony, demeanor, and so on. In contrast, a statistical model may be challenged on rational grounds because it is public" (p. 104).

Chance and Psychology

In psychology, the tendency to try to explain everything, to have our theories account for every bit of variability rather than just the systematic nonchance components of behavior, accounts for the existence of many unfalsifiable psychological theories, both "personal" theories and those that are ostensibly scientific. Practitioners of "psychohistory" are often guilty of committing this error. Every minor twist and turn in a famous individual's life is explained in these psychohistories, usually via psychoanalytic principles. The problem with most psychohistories is not that they explain too little, but that they explain too much. Rarely do they acknowledge the many chance factors that determine the course of a person's life.

An understanding of the role of chance is critical to the lay consumer of psychological information. Legitimate psychologists admit that their theories account for a portion of the variability in human behavior, but not for all of it. They openly acknowledge the chance factor. The "Phil Donahue guest" (Chapter 4) who has an answer for every single case, for every bit of human behavior, should engender not admiration, but suspicion. True scientists are not afraid to admit what they do not know. In short, another consumer rule for evaluating psychological claims is this: Before accepting a complicated explanation of an event, consider what part chance may play in its occurrence.

Coincidence

The tendency to seek explanations for essentially chance occurrences leads to much misunderstanding regarding the nature of coincidental events. Many people think that coincidences need special explanation. They do not understand that coincidences are bound to occur even if nothing other than chance is operating. Coincidences need no special explanation.

Webster's New World Dictionary defines *coincidence* as "an accidental remarkable occurrence of related or identical events." Since the same dictionary defines *accidental* as "occurring by chance," there is no problem here. A coincidence is merely an occurrence of related events that is due to chance. Unfortunately this is not how many people interpret what is meant by *coincidence*. The tendency to seek patterns and meanings in events, combined with the "remarkable" aspect of coincidences, leads many to overlook chance as an explanation. Instead, they seek elaborate theories in order to "understand" these events. How many times have you heard stories like this: "You know, the other day I was sitting around thinking about how I hadn't called old Uncle Bill down in Texas in a long time. And guess what? The next thing that happens . . . ring, ring. Yeah, you guessed it! It's old Uncle Bill on the phone. There must be something to this telepathy stuff, after all!" This is a fairly typical example of an elaborate explanation of a coincidental event. On any given day most of us probably think about several different distant people. How often do these people call us after we think of them? Almost never. Thus during a year we probably think about hundreds of people who do not call. Eventually, in the course of these hundreds of "negative trials," which we never recognize as such, someone is going to call after we think of her or him. The event is rare, but rare events do happen—purely by chance. No other explanation is necessary.

If people truly understood what *coincidence* meant (a remarkable occurrence that is due to chance), they would not fall prey to the fallacy of trying to develop systematic, nonchance explanations for these chance events. Yet, completely contrary to the dictionary definition, *coincidence* has come to imply to many people something that needs an explanation rather than something that can be explained by chance. For example, most of us have heard statements like "My goodness, what a coincidence! I wonder *why* that happened!" Marks and Kammann (1980) therefore suggested the neutral term *oddmatch* to signify two events whose co-occurrence strikes us as odd or strange. The term *oddmatch* does not specify if the co-occurrence is due to chance or has a systematic explanation.

One thing that contributes to the tendency to search for explanations of coincidental events is the mistaken idea that rare events never happen, that oddmatches are never due to chance. This fallacy is exacerbated because probabilities are sometimes stated in terms of odds, and because of the connotations that such statements have. Think of how we phrase the following: "Oh, goodness, that's very unlikely. The odds are 100 to 1 against that happening!" The manner in which we articulate such a statement strongly implies that it will never happen. Of course, we could say the same thing in a very different way, one that has very different connotations: "In 100 events of this type, this outcome *will* probably happen once." This alternative phrasing emphasizes that, although the event is rare, in the long run rare events *do* happen. In short, oddmatches do occur purely because of chance.

In fact, the laws of probability guarantee that, as the number of events increases, the probability that *some* oddmatch will occur becomes very high. Not only do the laws of chance allow oddmatches to happen, but they virtually *guarantee* them in the long run. Consider one of Marks and Kammann's examples. If you flipped five coins all at once and they all came up heads, you would probably consider this result to be an oddmatch, an unlikely event. You would be right. The probability that this happening in any one flip of five coins is 1/32 or .03. But if you flipped the five coins 100 times and asked how likely it is that in at least 1 of those 100 trials the coins would all come up heads, the answer would be .96. That is, in 100 trials, this rare event, this oddmatch, is *very likely* to happen.

Since many states have instituted lotteries, in which the winning numbers are usually drawn randomly, either by a computer or by some mechanical randomizing device, many statisticians and behavioral scientists have had occasion to chuckle to themselves when the inevitable has happened, that is, when the same winning number is drawn two weeks in a row. This provokes howls of protest from the public, who interpret the outcome as proof that the lottery is rigged or "crooked." The public's feeling that this outcome is proof of wrongdoing arises from the mistaken view that something this odd or unlikely cannot happen by chance alone. Of course, the reason the statisticians are chuckling is that chance works in just the opposite way. If lotteries go on long enough, consecutive identical winning numbers are bound to be drawn eventually. The fact that lottery commissions report such an outcome and do not cover it up, knowing that the public will protest loudly, is probably evidence that they are scrupulously honest!

Consider the many reports of the "remarkable" behavioral similarities of identical twins who have lived apart from each other. The presence of such similarities is often treated in the media as some kind of "paranormal" event, outside the bounds of normal scientific explanation (Wyatt, Posey, Welker, & Seamonds, 1984). Of course, there is nothing "remarkable" about their behavioral similarities at all. First, these individuals share the same genetic endowment. Second, even separated twins often end up in roughly similar environments (Farber, 1981). But there is a third factor operating that people often forget: chance. That is, reports of the similarities among some separated twins almost always fail to point out that some proportion of unrelated individuals will, merely by chance, match each other in a set of characteristics.

To get some idea of what the baseline probability of a behavioral match is, Wyatt et al. (1984) randomly paired 50 unrelated college students of the same sex and of roughly the same age. The students all filled out personality questionnaires and gave information on likes and dislikes. These researchers found that of the 25 pairs, there was 1 pair of women who were both Baptists, were both studying nursing, listed volleyball and tennis as their favorite sports, listed English as their favorite subject in school, listed shorthand as their least favorite subject, and preferred to visit historical places on vacations. The Wyatt et al. study demonstrates that a "remarkable" congruence as specific as this can occur in only 25 pairs of unrelated individuals, purely on the basis of chance. In short, chance alone can produce some "remarkable" results. Not all coincidences of this type need a special explanation.

Some years ago Ann Landers popularized a series of "eerie" coincidences between Presidents Abraham Lincoln and John Kennedy:

1. Lincoln was elected president in 1860; Kennedy was elected in 1960.
2. Lincoln and Kennedy were both concerned with civil rights.

3. *Lincoln* and *Kennedy* have seven letters each.
4. Lincoln had a secretary named Kennedy, and Kennedy had a secretary named Lincoln.
5. Both were succeeded by southerners named Johnson.
6. Both were assassinated by men with three names (John Wilkes Booth and Lee Harvey Oswald).
7. Booth and Oswald both espoused unpopular political ideas.
8. Booth shot Lincoln in a theater and hid in a warehouse; Oswald shot Kennedy from a warehouse and hid in a theater.

Of course, being coincidences, these conjunctions of events are not "eerie" at all. This was clearly demonstrated by University of Texas computer programmer John Leavy (1992), who ran a "spooky presidential coincidences contest" to demonstrate just how easy it is to generate lists like this for virtually *any* two presidents. For example, the Leavy article contains parallels between William Henry Harrison and Zachary Taylor, between Polk and Carter, Garfield and McKinley, Lincoln and Jackson, Nixon and Jefferson, Washington and Eisenhower, Grant and Nixon, and Madison and Wilson. Here, for example, are the "eerie" similarities between Garfield and McKinley:

1. McKinley and Garfield were both born and raised in Ohio.
2. McKinley and Garfield were both Civil War veterans.
3. McKinley and Garfield both served in the House of Representatives.
4. McKinley and Garfield both supported the gold standard and tariffs for the protection of American industry.
5. *McKinley* and *Garfield* both have eight letters.
6. McKinley and Garfield were both replaced by vice presidents from New York City (Theodore Roosevelt and Chester Alan Arthur).
7. *Chester Alan Arthur* and *Theodore Roosevelt* have seventeen letters each.
8. Both of the vice presidents wore mustaches.
9. McKinley and Garfield were both shot in September, in the first year of their current terms.
10. Both of their assassins, Charles Guiteau and Leon Czolgosz, had foreign-sounding names.

The lists for many other conjunctions of presidents are similar. In short, given the complexity of the interactions and events in a life that lasts several decades, it would be surprising if there were *not* some parallels between virtually any two individuals in what is perhaps a sample space of tens of thousands of events.

Personal Coincidences

Oddmatches that happen in our personal lives often have special meaning to us, and thus we are especially prone not to attribute them to chance. There are many reasons for this tendency. Some are motivational and emotional, but others are due to failures of probabilistic reasoning. We often do not recognize that oddmatches are actually just a small part of a much larger pool of "nonoddmatches." It may seem to some of us that oddmatches occur with great frequency. But do they?

Consider what an analysis of the oddmatches in your personal life would reveal (the following example is adapted from Marks & Kammann, 1980). Suppose on a given day you were involved in 100 distinct events. This does not seem an overestimate, considering the complexity of life in a modern industrial society. Indeed, it is probably a gross underestimate. You watch television, talk on the telephone, meet people, negotiate the route to work or to the store, do household chores, take in information while reading, complete complex tasks at work, and so on. All these events contain several components that are separately memorable. One hundred, then, is probably on the low side, but we will stick with it. An *oddmatch* is a remarkable conjunction of 2 events. How many possible different pairs of events are there in the 100 events of your typical day? Using a simple formula to obtain the number of combinations, we calculate that there are 4,950 different pairings of events possible in your typical day. This is true 365 days a year. Now, oddmatches are very memorable. You would probably remember for several years the day Uncle Bill called. Assume that you can remember all the oddmatches that happened to you in a ten-year period. Perhaps, then, you remember six or seven oddmatches (more or less, people differ in their criteria for oddness). What is the pool of nonoddmatches from which these six or seven oddmatches came? It is 4,950 pairs per day multiplied by 365 days per year multiplied by 10 years, or 18,067,500. In short, six odd matches happened to you in 10 years, but 18,067,494 things that *could* have been oddmatches also happened. The probability of an oddmatch happening in your life is .00000033. It hardly seems strange that 6 out of 18 million conjunctions of events in your life should be odd. Odd things do happen. They are rare, but they do happen. Chance guarantees it (recall the example of simultaneously flipping five coins). In our example, six odd things happened to you. They were probably coincidences: remarkable occurrences of related events that were due to chance.

Psychologists, statisticians, and other scientists have pointed out that many oddmatches are commonly thought to be more odd than they really are. In an article subtitled "Why the Long Arm of Coincidence Is Usually Not as Long as It Seems" (1972), Martin Gardner discussed the fact that many oddmatches are not as rare as is commonly believed. The famous "birthday problem" provides a good example of this. In a class of 23 people, what is the probability that 2 of them will have their birthday on the same day? What is the probability in a class of 35 people? Most people think that the odds are pretty low. Actually, in the class with 23 people, the odds are better than 50–50 that two people will have birthdays on the same day. And in the class of 35 students, the odds are very high (the probability is about .85). In short, many oddmatches are really not so odd after all.

Psychologists Ruma Falk and Don MacGregor (1983; Falk, 1989) have studied how people judge the surprisingness of events. One of the key findings of their studies was that we are egocentric when evaluating coincidences: people find coincidences that happen to themselves more surprising than equally unlikely coincidences that happen to other people. Falk and MacGregor (1983) speculated that one explanation for this finding was that "we seem unique to ourselves and fail to see how the events which happen to *us* could have happened to anyone. Said another way, we may not see how easily we could have been replaced in a set of events or circumstances by another individual" (p. 501). However, Falk and MacGregor argued that our egocentric tendency to see the events that happen to us as more "special" may have some negative consequences in our reasoning about our lives:

> By assigning a unique status to ourselves, we may come to believe that some events, while they happen infrequently to others, would happen even less frequently to us, like motor vehicle accidents. Such a bias in judgment could work against our taking adequate protective action or adopting an appropriate defensive attitude. On the other hand, when a seemingly rare combination of events happens in our own life, we may give it attention beyond what it is due, perhaps becoming preoccupied with attributing causality to something more chimerical than real. (p. 502)

The Gambler's Fallacy

The gambler's fallacy is the tendency for people to see links between events in the past and events in the future when the two are really independent. Two outcomes are independent when the occurrence of one does not affect the probability of the other. Most games of chance that use proper equipment have this property. For example, the number that comes up on a roulette wheel is independent of the outcome that preceded it. Half the numbers on a roulette wheel are red, and half are black (for purposes of simplification, we will ignore the green zero and double zero), so the odds are even (.50) that any given spin will come up red. Yet after five or six consecutive reds, many bettors switch to black, thinking that it is now more likely to come up. This is the gambler's fallacy: acting as if previous outcomes affect the probability of the next outcome when the events are independent. In this case, the bettors are wrong in their belief. The roulette wheel has no memory of what has happened previously. Even if 15 reds in a row come up, the probability of red's coming up on the next spin is still .50.

You can demonstrate a similar phenomenon in beliefs among the general public about coin flipping. Ask a group of people what the probability of obtaining heads is on the sixth flip after five heads in a row have occurred, and some people will answer that it is very unlikely. This again is the gambler's fallacy. Coin flips are independent. After five consecutive heads, coins still have only two sides, each equally likely of turning up in any given trial.

The gambler's fallacy is not restricted to the inexperienced or novice gambler. Research has shown that even habitual gamblers, who play games of chance over 20 hours a week, still display belief in the gambler's fallacy (Wagenaar, 1988). Also, it is important to realize that the gambler's fallacy is not restricted to games of chance. It operates in *any* domain in which chance plays a substantial role, that is, in almost *everything*. The genetic makeup of babies is an example. Psychologists, physicians, and marriage counselors often see couples who, after having two female children, are planning a third child because "We want a boy, and it's *bound* to be a boy this time." This, of course, is the gambler's fallacy. The probability of having a boy (approximately 50 percent) is exactly the same after having two girls as it was in the beginning. The two previous girls make it *no more likely* that the third baby will be a boy.

The gambler's fallacy operates in any domain that has a chance component, such as sporting events and stock markets (see Andreassen, 1987). For example, one group of psychologists (Gilovich, Vallone, & Tversky, 1985) has studied the belief in "streak shooting" or the "hot hand" in basketball, that is, the belief that a particular shooter can "get hot" and that after making a series of shots a player has a greater chance of making his next shot ("Get him the ball; he's hot"). The researchers ascertained that the belief in streak shooting was strong among both basketball fans and players. For example, on a questionnaire, 91 percent of a group of basketball fans believed that a player has a better chance of making a shot after having just made his last two or three shots than he does after having just missed his last two or three shots, and 84 percent of the fans believed that it is important to pass the ball to someone who has just made two or three shots in a row. The fans were asked to estimate, for a hypothetical player who shoots 50 percent from the field, what his field goal percentage would be after making a shot and what it would be after missing a shot. The fans estimated that after making a shot his percentage would be 61 percent and after missing a shot it would be 42 percent. The fans' strong beliefs in streak shooting were shared by most (but not all) of the players on the Philadelphia 76ers, who were interviewed by the researchers (see Gilovich et al., 1985).

But why are we discussing streak shooting here, under the heading of the gambler's fallacy? Because *there is no such thing as streak shooting!* Gilovich et al. (1985) studied the shooting statistics during the 1980–1981 season for the Philadelphia 76ers and the Boston Celtics. There were no sequential dependencies among the shots that the players took during the season. Let's see, nontechnically, what that means.

The gambler's fallacy is the belief that independent events are linked, that there are dependencies between events that are really not related. Statistically, the idea of streak shooting translates into the hypothesis that the probability of a hit (making a shot) after two or three consecutive hits is higher than the probability of a hit after two or three misses. Gilovich et al. (1985) calculated the probabilities and found that there was no evidence to support this hypothesis. For example, the data for Julius Erving (who took the most shots of anyone on the Philadelphia 76ers) showed that his probability of a hit after three consecutive hits was .48 and his probability of a hit after three previous misses was .52. Erving's probability of a hit after two consecutive hits was .52, compared to a probability of .51 after two consecutive misses. His probability of a hit after one previous hit was .53, compared to a probability of .51 after one miss. In short, Erving's probability of a hit was approximately .50 regardless of what had happened on his previous shots—no tendency toward streak shooting at all.

Data for other players were highly similar. Lionel Hollins had a field goal probability of .46 after two consecutive hits and a field goal probability of .49 after two consecutive misses. His probability of a hit after one hit was .46, exactly the same as his probability of a hit after one miss. Again, Hollins made approximately 47 percent of his shots regardless of what had happened on his previous shots. Data on free throws by the Boston Celtics showed the same thing. For example, Larry Bird made 88 percent of his free throws after making a free throw and made 91 percent of his free throws after missing a free throw. Nate Archibald made 83 percent of his free throws after making a free throw and made 82 percent of his free throws after missing a free throw. There are no streaks in free-throw shooting either. Belief in the "hot hand" is indeed an example of the gambler's fallacy, that is, believing that there are links among events that are really independent.

Interestingly, the gambler's fallacy appears to be another instance—like "intuitive physics," discussed in Chapter 6—in which mere experience does not reveal to people the true nature of the world. Gilovich et al. (1985) examined the performance of college basketball players who were practicing shots from about 15 feet on an open court (i.e., there were no defenders). They had the players make bets on 100 shots. The players were guaranteed to win because they had made about 50 percent of their shots from that distance, and the bets were structured so that the players won more when they made the shot than they lost when they missed the shot. However, the players could choose to make high bets (win a lot, lose a lot) or low bets (win a little, lose a little) before each shot. Obviously the players would do better if they could predict their own performance. That is, they should bet high when they thought the probability of making the shot was high and bet low when they thought the probability of making the shot was low. The results of this experiment indicated that, as with the professional players, there was no "hot hand": the probability of making a shot after one or more made shots was no higher than the probability of making a shot after a miss. However, the players *thought* there was such a thing as a hot hand. They bet more on the next shot after they had made a shot than they bet after they had missed a shot. As a result, the players were *absolutely unable to predict their own performance*: their predictions were no better than chance.

The gambler's fallacy stems from many mistaken beliefs about probability. One is the belief that if a process is truly random, no sequence, not even a small one (six coin flips, for instance), should display runs or patterns. People routinely underestimate the likelihood of runs (HHHH) and patterns (HHTTHHTTHHTT) in a random sequence. The tendency to underestimate such sequences relates to our previous discussion of coincidence. Many people think that every oddmatch needs a nonchance explanation because it could not come about simply by chance. They do not realize that purely chance oddmatches are much more likely than they think. For this reason people cannot generate truly random sequences when they try to do so. The sequences that they generate tend to have too few runs and patterns. When generating such sequences, people alternate their choices too much in a mistaken effort to destroy any structure that might appear (Lopes & Oden, 1987).

Those who claim to have psychic powers can easily exploit this tendency. Consider a demonstration sometimes conducted in college psychology classes. A student is told to prepare a list of 200 numbers by "randomly" choosing from the numbers 1, 2, and 3 over and over again. After it is completed, the list of "random" numbers is kept out of view of the instructor. The student is now told to concentrate on the first number on the list, and the instructor tries to guess what the number is. After the instructor guesses, the student tells the class and the instructor the correct choice. A record is kept of whether the instructor's guess matched, and the process continues until the complete record of 200 matches and nonmatches is recorded. Before the procedure begins, the instructor announces that she or he will demonstrate "psychic powers" by reading the subject's mind during the experiment. The class is asked what level of performance—that is, percentage of "hits"—would constitute empirically solid evidence of psychic powers. Usually a student who has taken a statistics course volunteers that, since a result of 33 percent hits could be expected purely on the basis of chance, the instructor would have to achieve a larger proportion than this, probably at least 40 percent, before one should believe that she or he has psychic powers. The class usually understands and agrees with this argument. The demonstration is then conducted, and a result of more than 40 percent hits is obtained, to the surprise of many.

The students then learn some lessons about randomness and about how easy it is to fake "psychic powers." The instructor in this example merely takes advantage of the fact that people do not generate enough runs: they alternate too much when producing "random" numbers. In a truly random sequence of numbers, what should the probability of a 2 be after three consecutive 2's? One third, the same as the probability of a 1 or a 3. But this is not how most people generate such numbers. After even a small run, they tend to alternate numbers in order to produce a "representative" sequence. Thus, on each trial in our example, the instructor merely picks one of the two numbers that the student did not pick on the previous trial. Thus, if on the previous trial the student generated a 2, the instructor picks a 1 or a 3 for the next trial. If on the previous trial the subject generated a three, the instructor picks a 1 or a 2 on the next trial. This simple procedure usually ensures a percentage of hits greater than 33 percent—greater than chance accuracy without a hint of "psychic power." Many legitimate magicians and some fraudulent magicians who pose as "psychics" similarly exploit people's mistaken ideas about chance and randomness.

The Conjunction Fallacy

There is a basic rule of probability that is easily stated and readily understood: The probability that event A and event B will *both* occur must be less than the simple probability of A or the simple probability of B. This is the conjunction rule, that the co-occurrence of two events must be less probable than the occurrence of either of the two events singly. Stated in this way, the rule is easy to understand, and most people readily assent to it. However, when we move from the neutral world of events A and B to social and personal inferences, the conjunction rule sometimes gets lost in the shuffle. Probabilistic reasoning is not as firmly ingrained as some of the other strategies that are used for thinking about social and personal events.

Tversky and Kahneman (1983) studied the breakdown of the conjunction rule by giving subjects a description of a person, such as the following:

Linda is 31 years old, single, outspoken, and very bright. She majored in philosophy. As a student, she was deeply concerned about issues of discrimination and social justice and also participated in antinuclear demonstrations.

The subjects were then presented with several possible facts about Linda and were asked to evaluate their probability in various ways. Some of the statements about Linda were

1. Linda works in a bookstore and takes yoga classes.
2. Linda is active in the feminist movement.
3. Linda is a psychiatric social worker.
4. Linda is a bank teller.
5. Linda is an insurance salesperson.
6. Linda is a bank teller and is active in the feminist movement.

It is clear that statement 6 is the conjunction of 2 and 4. As such, the probability of 6 cannot be greater than that of either 2 or 4. Nevertheless, the majority of the subjects who assess the probabilities of these statements incorrectly rate 6 as more probable than 4. The reason is that the thinking of most subjects is dominated by another strategy of attribution and judgment called the *representativeness strategy*. Subjects using this strategy simply attempt to match the attributes of the instance being evaluated (Linda's description) to the attributes of a general class (bank tellers). The greater the overlap between the attributes (the more "representative" the instance is of the class), the higher the probability evaluation is.

In many cases this is a fine general strategy for arriving at gross probability estimates. However, this reasoning goes astray when it comes into conflict with a probability rule that should dominate it. This is precisely what happens in many conjunction situations of the type studied by Tversky and Kahneman. In this situation, example 6 is judged more probable because the addition of "active in the feminist movement" seems more congruent with the description of Linda. As a result, 6 has more overlap with Linda's description than does 4, which does not seem to overlap at all. In this case, representativeness, a generally useful rule, leads to a serious error in reasoning because it masks a probabilistic rule that dominates it. If Linda is a bank teller and is active in the feminist movement (6), she, of course, is also a bank teller (4). Alternative 6 can never be more probable than 4. In fact, since all feminist bank tellers are bank tellers and since not all bank tellers are feminist bank tellers, then alternative 4 must be considerably more probable than 6. Many subjects acknowledge their error when given this explanation but still find alternative 6 alluring. The conjunction fallacy is a true cognitive illusion. People find the incorrect alternative attractive even when they know it is incorrect.

The conjunction fallacy is also displayed by people who have much formal experience in making probabilistic assessments. Groups of physicians in the Boston area were given a case description such as "A 55-year-old woman had a pulmonary embolism documented angiographically ten days after a cholecystec-tomy." They then had to make probability assessments for a list of conditions (with the warning that patients could naturally have more than one of the conditions) that the patient might have:

1. Dyspnea and hemiparesis
2. Calf pain
3. Pleuritic chest pain
4. Syncope and tachycardia
5. Hemiparesis
6. Hemoptysis

Clearly, 1 is a conjunction of alternative 5, hemiparesis (partial paralysis), and another condition, dyspnea (shortness of breath). As such, alternative 1 cannot be more probable than 5. Yet the physicians did judge 1 as being more probable than 5, thus demonstrating the conjunction fallacy. The reason is again representative-ness. Hemiparesis is an atypical symptom for this patient's condition, whereas dys-pnea is very typical. Therefore the conjunction seemed to be more representative of the patient's condition and was thus judged more probable even though every patient who displays hemiparesis and dyspnea also displays hemiparesis. In other words, the probability of 5 must always be greater than that of 1. That this exam-ple again demonstrates a true cognitive illusion was apparent in a group discus-sion of the conjunction fallacy by 24 physicians at Stanford Hospital. The physi-cians immediately recognized the fallacy after an explanation was given and were dismayed by having been lured into such an elementary error of reasoning. The tendency to use the representativeness strategy is stronger than the tendency to use the conjunction rule of probability, even for people who know that the latter should dominate the former.

Avoiding the conjunction fallacy is important when attempting to evaluate hy-potheses and theoretical explanations. This fallacy contributes to the staying power of many unfalsifiable theories that account for complex outcomes by a post hoc stringing together of explanations. Overuse of the representativeness strategy often makes these complex post hoc explanations seem plausible, even when a proper application of the conjunction rule would render them highly improbable. Take, for example, the field of psychohistory again. Nearly all psychohistories, if written by a minimally competent practitioner, sound plausible. Of course, as a chain of conceptual events that "explain" a person's life from early childhood to the time of their adult achievements, the probability that any such psychohistory is accurate is incredibly small. The conjunction rule dictates that the probabilities of all the linked events must be multiplied together to yield the probability of the entire scenario. For example, the probability of four events, each with a probability of .20, *all* happening is .0016. However, if many of the linked conceptual events are seen as representative, the overall scenario may be incorrectly viewed as highly probable, just as the feminist bank-teller alternative in our example was incorrectly given a greatly overestimated probability as a hypothesis.

A Final Word About Statistics and Probability

These, then, are just a few of the shortcomings in statistical reasoning that obscure an understanding of psychology. More complete and detailed coverage is provided in Nisbett and Ross's book *Human Inference: Strategies and Shortcomings of Social Judgment* (1980) and the book *Judgment Under Uncertainty: Heuristics and Biases* (1982), edited by Kahneman, Slovic, and Tversky. Popular introductions to a lot of these ideas (and good places to start for those who lack any mathematics training) are contained in John Paulos's book *Innumeracy: Mathematical Illiteracy and Its Consequences* (1988) and in Tom Gilovich's *How We Know What Isn't So: The Fallibility of Human Reason in Everyday Life* (1991). Somewhat more technical, but still very readable, introductions are also contained in Robyn Dawes's *Rational Choice in an Uncertain World* (1988) and in Jonathan Barons's *Thinking and Deciding* (1994).

The probabilistic thinking skills discussed in this chapter are of tremendous practical significance. Because of inadequately developed probabilistic thinking abilities, physicians choose less effective medical treatments (McNeil, Pauker, Sox, & Tversky, 1982; Sutherland, 1992); people fail to accurately assess risks in their environment (Lichtenstein et al., 1978; Yates, 1992); information is misused in legal proceedings (Saks & Kidd, 1980–1981), millions of dollars are spent on unneeded projects by government and private industry (Dawes, 1988, pp. 23–24); animals are hunted to extinction (Gilovich, 1991, p. 5); unnecessary surgery is performed (Dawes, 1988, pp. 73–75); and costly financial misjudgments are made (Etzioni, 1988; Fridson, 1993; Thaler, 1992; Willis, 1990).

Of course, a comprehensive discussion of statistical reasoning cannot be carried out in a single chapter. Our goal was much more modest: to emphasize the importance of statistics to a thorough understanding of psychology. Unfortunately there is no simple rule to follow when confronted with statistical information. Unlike some of the other components of scientific thinking that are more easily acquired, functional reasoning skills in statistics probably require some type of formal study. Fortunately most universities and community colleges now offer introductory-level statistics courses that require no previous college mathematics. Before taking such a course, the reader can begin with the books I have recommended.

While many scientists sincerely wish to make scientific knowledge accessible to the general public, it is intellectually irresponsible to suggest that a deep understanding of a particular subject can be obtained by the layperson when that understanding is crucially dependent on certain technical information that is available only through formal study. Such is the case with statistics and psychology. Psychologist Alan Boneau (1990) recently surveyed authors of psychology textbooks, asking them to list the most important terms and concepts that students need to learn in psychology. Approximately 40 percent of the 100 terms and concepts that were listed most frequently were in the areas of statistics and methodology! No one can be a competent contemporary psychologist without being fully conversant with statistics and probability.

Clearly one of the goals of this book is to make research in the discipline of psychology more accessible to the general reader. However, the empirical methods and techniques of theory construction in psychology are so intertwined with statistics (as is the case in many other fields, such as economics, sociology, and genetics) that it would be wrong to imply that one can thoroughly understand the field without having some statistical knowledge. Thus, although this chapter has served as an extremely sketchy lesson in statistical thinking, its main purpose has been to highlight the existence of an area of expertise that is critical to a full understanding of psychology.

Chapter 11

THE RODNEY DANGERFIELD OF THE SCIENCES

Consider some studies in the scientific literature. See if you can guess what they all have in common. In an article published in the journal *Circulation Research* in 1960, Scher, Young, and Meredith attempted to determine how many basic voltage generators are necessary to account for the voltages recorded on the human body surface during electrocardiographic recording. Ziegler, Hassanein, and Hassanein reported in the *Journal of Chronic Diseases* in 1972 a study in which they attempted to differentiate several types of headaches based on 27 different symptom variables. The 1966 volume of the journal *Econometrica* contains an article by Adelman and Morris in which they attempt to trace the relationship between per capita gross national product and various social and political variables. The *Journal of the Association for Computing Machinery* published an article by Sackman and Munson in 1964 in which the authors attempted to develop a model of how computer operating time was determined by system capacity variables. Twenty years ago, Lee Cady of New York University reported on an investigation in which the relative importance of various factors associated with coronary heart disease, such as blood pressure, family history, blood lipids, and body weight, were studied. Imbrie and Van Andel reported in the 1964 volume of the *Geological Society of America Bulletin* a study of the heavy mineral composition of sediment from the Gulf of California. Finally, in 1973 Redman published a paper in *American Antiquity* on productive archaeological research designs.

Stumped? Well, don't worry. Actually, the connection is not very obvious from these brief descriptions. These examples were chosen because the connection between them is indirect. The connection between all these articles is through the discipline of psychology. You see, what these studies in cardiology, computer science, economics, chronic disease, geology, and archaeology have in common is their extensive use of a statistical data analysis technique that was developed by psychologists. The technique is called *factor analysis*, and it traces back to a paper published in 1904 in the *American Journal of Psychology* by Charles Spearman, a psychologist at the University of London.

Factor analysis is a complex statistical technique, but it accomplishes a task that is fundamental to many sciences: it determines the degree to which sets of measured variables cluster together. Factor-analytic techniques are the foundation of many theories of intelligence (the psychological problem that was the focus of Spearman's original paper), and they have undergone considerable development and refinement since Spearman's day. Psychologists such as L. L. Thurstone and Godfrey Thomson were important contributors to the subsequent refinements of factor-analytic techniques.

It was soon recognized that, conceptually, factor analysis is in no way strictly limited to the psychological problems that spurred its development. Because it deals with problems of classification and dimensionality that are fundamental to many sciences, factor analysis has been used extensively in such diverse fields as medicine, metallurgy, biology, and paleontology. The example of factor analysis is not atypical in this respect. Yet the fact that psychologists have always been important contributors to developments in statistical methods (Asher, 1990; Townsend & Kadlec, 1990) is not generally known. Many people would never in their wildest dreams imagine that a "hard" science like biology, chemistry, or metallurgy would actually use a statistical technique developed by psychologists. ("Psychologists? You mean rats and people on couches, don't you? Statistics isn't part of psychology!")

The shocked reaction to the fact that psychologists have developed methodologies and statistics that are used by other sciences reflects the problem that is the focus of this chapter: psychology's public image. While there is a great public fascination with "psychological" topics ("Oh, did you hear that Lady Di is anorexic? Yes, it's true! A psychologist in *People* magazine said so!"), most judgments about the field and its accomplishments are resoundingly negative. Psychologists are aware of their discipline's image problem, but most feel that there is little they can do about it, so they simply ignore it. This is a mistake. Psychology's image problem is multifaceted and is damaging both to the public and to the field itself. As the mass media become more and more influential in determining public perceptions (for example, fictional TV "docudramas" become the true history for a public that does not read), ignoring psychology's image problem threatens to make it worse.

Rodney Dangerfield is a popular comedian whose trademark is the plaintive cry, "I don't get no respect!" In a way this is a fitting summary of psychology's status in the public mind. This chapter will touch on some of the reasons that psychology appears to be the Rodney Dangerfield of the sciences.

PSYCHOLOGY'S "IMAGE" PROBLEM

Some of these reasons have already been discussed. For example, the Freud problem discussed in Chapter 1 undoubtedly contributes to the low esteem in which psychology is held. To the extent that the public knows any reputable psychologists at all, Freud and Skinner are those psychologists. The distorted versions of their ideas that circulate among the public must contribute to the idea that psychology is a frivolous field indeed. There would appear to be little hope for a field when one of its most renowned scholars is said to have claimed that we have no minds and that we are just like rats. Of course, Skinner did not deny that we think, and many principles of operant conditioning that he developed from work with animals *have* been shown to generalize to human behavior. However, the public is little aware of any of these facts.

Distorted ideas from Freudian doctrine also contribute to lowering the public esteem of psychology. Aside from the fact that many of the popularized versions of these ideas are grossly inaccurate, it is generally unknown that the number of orthodox Freudians in the field of psychology is extremely small.

The layperson's knowledge of reputable psychological research, outside of the work of Freud and Skinner, is virtually nonexistent. One way to confirm this fact is to look in your local bookstore to see what material on psychology is available to the general public. Inspection will reveal that the material generally falls into three categories. First, there are a few "classics." Skinner's controversial *Beyond Freedom and Dignity* and a few books on or by Freud will be there, as well as some of the more well-known works of Carl Jung, Erik Erikson, and Erich Fromm. Whether a particular bookstore goes beyond this small set of classics will depend on its quality, of course, but the legitimate psychology in many stores stops with the small set mentioned here.

Psychology and Parapsychology

The second class of material found in most stores might be called pseudoscience masquerading as psychology, that is, the seemingly never-ending list of so-called paranormal phenomena such as telepathy, clairvoyance, psychokinesis, precognition, reincarnation, biorhythms, astral projection, pyramid power, plant communication, psychic surgery, and so on. The presence of a great body of this material in the psychology sections of bookstores undoubtedly contributes to, and also reflects, the widespread misconception that psychologists are the people who have confirmed the existence of such phenomena. There is a bitter irony for psychology in this misconception. In fact, the relationship between psychology and the "paranormal" is easily stated. These phenomena are simply not an area of active research interest in modern psychology. The reason, however, is a surprise to many people.

The statement that the study of ESP and other "paranormal" abilities is not accepted as part of the discipline of psychology will undoubtedly provoke the ire of many readers. Surveys have consistently shown that more than 50 percent of the general public believes in the existence of such phenomena and often holds these beliefs with considerable fervor. Historical studies and survey research have suggested why these beliefs are held so strongly (Bainbridge & Stark, 1980; Gardner, 1981; Grimmer, 1992; Moore, 1977; Stanovich, 1989). A materialist culture tends to weaken the traditional religious beliefs of many people, who then seek some other form of transcendental outlet. Like most religions many of the so-called paranormal phenomena seem to promise things such as life after death, and for some people they serve the same need for transcendence. It should not be surprising, then, that the bearer of the bad tidings that research in psychology does not validate ESP is usually not greeted with enthusiasm. The statement that psychology does not consider ESP a viable research area invariably upsets "believers" and often provokes charges that psychologists are dogmatic in "banishing" certain topics from their discipline. Psychologists do not contribute to public understanding when they throw up their hands and fail to deal seriously with these objections. The public deserves a careful and clear explanation of why such objections are ill founded.

Scientists do not determine by edict which topics to investigate. No proclamation goes out declaring what can and cannot be studied. Areas of investigation arise and are expanded or terminated according to a natural selection process that operates on ideas and methods. Those that lead to fruitful theories and empirical discoveries are taken up by a large number of scientists. Those that lead to theoretical dead ends or that do not yield replicable or interesting observations are dropped. This natural selection of ideas and methods is what leads science closer to the truth.

The reason that ESP, for example, is not considered a viable topic in contemporary psychology is simply that its investigation has not proved fruitful. Therefore very few psychologists are interested in it. It is important here to emphasize the word *contemporary,* because the topic of ESP was of greater interest to psychologists some years ago, before the current bulk of negative evidence had accumulated. As history shows, research areas are not declared invalid by governing authorities; they are merely winnowed out in the competing environment of ideas.

ESP was never declared an invalid topic in psychology. The evidence of this fact is clear and publicly available. Many papers investigating ESP *have* appeared in legitimate psychological journals over the years. Parapsychologists who thrive on media exposure like to give the impression that the area is somehow new, thus implying that startling new discoveries are just around the corner. The truth is much less exciting.

The study of ESP is actually as old as psychology itself. It is not a new area of investigation. It has been as well studied as many of the currently viable topics in the psychological literature. The results of the many studies that have appeared in legitimate psychological journals have been overwhelmingly negative. After more than ninety years of study, there still does not exist one example of an ESP phenomenon that is replicable under controlled conditions. This simple but basic scientific criterion has not been met despite dozens of studies conducted over many decades. Many parapsychologists and believers themselves are even in agreement on this point (see Alcock, 1981, 1990; Druckman & Swets, 1988; Krippner, 1977). For this reason alone the topic is now of little interest to psychology.

It is sometimes mistakenly suggested that scientists deny the existence of such phenomena because they violate currently accepted theories of nature. From our previous discussion of the scientific process in Chapters 1 and 2, it should be clear that this claim is false. All scientists are in the *business* of overturning currently accepted theories of nature, for it is only by changing and refining our current views, while maintaining, of course, the connectivity principle, that we can hope to get nearer the truth. When a new phenomenon contradicts currently accepted knowledge, scientists question it and seek alternative explanations for it. But this is not the reason that psychologists do not believe in the existence of ESP. The reason is simpler. There is just no scientific evidence for it. In short, there is no demonstrated phenomenon that needs scientific explanation (see Alcock, 1981, 1984, 1990; Hines, 1988; Kurtz, 1987).

And now the irony. Psychologists have played a prominent role in attempts to assess claims of paranormal abilities. The importance of their contribution is probably second only to that of the professional magicians, who have clearly done the most to expose the fraudulent nature of most purported demonstrations of paranormal abilities (Randi, 1980, 1987). Three of the most important books on the state of the evidence on paranormal abilities were written by psychologists (James Alcock of York University in Canada, 1990; C. E. M. Hansel of the University of Swansea in Wales, 1980; and David Marks and Richard Kammann of the University of Otago in New Zealand, 1980). The training that psychologists receive in the controls necessary in human experimentation is far more relevant to the assessment of ESP claims than that received by other scientists.

The irony, then, is obvious. Psychology, the discipline that has probably contributed most to the accurate assessment of ESP claims, is the field that is most closely associated with such pseudosciences in the public mind. Psychology suffers greatly from this "guilt-by-association" phenomenon. As will be discussed in greater detail later, psychology is often the victim of a "double whammy." Here is just one example. The assumption that anything goes in psychology, that it is a field without scientific mechanisms for deciding among knowledge claims, leads to its being associated with pseudosciences such as ESP. However, if psychologists ever become successful in getting the public to recognize these pseudosciences for what they really are, the pseudosciences' association with psychology will be seen as confirmation that psychology is indeed not a science!

The Self-Help Literature

The third category in bookstore psychology is the so-called self-help literature. There are, of course, many different genres within this category. Some books are spiritually uplifting tracts written with the purpose of generally increasing feelings of self-worth and competence. Others attempt to package familiar bromides about human behavior in new ways. A few (but all too few) are authored by responsible psychologists writing for the general public. Many that are not in the latter category vie for uniqueness by presenting new "therapies" that are usually designed not only to correct specific behavioral problems but also to help satisfy general human wants (making more money, losing more weight, and having better sex are the "big three"), thereby ensuring larger book sales. These so-called new therapies are rarely based on any type of controlled experimental investigation. They usually rest on "personal experience," or on a few case histories if the author is a clinician.

The many behavioral and cognitive therapies that have emerged after painstaking psychological investigation as having demonstrated effectiveness are usually poorly represented on the bookshelves. The situation is even worse in the electronic media. Radio and TV carry virtually no reports of legitimate psychology and instead present purveyors of bogus "therapies" and publicity-seeking media "personalities" who have no connection to the actual field of psychology. The main reason is that the legitimate psychological therapies do not claim to provide an instant cure or improvement, nor do they guarantee success or claim a vast generality for their effects ("Not only will you quit smoking, but every aspect of your life will improve!").

Psychologist Gerald Rosen (1987) analyzed the self-help literature and warned that "commercial considerations rather than professional standards, have been influencing the development of treatment books" (p. 46). He criticized psychologists themselves for publishing misleading self-help books. For example, Rosen quoted a scientific paper by two obesity researchers in which they concluded, "We remain a long way from any semblance of justification of complacency in weight regulation; significant poundage losses are still in the minority, and long-term maintenance has remained unexamined" (p. 46). Yet in the same year these same two psychologists published a self-help book titled *Permanent Weight Control!*

The public is largely unaware that the publishing industry provides no quality controls for readers of the self-help literature. Fridson (1993) described the case of a writer of pop psychology who wrote best-selling books on careers. The writer had a column in *Forbes* magazine and appeared on television programs such as the *Phil Donahue Show*. It was then discovered that the writer did not have the Ph.D. degree that he claimed to have (he actually had a doctorate from an unaccredited correspondence school). Further investigation revealed that some of the 8,000 interviews that the author claimed to have conducted were fictitious. When questioned about the ethics of marketing misleading books by someone with bogus credentials, one of this author's publishers said that it "had seen no need to check out the would-be psychologist's research methods" (Fridson, 1993, p. 144), and the other defended its actions by arguing that "ninety-nine percent of what we do is based on faith" (p. 144). The reader who has digested this book will now have a valuable supplement to faith: knowledge of the logic of the empirical methods of modern science.

The self-help literature, which accounts for a substantial portion of the book market in the United States, has many unfortunate effects on the general perception of psychology. First, as with the Freud problem, it creates confusion concerning the problems that dominate the attention of psychologists. For example, although there is a substantial number of psychologists engaged in providing therapy for problems of obesity and sexuality and also in researching these problems, the actual number is far less than that suggested by their representation in the self-help literature. This misrepresentation also contributes to the public's view that most psychologists are engaged in treatment of and research on abnormal behavior. In fact, most psychological research is directed at nonpathological behavior that is typical of all humans.

Beyond the content confusion, the self-help literature creates an inaccurate impression of the methods and goals of psychology. As we showed in Chapter 4, the science of psychology does not consider a few case studies, testimonials, and "personal experiences"—that is, the database for most of the self-help "therapies"—adequate empirical evidence to support the efficacy of a therapy. The self-help literature misleads the public by implying that this is the type of database on which most psychological conclusions rest. As illustrated in Chapter 8, the confirmation of a theory must rest on many different types of evidence, and case studies yield the weakest type of data. It is a fundamental mistake to view such data as definitive proof of a particular theory or therapy.

Recipe Knowledge

Finally, the self-help literature creates confusion about the goals of psychology and about the type of knowledge that most psychological investigations seek. Psychologist Leigh Shaffer (1981) suggested that this literature strongly implies that psychological researchers seek what has been termed *recipe knowledge*. Recipe knowledge is the knowledge of how to use something without knowledge of the fundamental principles that govern its functioning. For example, most people know many things about how to use a telephone. They know how to dial, how to get information, how to make long-distance connections, and so on. But many are completely ignorant of the physical principles on which the operation of the telephone is based. They do not know how it does what it does; they only know that they can make it work. This is recipe knowledge of the telephone. Our knowledge of many technological products in our society is also recipe knowledge.

Of course, this is not an entirely negative thing. Indeed, most technological products have been designed to be used without knowledge of all the principles on which they are based. In fact, the idea of recipe knowledge provides one way of conceptualizing the difference between basic and applied research. The basic researcher seeks to uncover the fundamental principles of nature without necessarily worrying about whether they can be turned into recipe knowledge. The applied researcher is more interested in translating basic principles into a product that requires only recipe knowledge.

Most self-help literature provides only recipe knowledge about human behavior. It usually boils down to the form "Do X and you will become more Y," or "Do Z and person A will react more B." Now, there is nothing inherently wrong here, assuming, of course, that the recipes provided are correct (which is usually not a safe assumption). Many legitimate psychotherapies also provide much recipe knowledge. However, a problem arises when people mistakenly view recipe knowledge as the ultimate goal of all psychological research. While a number of psychological researchers do work on turning basic behavioral principles into usable psychotherapeutic techniques, health-maintaining behavior programs, or models of efficient industrial organization, psychological research is largely basic research aimed at uncovering general facts and theories about behavior. Here we have another reason why psychological research may seem "strange" to the outsider. Investigations of basic principles often look very different from studies focused on developing applications.

We would consider it silly to walk into a molecular biology laboratory and ask a researcher whether we should take two or three aspirins for a headache. The reason is not that molecular biology has nothing to do with aspirin. Future developments in pain relievers will probably involve knowledge from this area of science. It is silly to ask this question because the molecular biologist is simply not working at the recipe level that deals with whether to take two aspirins or three. The researcher is concerned with fundamental facts about the molecular level of biological substances. These facts could lead to recipe knowledge in any number of areas, but the transformation to recipe knowledge will probably not be accomplished by the same investigator who uncovered the basic facts at the molecular level, nor will it be accomplished by use of the same methods that led to the original discoveries.

Thus, because the self-help literature has led people to believe that most psychologists work at developing recipe knowledge, much of the basic research that psychologists conduct often appears strange. What did Wrightsman's study of Wallace supporters (Chapter 8) have to do with telling people how to lose weight? Nothing, of course. His intent clearly was not to develop recipe knowledge of any kind. Wrightsman did uncover a basic fact about expressed political attitudes and behavior. This type of knowledge is fundamental to an accurate understanding of exactly how our democratic society works. Perhaps certain types of recipe knowledge will one day develop from it. In fact, social science data and theories are already becoming increasingly prevalent in the political arena. The techniques of survey research (developed in part by psychologists) are now very important in both political campaigns and government. Similarly, what did Hecht's data about subjects looking at red lights in a dark room have to do with helping my sex life? Again, nothing. Hecht was interested in uncovering basic laws about the way the visual system adapts to darkness. In this case, though, the basic principles were eventually translated into recipe knowledge of how to deal with some specific problems, such as night blindness due to vitamin deficiency.

Thus the self-help literature has two unfortunate side effects on the public perception of psychology. The range of problems addressed in this literature does not necessarily represent the focus of contemporary psychology. Instead, it reflects, quite naturally, what people want to read about. Students of psychology are often not sufficiently aware that publishing is a commercial endeavor. Market forces determine what appears on the bookshelves. However, the focus of science is not determined in the same way. Thus, in all sciences, and in psychology in particular, there is usually a gap between the ideas that are productive for scientists and those that can be packaged to sell to the public.

Finally, the self-help literature presents psychology as purely recipe knowledge. While this is not entirely inaccurate, it does not reflect the large amount of basic research that goes on in psychology.

Psychology and the Media

Of course, some psychologists *are* concerned about topics such as obesity and sexuality. These are active research areas in psychology. But the results of these investigations have rarely led to the "breakthroughs" that make for best-sellers. Furthermore, psychologists are often very concerned that their findings not be inappropriately extrapolated. For example, Judith Rodin of Yale University received the American Psychological Association's Early Career Award in 1979 for her studies of the complex factors that contribute to excessive weight. Researchers in the 1960s and 1970s had discovered one factor that was termed *the internal-external distinction*. It had been found that the eating behavior of normal-weight individuals was more under the control of internal stimuli, and that the eating behavior of overweight individuals was more responsive to external cues, such as the sight and smell of food or the passage of time.

Rodin (1981) discovered, though, that this distinction reflected only a weak probabilistic trend (see Chapter 10), and that it was a mistake to imply a strict distinction between internally oriented normal-weight people and externally oriented obese people. In her studies, she learned that the internal-external dimension interacted in some very complex ways with the other factors (for instance, metabolic rate) that also cause obesity (multiple causation again, see Chapter 9). Her summary of this research amply reflects the complexity of the issues:

> I would like to reiterate that onset and degree of overweight are determined by a combination of genetic, metabolic, psychological, and environmental events. Considerable data arguing against the simplistic notion that all overweight people are externally responsive and lack internal sensitivity, and that people of average weight show the opposite pattern, have been reviewed. It may never be possible to find the "magic bullet," since obesity is not a single syndrome, has no single cause, and therefore probably does not have a single cure. (p. 370)

Although this analysis is scientifically quite accurate, it is not the stuff of which best-sellers are made.

Some unfortunate consequences arise because most psychologists are well aware of their discipline's image problem. Here we can see another example of the "double whammies" that plague the field. Many psychologists are very concerned about disassociating their field from the self-help books and pseudosciences that partially define it for the public. This concern has made many psychologists extremely wary about drawing firm conclusions regarding solutions to pressing human problems. Note the tentativeness of Rodin's conclusion above. This reluctance to claim special knowledge is virtually built in to the training of research psychologists in most graduate schools. Research psychology is one of the most self-critical fields. The psychology journals are strewn with papers warning about all the critical methodological issues we have covered in previous chapters (the trap of inferring causation from correlation, the need for converging evidence, the need to test alternative explanations, and so on).

Thus conservatism regarding the communication of psychological findings is deeply ingrained in most psychological researchers. Psychologists are therefore quite reluctant to claim that they have the answers to pressing social problems. This reluctance is, of course, often well advised (as in Rodin's case, for example). The problems surrounding human behavior are complex, and it is not easy to study them. However, some unfortunate side effects result when psychology interacts with the media.

The peculiar logic of the media dictates that if the public is interested in a particular psychological question, the media will deliver a story whether or not there is one to tell. A scientist who tells a reporter, "I'm sorry, but that is a complex question, and the data are not yet in. I wouldn't want to comment on it," by no means terminates the reporter's search for an answer. The investigator will simply continue until he or she finds a scientist (or, often, in the case of psychology, *anyone* who can be quoted as an "authority") who is less conservative about coming to conclusions.

Kelly, Rotton, and Culver (1985) discussed the way this unfortunate "media logic" has worked to publicize so-called lunar effects—the belief that the phases of the moon can affect human behavior, especially abnormal behavior. These researchers analyzed the results from 37 different studies and found that there was no evidence of lunar effects on human behavior. They found instead that it would make more sense to be studying "media effects," that is, how the media can create belief in nonexistent phenomena. Kelly et al. (1985) pointed directly to the media logic we have just discussed:

> Newspapers, television programs, and radio shows favor individuals who claim that a full moon influences behavior. . . . When reporters call us on the phone, they would probably be happier if we assure them by saying "The streets are full of loonies when the moon is full." Unfortunately, when one scientist doesn't give them a quotation that can be turned into an interesting headline, they can always find an "expert" who will provide the quotation they need. (p. 133)

Journalism professor Curtis MacDougall, in his book *Superstition and the Press* (1983), gave an example of media logic when he quoted a reporter who routinely wrote stories about "psychic powers." When asked whether he actually thought that there was evidence indicating that such powers existed, the reporter replied, "I don't have to believe in it. All I need is 2 Ph.D.'s who will tell me it's so and I have a story" (p. 558). This example illustrates why reliance on peer-reviewed journals for scientific information has been emphasized in this book. It is the only protection that the consumer of scientific information has. Television talk shows, for example, contain no such protection. They work on exactly the logic in the MacDougall quote: if someone will say it, and people are interested in it, then it gets on television (see Burnham, 1987). Proof, truth, evidence, logic, justification, data, and so on have absolutely nothing to do with television talk shows. They are for *entertainment,* period. For information, look elsewhere.

The media selection process that presents science to the public has the following logic: Scientists who are cautious about stating opinions are rarely quoted. Only those more willing to go out on a limb become public figures. Again, this is not always a bad thing. For example, Carl Sagan and Stephen Gould sometimes go a little too far in the opinion of their more conservative colleagues, but their vast contributions to the public understanding of astronomy and biology undoubtedly more than compensate for any minor inaccuracies that they may have conveyed.

The situation in psychology, however, is not so benign. Most media psychologists, unlike Sagan and Gould, have absolutely no standing among researchers in their field. Yet one survey of Kansas college freshmen (Davis, Thomas, & Weaver, 1982) yielded the name of Joyce Brothers as one of the ten most important contemporary psychologists, right up there with Skinner and Piaget! This difference in psychology is due to a combination of factors. People want the answers to questions concerning human beings much more than they want the answers to questions about other aspects of nature. People want to know how to lose weight, whether psychological therapies actually work, whether absence does make the heart grow fonder, or how to increase the academic achievement of their children much more than they want to know what is the composition of the rings of Saturn or whether a black hole in space is really possible. Combine the fact that answers are sought more urgently of psychology with the reality that the answers to these complex questions are harder to come by, and psychology's problem becomes clear.

In other disciplines the media selection process weeds out more conservative scientists and replaces them with scientists who are a little looser with their conclusions. Unfortunately, in psychology, the scientists are often weeded out altogether! Child psychologist David Elkind (1987) lamented this situation when he reviewed two books on child development that were scientifically sound and also packed full of useful information: "It says something about our society when a book on child rearing by a comedian resides on the best-seller lists for months while these two wise, well-written books by established authorities in the field will, in all likelihood, go largely unread" (p. 67).

The scientifically justified conservatism of psychologists when faced by media representatives creates a void because a tentative statement does not make a story. But justified or not, the void does not remain a void for long. Into it rush all the self-help gurus and psychic charlatans who, bursting forth on TV and radio talk shows, become associated with psychology in the public mind. In short, the conservatism backfires. By exercising proper scientific caution in presenting the results of research to the public, psychology helps to create an image for itself that subsequently leads to its devaluation by both the public and other scientists (see Pallak & Kilburg, 1986). This, then, is the double whammy, and there seems to be no easy way for psychology to avoid it.

Psychologist Robert McCall (1988) carefully analyzed some of the differences between the media reporting of psychology and their reporting of other sciences. He noted that, whereas articles about physics, astronomy, and medicine are typically written by trained science writers, those about the behavioral sciences "tend to be written by a great variety of reporters who seek information pertaining to a news event (for instance, economic or crime reports, day care licensing, low student test scores), not the latest research report" (p. 91). Thus not only is the reporter different, but the stories originate from different sources. In the physical sciences the direction tends to be from science to public; a finding or a theory originates within the discipline and then is reported to the public. In psychology, the direction is often reversed; the public is concerned about something and turns to psychology for answers to its questions. When psychology then fails to give simple answers to society's complex questions, it is devalued and criticized. But consider what the asymmetry in the source of the question would amount to on a personal level. What if I asked you to talk for ten minutes on one of your favorite interests (such as music, books, sports, or art)? You would probably do this easily. Furthermore, you would be fluent and would seem intelligent. Try it. Now

I want you to talk for ten minutes about the origins of the European Economic Community. Chances are that you cannot do so with much fluency and probably not for ten minutes.

This example precisely reflects the differences in how the media approach different sciences. The physical sciences are often asked by trained science reporters what they have recently discovered that is interesting. This is easy for any scientist, including psychologists, to talk about. In contrast, a nonspecialist reporter may well call up a psychologist and ask, "How do children react to stories about AIDS?" and will be disappointed when the psychologist has little to say. The important difference is that this question is the reporter's, not the psychologist's. The psychologist is in the same position as you were in when I asked you to speak about the European Economic Community.

Sometimes when reporting on "psychological" topics, the media dispense with even the *pretense* of scientific validity. Consider, as an example of media reporting of psychology, an article in the June 20, 1994, issue of *Newsweek*. After spending one column hyping a new therapy, "eye movement desensitization and reprocessing"—for example, quoting *another* newsmagazine which called the therapy "a miracle cure"—the *Newsweek* article tells us, "Unfortunately, the excitement is based largely on testimonials [see Chapter 4]. Proponents have yet to show scientifically that EMDR has unique advantages over other forms of therapy" (Cowley & Biddle, 1994, p. 70). Then what, one may ask, is the rationale for publishing this story? To emphasize how bad the media problem is for psychology, we need only ponder the source of the report of this unvalidated therapy. *Newsweek* magazine is not a supermarket tabloid. One may rightfully ask: *What possible purpose is served by printing a story on an unvalidated therapy in a national magazine that will be read by millions of people,* many of whom are desperately seeking cures for a variety of maladies?

McCall (1988) discussed how science writing as a separate journalistic specialty developed in the 1960s because of the need to cover the first manned space shots. The original core of science writers that developed at this time had a large influence and, unfortunately, were uninformed about the behavioral sciences. McCall quoted one veteran science writer's attitude: "I'm not very well equipped to evaluate sociology, but it can't hurt anybody so I figure it's not going to do much damage if I get it a little screwed up" (p. 92). But, as McCall pointed out, "Not only may social and behavioral scientists be asked to apply their research results to practical issues more than other scientists, but also the general public may be more able to act on those suggestions without professional control or guidance. Consequently, getting behavioral science 'a little screwed up' may hurt people more, not less, than reporting errors in stories on other disciplines" (p. 92).

McCall (1988) concluded:

> Press coverage of the social and behavioral sciences is different from coverage of other disciplines. The social and behavioral sciences are less likely to be covered by trained science writers; the topics are more popular with editors and readers; researchers may be asked more frequently to generalize beyond the research to

specific events or applications in society; commonplace terminology may be more easily misinterpreted or mistranslated; findings may be held up to a criterion of "common sense" not applied to other disciplines; and such reports may compete with nonscientific sources of information. (p. 92)

PSYCHOLOGY AND OTHER DISCIPLINES

Psychology, of course, does not have a monopoly on studying behavior. Many other allied disciplines, using a variety of different techniques and theoretical perspectives, also contribute to our knowledge. Many problems concerning behavior call for an interdisciplinary approach. However, a frustrating fact that most psychologists must live with is that, when work on an interdisciplinary problem is publicized, the contributions of psychologists are often usurped by other fields.

There are many examples of scientific contributions by psychologists that have been ignored, minimized, or partially attributed to other disciplines. For instance, the first major survey of the evidence on television's effects on children's behavior was conducted under the aegis of the U.S. Surgeon General, so it is not surprising that the American Medical Association (AMA) passed a resolution to reaffirm the survey's findings of a suggested causal link and to bring the conclusions more publicity. Again, there is nothing wrong here, but an unintended consequence of the repeated association of the findings on televised violence with the AMA is that it has undoubtedly created the impression that the medical profession conducted the scientific research that established the results. In fact, the vast majority of the research studies on the effects of television violence on children's behavior has been done by psychologists.

One of the reasons that the work of psychologists is often ascribed to other disciplines is that the word *psychologist* has, over the years, become ambiguous. Many research psychologists commonly append their research specialty to the word *psychologist* when labeling themselves, calling themselves, for example, physiological psychologists, cognitive psychologists, industrial psychologists, or neuropsychologists. Some use a label that does not contain a derivative of the word *psychology* at all, for example, neuroscientist, cognitive scientist, sociobiologist, artificial intelligence specialist, and ethologist. Both of these practices—in conjunction with the media's bias that "psychology isn't a science"—lead to the misattribution of accomplishments by psychologists: the work of physiological psychologists is attributed to biology, the work of cognitive psychologists is attributed to computer science, the work of industrial psychologists is attributed to engineering and business, and so on.

Psychologist Frederick King (1993), the director of the Yerkes Primate Research Center at Emory University, told of taking time to explain to a reporter the importance of animal models in the study of human neurological disorders. After listening to the long explanation by King, who had contributed for years to the research literature on the neurological and behavioral problems of epilepsy, the reporter asked, "How do you know anything about epilepsy? You're just a psychologist."

Consider another example. In my files I have a form from the library for the blind and handicapped of a large county in Michigan. The form is a certificate of eligibility, and at the bottom of it is a list of the various handicapping conditions that qualify one to use the library. The last category listed is reading disability. Next to it, in large block letters, is the statement, "If this disability is checked, a medical or osteopathic doctor must sign." To an educational psychologist, this requirement is laughably ironic. In all likelihood, nothing has done more to hinder the scientific study of reading disability than unwarranted medical speculation about the condition. It has taken this field decades to rid itself of the many incorrect physiological explanations that sprouted from the few uncontrolled case studies that were at one time introduced into medical literature. In 1957 a medical dictionary defined *dyslexia* as "an inability to read . . . due to central lesion," even though no such central lesion had ever been identified!

The definition and explanation of *reading disability* is still a difficult area of research, but recently some scientific consensus has been achieved. Progress has been slow because the study of reading disabilities is intertwined with difficult issues, such as how to define achievement deficits, random versus systematic differences in performance profiles, the relationship between various aptitudes, and the procedures for avoiding statistical artifacts (McKinney, 1987; Reynolds, 1985; Shepard, 1980; Stanovich & Siegel, 1994; Swanson, 1991). Almost all the pertinent issues are behavioral, not medical. Undoubtedly we will eventually find that distinct physiological conditions are responsible for some reading disabilities (Galaburda, 1994), but currently the knowledge of a medical practitioner is virtually irrelevant to the diagnosis and treatment of this educational and psychological problem; yet the form from this library still reflects the implicit assumption that medical expertise is more valuable than behavioral expertise.

This example is extreme, but the pattern of legitimate medical diagnoses' sliding over into the area of behavioral explanation and remediation has been repeated quite often. For years physicians informed parents of children born with Down syndrome that their children were not educable and should be institutionalized. This practice continued long after behavioral scientists in psychology and other disciplines had demonstrated that the aptitude of these children had been markedly underestimated (Rynders & Horrobin, 1990) and that institutionalization was not the appropriate treatment.

In the late 1970s several cases involving the use of standardized tests were adjudicated in the courts. One such case, *PASE v. Hannon,* involved the issue of cultural bias in intelligence tests. The judge in the case felt that the only way to arrive at a decision was to inspect each test item himself and to trust his own intuition. He had no reservations about his ability to make an accurate judgment and, in his legal opinion, cited his own view of each question on the tests involved (Bersoff, 1981, 1982). He concluded that eight items in one test and a single item in another may have been biased. The judge did not realize that the issue in question is an empirical one that can be answered by use of the scientific method. Personal opinion is not only irrelevant but may be extremely misleading. The determination of bias in test items involves complex statistical procedures and the collection of many data. Psychologists have been prominent in collecting the necessary data and developing the necessary statistical techniques for their evaluation.

Ironically, given the judge's action, research has in fact revealed that the layperson's intuitive judgment about which items are culturally biased is often markedly inaccurate. Many items that are judged to be fair are in fact biased against various racial and sociocultural groups, and many that are thought to be unfair are actually statistically unbiased (Sandoval & Miille, 1980). For example, the Wechsler Adult Intelligence Scale has been criticized in Canada because some of the items on one of its subscales (Information) clearly seem to be biased in favor of U.S. citizens. One item, for instance, asks the respondent to name four men who have been president of the United States since 1950. Thus some of the items have been "Canadianized" for administration in Canada (Violato, 1984, 1986). The "presidents" item, for example, was changed to "Name four men who have been prime minister of Canada since 1900." However, there was one little problem with this obvious, "commonsense" change: Canadian citizens do better on the "presidents" version than on the "prime ministers" version!

Physicists and the Paranormal: Another Example

People are duly impressed when a physicist announces to the media that she or he has verified that a "psychic" has bent a spoon using "mindpower" or that a remote scene has been described by a person who has never been there. The prestige of physics among the sciences automatically confers legitimacy on these claims. It is rarely pointed out that physicists are not routinely trained in the procedures necessary to evaluate claims of psychic abilities. Fundamentally, evaluating these claims involves the assessment of alternative explanations of a behavioral performance. The controls and methodological procedures necessary in such an evaluation are precisely the things that psychologists are trained in. This is the reason that psychic charlatans like Uri Geller are much more wary of experimental psychology laboratories than of solid-state physics centers. Nevertheless, psychology's image problem and the halo that surrounds physics make it inconceivable to many that a psychologist may possess methodological techniques and training that a physicist lacks.

Consider Russel Targ and Harold Puthoff, two senior physicists at SRI International's Radio Physics Laboratory. In the mid-1970s they excited the world and garnered enormous media attention with their claims that they had scientifically demonstrated the existence of remote viewing, the ability to see scenes that are not physically present. Years later much less publicity was given to the fact that three psychologists had uncovered serious flaws in the research design used to test this claim and had demonstrated that, when proper controls were applied, remote viewing did not occur.

In their studies Targ and Puthoff had assigned one experimenter to remain with the subject in the SRI labs. Another experimenter went with other observers to a location chosen from a previously compiled list. At the synchronized moment when the observing team arrived at the location, the experimenter back at SRI told the subject to begin describing the scene. The description was recorded, a transcript was made, and the viewer was provided feedback about his or her performance. This procedure was followed for several target locations over a period of days. An independent judge then received a list of the target locations, which he visited, as well as the transcripts of the "remote" descriptions. The independent judge attempted to match the locations with the transcripts. It was found that the descriptions matched the locations with greater than chance accuracy. This was the basis for the claim that information from the scenes had been detected by an individual not actually there.

After these results appeared, with much fanfare, in books, on television talk shows, and in the popular press, two psychologists at the University of Otago in New Zealand attempted to replicate the experiment. When numerous experiments failed to reveal any evidence of remote viewing, the two researchers, David Marks and Richard Kammann (1980), attempted to obtain more detailed information about the procedures used at SRI and about the actual transcripts that had been the database of the SRI experiments. The independent judge had information about the order in which the targets had been visited because the targets were listed in chronological sequence. Having information about order turned out to be a fatal flaw because the transcripts contained references to targets that had been visited on earlier trials. For example, in the transcript of the seventh trial, the subject made reference to a marina that had been at a previous location. This cue would obviously signal the judge that the seventh transcript went with a location that occurred after the marina. In fact, the transcripts were riddled with such cues. By using this information, the judge could make better than chance matches even without visiting the target locations.

Marks and Kammann confirmed this flaw by having a set of judges who had never seen the locations try to match the transcripts with the target list. All the judges were able to match the transcripts to the list with better than chance accuracy. Marks and Kammann then repeated the experiment after taking the order cues out of the transcripts. The judges visited the locations and tried to match the transcripts as before. The matches obtained this time did not exceed what would be expected on the basis of chance. A similar flaw in the remote viewing experiments was uncovered by University of Oregon psychologist Ray Hyman (1984–1985).

The evidence supporting remote viewing that had been trumpeted to the public by an eager media, reinforced by association with a major research institute, and given credibility by the fact that the investigators were physicists, had actually been obtained because of a simple methodological flaw. The point of this example is not that one would have to be a psychologist to detect the flaw in the Targ-Puthoff experiments. Obviously anyone prone to careful thought about alternative explanations might have uncovered it. It undoubtedly is the case, though, that someone trained in the research techniques of psychology is more likely to detect such errors, simply because they represent the type of problem in research design that a behavioral scientist deals with every day in the lab.

Our Own Worst Enemies

Lest it appear that we are blaming everyone else for psychology's image problems, it is about time that we acknowledge the contribution of psychologists themselves to confusion about their field. Gerald Rosen (1987) documented examples of how psychologists have contributed irresponsibly to the self-help literature. Psychologist Roy Baumeister (1987) argued that psychologists have not taken their role as public communicators seriously, and that only a few have chosen to put legitimate psychological research in a form accessible to the layperson. He stated that we mock the public "for relying on Freud when they need some psychological ideas, but we certainly cannot expect them to read our journals, and we do not offer them any other means of access" (p. 699). Baumeister was right. There are very few rewards for the legitimate psychologist who tries to communicate actual psychology to the public. Although the American Psychological Association and the American Psychological Society are making more efforts to facilitate public communication, psychology needs to make much more of an effort in this domain. Otherwise, we will have only ourselves to blame for the misunderstanding of our discipline.

And finally, there is the phenomenon of antiscientific attitudes within parts of psychology itself. For example, some groups of psychotherapists have traditionally resisted scientific evaluations of their treatments. Columnist and psychotherapist Charles Krauthammer (1985) wrote of how this attitude presents a serious threat to the integrity of psychotherapy. First, there is the proliferation of therapies that has occurred because of reluctance to winnow out those that do not work. Such a proliferation not only removes a critical consumer protection but promotes confusion in the field: "Psychotherapy has come upon this state of confusion because . . . it permits too few deaths among its schools. It is incapable of killing its own. Psychotherapy is dying of dilution." Krauthammer was here lamenting about how the failure to use the falsification strategy stymies scientific progress.

Finally, Krauthammer pointed to the inconsistency of a therapeutic community that, on one hand, argues against scientific evaluation because it is "more art than science," in the common phrase, but still is greatly concerned about what he called the 800-pound gorilla: reimbursement for services by government and private health insurers. Krauthammer exposed the inconsistency of these attitudes within the psychotherapy community: "As long as psychotherapies resist pressure to produce scientific evidence that they work, the economic squeeze will tighten. After all, if psychotherapy is really an art, it should be supported by the National Endowment for the Humanities, not by Medicare."

Some readers of earlier editions of this book have commented that they thought I had "let psychologists get off too easy" by not emphasizing more strongly that unprofessional behavior and antiscientific attitudes among psychologists themselves contribute greatly to the discipline's image problem. My task of providing more balance on this point has been made easier by the publication, in 1994, of Robyn Dawes's *House of Cards: Psychology and Psychotherapy Built on Myth*. If anyone doubts that psychologists themselves have contributed greatly to the field's dilemmas, they need only read this book. In this courageous work, Dawes (1994) did not hesitate to air psychology's dirty linen, at the same time arguing that the scientific attitude toward human problems that is at the heart of the *true* discipline of psychology is of great utility to society (although its potential is still largely untapped). For example, Dawes argued that "there really is a science of psychology that has been developed with much work by many people over many years, but it is being increasingly ignored, derogated, and contradicted by the behavior of professionals—who, of course, give lip service to its existence" (p. vii).

What Dawes (1994) objected to is the historical trend of the field to become more concerned about so-called guild issues, such as licensure, than about scientific issues—a trend observable in the behavior of its oldest organization, the American Psychological Association (APA). In principle, there is nothing wrong with imposing licensure requirements that protect the unique expertise that the study of psychology conveys. But the field does seem to have lost sight of what *is* unique about it. Recall our discussion at the very beginning of this book, in Chapter 1. The unique aspect of the field of psychology is that it brings the tools of the scientific method to the study of behavior. In contrast, the study of psychology does not convey any specific "intuitive" powers to "read people." Indeed, there has been voluminous research on just this point. Recall the discussion of actuarial versus clinical prediction in the previous chapter. The research of forty years on this topic has consistently indicated that, in predicting just about any relevant psychological outcome, a quantification of relevant variables makes better predictions of human behavior than do trained clinicians (Dawes et al., 1989; Faust et al., 1988; Goldberg, 1959, 1968, 1991; Meehl, 1954; Sawyer, 1966). Furthermore, even in the realm of psychotherapeutic outcome itself (rather than the prediction of outcomes), research evidence indicates that neither the training leading to licensure as a psychologist nor years of experience as a clinical psychologist lead to a better therapeutic outcome. Much research has been conducted on this issue, and it consistently indicates that the therapeutic results of nonpsychologist practitioners (e.g., social work professionals) are equal to those of licensed clinical psychologists (Landman & Dawes, 1982; Smith et al., 1980). Indeed, the results of completely uncredentialed paraprofessionals are equal to those of licensed clinical psychologists (Berman & Norton, 1985; Christensen & Jacobson, 1994). Finally, there is no evidence that experience in psychotherapy leads to better outcomes. Years of experience as a psychotherapist are uncorrelated with therapeutic outcome (Christensen & Jacobson, 1994; Landman & Dawes, 1982; Smith et al., 1980).

If the field of psychology were true to its principles of relying on empirical evidence to guide its actions, then it would be publicizing such findings and thus helping the nation to find lower cost ways to meet its mental health needs. As Dawes (1994) argued:

> These results have very strong implications for public policy in the mental health area. We should not be pouring out resources and money to support high-priced people who do not help others better than those with far less training would, and whose judgments and predictions are actually worse than the simplest statistical conclusion based on "obvious" variables. Instead, we should take seriously the findings that the effectiveness of therapy is unrelated to the training or credentials of the therapist. We should take seriously the findings that the best predictors of future behavior are past behavior and performance on carefully standardized tests, not responses to inkblot tests or impressions gained in interviews, even though no prediction is as good as we might wish it to be. The conclusion is that in attempting to alleviate psychological suffering, we should rely much more

than we do on scientifically sound, community-based programs and on "parapro-fessionals," who can have extensive contact with those suffering at no greater expense than is currently incurred by paying those claiming to be experts. (p. 5)

Instead of following this course, the field of psychology justifies licensure requirements based on the scientific status of psychology and then uses licensure to protect the unscientific behavior of psychological practitioners. For example, one thing that a well-trained psychologist should know is that we can be reasonably confident only in *aggregate* predictions. In contrast, predicting the behavior of *particular* individuals is fraught with uncertainty (see Chapter 10) and is something no competent psychologist should attempt without the strongest of caveats, if at all. As Dawes (1994) noted:

> A mental health expert who expresses a confident opinion about the probable future behavior of a single individual (for example, to engage in violent acts) is by definition incompetent, because the research has demonstrated that neither a mental health expert nor anyone else can make such a prediction with accuracy sufficient to warrant much confidence. (Professionals often state that their professional role "requires" them to make such judgments, however much they personally appreciate the uncertainty involved. No, they are not required—they volunteer.) (p. vii)

In short, the American Psychological Association has fostered an ethos surrounding clinical psychology which suggests that psychologists can be trained to acquire an "intuitive insight" into the behavior of individual people which the research evidence does not support. When pushed to defend licensure requirements as anything more than restraint of trade, however, the organization uses its scientific credentials as a weapon (one president of the APA, defending the organization from attack, said "Our scientific base is what sets us apart from the social workers, the counselors, and the Gypsies"; Dawes, 1994, p. 21). But the very methods that the field holds up to justify its scientific status have revealed that the implication that licensed psychologists have a unique "clinical insight" is false. It is such intellectual duplicity on the part of the APA that spawned Dawes's book and that in part led to the formation of the American Psychological Society in the 1980s by psychologists tired of an APA that was more concerned about Blue Cross payments than with science.

ISN'T EVERYONE A PSYCHOLOGIST? IMPLICIT THEORIES OF BEHAVIOR

We all have theories about human behavior. It is hard to see how we could get through life if we did not. In this sense we are all psychologists. It is very important, though, to distinguish between this individual psychology and the type of knowledge produced by the science of psychology. The distinction is critical because the two are often deliberately confused in popular writings about psychology, as we shall see.

In what ways is our personal psychological knowledge different from the knowledge gained from a scientific study of behavior? We have already discussed several. Much of our personal psychological knowledge is recipe knowledge. We do certain things because we think they will lead others to behave in a certain way. We behave in particular ways because we think that certain behavior will help us achieve our goals. But it is not the mere presence of recipe knowledge that distinguishes personal psychology from scientific psychology, which also contains recipe knowledge. Psychotherapies, to varying degrees, provide recipe knowledge about which behaviors and environments will lead to the solution of personal problems or to a more fulfilling life. The main difference here is that the science of psychology seeks to validate its recipe knowledge empirically.

Scientific evaluation is systematic and controlled in ways that individual validation procedures can never be. Indeed, psychological research on decision making has indicated that humans have difficulty detecting correlations in their behavioral environment that run counter to their accepted beliefs (see Baron, 1994; Nisbett & Ross, 1980). We see what we want to see. Psychologists have uncovered many of the reasons, but they need not concern us here. Even if we wanted to evaluate personal recipe knowledge on an individual basis, built-in biases that make us less than adequate observers of behavioral phenomena would make it extremely difficult. The scientific method has evolved to avoid the biases of any single human observer. The implication here is a simple one. The recipe knowledge generated by the science of psychology is more likely to be accurate because it has undergone validation procedures more stringent than those to which personal recipe knowledge is exposed.

As discussed earlier in this chapter, the differences between personal and scientific psychologies go beyond the validation of recipe knowledge. Science always aspires to more than recipe knowledge of the natural world. Scientists seek more general, underlying principles that explain why the recipes work. But many people desire no more insight into human behavior than that provided by recipe knowledge. Indeed, the idea of investigating the underlying causes of behavior actually frightens some people, and they actively avoid such knowledge.

The personal psychologies of some people, however, *are* similar to scientific psychology in seeking to explain recipe knowledge in terms of more basic psychological principles and theories. These personal theories, though, often depart from scientific theories in important ways. We have already mentioned that they are often unfalsifiable. Rather than being coherently constructed, many people's personal psychological theories are merely a mixture of platitudes and clichés, often mutually contradictory, that are used on the appropriate occasion. They reassure people that an explanation does exist and, furthermore, that the danger of a seriously contradictory event—one that would deeply shake the foundations of a person's beliefs—is unlikely to occur. Somehow the net of clichés will be stretched, no matter how far, to explain whatever happens. As discussed in Chapter 2, while this may indeed be comforting, comfort is all that theories constructed in this way provide. In explaining everything post hoc, these theories predict nothing. By making no predictions, they tell us nothing. Theories in the discipline of psychology must meet the falsifiability criterion, and in doing so, they depart from the personal psychological theories of many laypeople. Theories in psychology can be proved wrong, and therefore they contain a mechanism for growth and advancement that is missing from many personal theories.

Some personal theories, however, are not merely unfalsifiable, jerry-built sets of clichés. Some people do hold to implicit psychological theories that are structured in a reasonably coherent manner and that are indeed potentially falsifiable. However, a personal psychological theory of this type still suffers from some of the same difficulties as personal recipe knowledge. While the theory may be coherent and potentially falsifiable, there remains the problem of evaluating the data that could lead to the revision of the theory. An individual's observations are simply not structured in the controlled manner of the scientific method. They are subject to biased interpretations and are acquired in an intermittent way that leads to errors in probabilistic reasoning (see Chapter 10; Nisbett & Ross, 1980). Indeed, we saw in Chapter 6 that people's intuitive theories about motion in the natural world are often very wrong, despite years of experience with moving objects. In the more variable area of human behavior, the situation is bound to be much worse.

THE SOURCE OF RESISTANCE TO SCIENTIFIC PSYCHOLOGY

· *Conflict of Interest*

For all these reasons, it is important not to confuse the idea of a personal psychological theory with the knowledge generated by the science of psychology. Such a confusion is often deliberately fostered in order to undermine the status of psychology in the public mind. The idea that "everyone's a psychologist" is true if it is understood to mean simply that we all have implicit psychological theories. But it is often subtly distorted to imply that psychology is not a science.

We discussed in Chapter 1 why the idea of a scientific psychology is threatening to some people. A maturing science of behavior will change the kinds of individuals, groups, and organizations that serve as sources of psychological information. It is natural that individuals who have long served as commentators on human psychology and behavior will resist any threatened reduction in their authoritative role. Chapter 1 described how the advance of science has continually usurped the authority of other groups to make claims about the nature of the world. The movement of the planets, the nature of matter, and the causes of disease were all once the provinces of theologians, philosophers, and generalist writers. Astronomy, physics, medicine, genetics, and other sciences have gradually wrested these topics away and placed them squarely within the domain of the scientific specialist.

Many religions, for example, have gradually evolved away from claiming special knowledge of the structure of the universe. The titanic battles between science and religion have passed into history, with the exception of some localized flare-ups such as the creationism issue. Scientists uncover the structure of the natural world. Many religions provide guidance and commentary on the moral implications of the uses of these discoveries, but they no longer contest with scientists for the right to determine what the discoveries are. The right to adjudicate claims about the nature of the world has unquestionably passed to scientists. This by no means implies that there is nothing left for theologians or philosophers to do. On the contrary, scientific discoveries constantly raise new moral, ethical, and metaphysical questions that a rational and intelligent society should be debating with vigor. The discussion of these important questions will benefit greatly from the expertise of all who believe in the rational and humane exchange of ideas, and scientists are only one part of this group.

The issue, then, is the changing criteria of belief evaluation. Few newspaper editorials ever come out with strong stands on the composition of the rings of Saturn. Why? No censor would prevent such an editorial. Clearly the reason it is not written is that it would be futile. Society knows that scientists, not editorial writers, determine such things. Only a hundred years ago, newspapers and preachers in the pulpit did comment vociferously on the origins of species in the animal kingdom. These comments have largely disappeared because science has destroyed the conditions that would allow them to be believed by rational thinkers. Psychology threatens to destroy those conditions in another large domain of nature. A hundred years from now, newspaper editorials entitled "Heredity or Environment in Early Childhood Growth?" may sound as silly and dated as Archbishop Ussher's statement that the world was created in 4004 B.C.

Some people find it difficult to accept such a state of affairs when it comes to psychology. They cling tenaciously to their right to declare their own opinions about human behavior even when these opinions contradict the facts. Of course, the correct term here is really not *right,* because, obviously, in a free society, everyone has the *right* to voice opinions, regardless of their accuracy. It is important to understand that what many people want is much *more* than simply the right to declare their opinions about human behavior. What they really want is *the conditions that are necessary for what they say to be believed.* When they make a statement about human psychology, they want the environment to be conducive to belief in their opinion. This is the reason that there are always proponents of the "anything goes" view of psychology, that is, the idea that psychological claims cannot be decided by empirical means and are simply a matter of opinion. But science is always a threat to the "anything goes" view, because it has a set of strict requirements for determining whether a knowledge claim is to be believed. In short, anything does not go in science. This ability to rule out false theories and facts accounts for scientific progress.

In short, a lot of the resistance to scientific psychology is due to what might be termed *conflict of interest.* As discussed in earlier chapters, many pseudosciences are multi-million-dollar industries that thrive on the fact that the public is unaware that statements about behavior can be empirically tested (there are 20 times more astrologers in the United States than astronomers; Gilovich, 1991, p. 2). The public is also unaware that many of the claims that are the basis of these industries (such as astrological prediction, subliminal weight loss, biorhythms, the efficacy of laetrile, and psychic surgery) have been tested and found to be false. A subcommittee of the U.S. Congress has estimated that $10 billion is spent annually on medical quackery, an amount that dwarfs the sum that is spent on legitimate medical research (U.S. Congress, 1984).

Many purveyors of pseudosciences and bogus therapies depend on an atmosphere of "anything goes" surrounding psychology. It provides a perfect environment for feeding on public gullibility, because the public has no consumer protection if "anything goes." As attorney Peter Huber (1990) argued, "[At] the fringes of science and beyond . . . assorted believers in homeopathic medicine and the curative powers of crystals and pyramids . . . must discredit orthodox science to build their own cases for unorthodox nostrums" (p. 97). Those selling pseudoscience have a vested interest in obscuring the fact that there are mechanisms for *testing* behavioral claims. As Michael Ghiselin (1989) warned, "What is going on here is quite straightforward. People are trying to sell a given point of view. Those who know how to evaluate the product are not the same as those to whom it is being marketed" (p. 139). In the domain of behavioral claims and therapies, psychologists are the ones who "know how to evaluate the product." This is the reason for the continued opposition of the pseudoscience industry to the authority of scientific psychology to pass judgment on behavioral claims. However, the purveyors of pseudoscience often do not need to do direct battle with psychology. They simply do an end run around psychology and go straight to the media with their claims. The media make it very easy for cranks, quacks, and pseudoscientists to do an end run around scientific psychology. Phil Donahue, Oprah, Geraldo, Maury, and the plethora of other talk shows that have inundated the airwaves in the 1990s do not ask their guests to produce their bibliographies of scientific research. If these guests are "interesting," they are simply put on the show.

Similar types of conflict of interest do plague other sciences, however. Psychology is not unique in this respect. Established industries often have a vested interest in obscuring the findings of science and the scientific mechanisms of public criticism. The strategy used by established industries is more often to confuse and confound, to muddy the waters, and to turn clear distinctions into blandness so that the public feels that there are no differences on which to base a choice. The area of nutrition provides a good example. Dietician Jayne Hurley (1990) described how the representatives of the food industry (e.g., the Cattleman's Association, the Egg Council, and the Pork Producers) like dieticians to use vague phrases like "moderation of food intake may be the key to many nutritional problems," because such phrasing does not suggest any specific actions that consumers should take. The industry knows that words like *moderation* implicitly encourage people to continue their current eating habits. Hurley (1990) argued, "Balance and 'moderation' is a smokescreen that food manufacturers use to avoid tougher advice to cut down on fat, salt, etc. It's a favorite of the food industry because it's so vague, and it doesn't suggest that our diets need to change. . . . 'Moderation'? That means something different to everybody, which is why the food industry loves it" (p. 8). Similarly the industry loves the idea of the "four basic food groups" because it makes no distinctions among foods and focuses people's attention on getting enough food rather than on getting too much. As Hurley pointed out, "Most Americans suffer not from eating too little, but from eating too much—saturated fat, cholesterol, salt, and sugar. What does the Basic Four have to say about those excesses? Not a peep. Is turkey breast better than a hot dog? Is skim milk better than whole? Is whole wheat bread better than white? Not in the eyes of the Basic Four" (p. 8).

The situation in which Hurley found herself is not unlike that of the psychologist. Hurley was trying to replace ingrained "folk wisdom"—most of which is wrong—with scientific ideas about diet and nutrition. However, powerful forces (the food industries) have a vested interest in convincing the public that they do not *need* modern scientific nutritional information because, after all, their common sense about what to eat (e.g., the four basic food groups) is as good as any scientific information. In addition, folk wisdom often contains a lot of wishful thinking: people want to believe that the world is the way they wish it to be rather than the way it is. Science has the unenviable task of often having to tell the public that the nature of the world is somewhat different from how they wish it to be ("No, that fast-food lunch is *not* good for your health"). The media, which could help in this situation (by telling people what is true rather than what they want to hear), only make it worse with their focus on what will "entertain" rather than on what will inform (Postman, 1985).

Science, then, does rule out the special-knowledge claims of those proposing statements that do not meet the necessary tests. In this book, we have briefly touched on what are considered adequate and inadequate tests in science. Introspection, personal experience, and testimonials are all considered inadequate tests of claims about the nature of human behavior. Thus it should not be surprising that conflict arises because these are precisely the types of evidence that nonpsychologist commentators have been using to support their statements about human behavior since long before a discipline of psychology existed.

However, it should not be thought that I am recommending a dour, spoilsport role for the science of psychology. Quite the contrary. The actual findings of legitimate psychology are vastly more interesting and exciting than the repetitious gee-whiz pseudoscience of the media. Further, it should not be thought that scientists are against fantasy and imagination. Again, on the contrary, scientists have nothing against fantasy, imagination, and flights of fancy—in their proper contexts. Peter Medawar (1990) addressed this point:

> I am quite a believer in hot air in its proper place. I believe that most people psychologically need to be what Paul Jennings calls "bunkrapt." (You may remember Paul Jennings' typewriter when he was trying to write "bankrupt" wrote "bunkrapt.") Everybody needs to be bunkrapt, and I prefer to be bunkrapt by listening to Wagner's music dramas or reading Tolkien's novels. It must not spill over into science. (p. 5)

If we stop and think for a minute, most of us would agree with Medawar's point. We want fancy and fantasy when we go to the movies or the theater—but not when we go to the doctor's office, buy insurance, register our children for child care, fly in an airplane, or have our car serviced. We could add to this list going to a psychotherapist, having our learning-disabled child tested by a school psychologist, or taking a friend to suicide prevention counseling at the university psychology clinic. Psychology, like other sciences, must remove fantasy, unfounded opinion, "common sense," commercial advertising claims, the advice of "gurus," testimonials, and wishful thinking from its search for the truth.

It is difficult for a science to have to tell parts of society that their thoughts and opinions are needed—but not here. Psychology is the latest of the sciences to be in this delicate position. The difference in time period for psychology, however, is relevant. Most sciences came of age during periods of elite control of the structures of society, when the opinion of the ordinary person made no difference. Psychology, on the other hand, is emerging in a media age of universal suffrage and ignores public opinion at its own peril. Cuts in behavioral science budgets during the 1980s should serve as a warning against the folly of leaving communication about psychology in the hands of those hostile to the discipline.

Moral and Philosophical Objections to Psychology

Many psychologists are now taking greater pains to remedy the discipline's lamentable record in public communication (Pallak & Kilburg, 1986). As more psychologists take on a public communication role, the conflicts with those who confuse personal and scientific psychology are bound to increase. Jacob Bronowski (1974) stated this point most bluntly in the context of science in general:

> Criticism of science that I hear comes from people who have really made no attempt to grapple with it. So I think as little of it as I think of Jeremy Bentham's disdain for poetry, since I know that, though he was a great man, he did not understand what poetry was about. . . . I am sorry if that sounds high-handed. But man did not get where he is by cutting out the hard intellectual work, and drawing his judgments from the pit of his stomach. (pp. 402–403)

Our discussion thus far has implied that resistance to a scientific psychology is due to what might be called a conflict of interest. A scientific psychology threatens the legitimacy of the knowledge claims of people who have been seen as authorities on behavior but who are not trained as psychologists. This, however, should not be taken to mean that conflict of interest is the only reason for resistance to the idea of a scientific psychology. Objections can also spring from those with sincerely held philosophical beliefs.

What is to be said about those with sincere philosophical or ethical objections to the idea of a science of human behavior? One objection frequently heard is that the scientific study of behavior diminishes or dehumanizes people. There is really no way to refute such objections since they often arise from different metaphysical orientations or deep feelings about the nature of the universe that are not altered by rational discussion. Psychologists can show respect for these beliefs by taking them seriously enough to state clearly why they reject them. Psychologists may state that their discipline is strongly affected by historical precedent. It was often thought that a detailed knowledge of the structure of the world would diminish our wonder in and curiosity about the universe, but this has turned out not to be true. Each new scientific discovery has increased our understanding of, curiosity about, and respect for nature and our desire to know more.

Also, our understanding of nature has often freed us from cruel superstition. Biologist Michael Ghiselin (1989) asked us to consider how scientific views of birth defects have changed our behavior and attitudes. Before the nineteenth-century work of French zoologist Étienne Geoffroy Saint-Hilaire, there was no natural explanation of birth defects, and they were often attributed to supernatural causes: "The birth of a deformed infant was interpreted as punishment for some kind of sin on the part of the mother" (p. 195). (That is, a "just world" was assumed to explain this outcome, rather than chance; see Chapter 10.) As Ghiselin argued, "The world is better off when we need not blame ourselves or others when accidents are misinterpreted as the consequence of sin. And understanding what goes on in the world around us provides a wholesome sense of confidence if it allows us to tell a legitimate fear from one grounded on ignorance" (p. 195).

Philosopher Charles Frankel (1973) has addressed the philosophical objections to science that are still sometimes heard:

> Indeed, it is passing difficult to understand why the myth persists among many educated people that rational inquiry thins out the world or deprives human experience of its extra dimensions of meaning. Thanks to science, the present world makes available to those who will do their homework subatomic particles, DNA, marginal utilities, relative deprivations, the Minoan culture, the story of evolution. This adds immeasurably to the import to be found in daily existence, to the connections to be drawn, to the implications to be read, to the "unseen things" to be adduced. What science and rational methods have done to "denude" nature is, first, to have introduced ideas for dealing with it that require specialized study and that are not easily available to the man on the run, and, second, to have deprived nature of her anthropomorphic and animistic qualities. (p. 928)

Psychologists simply believe that the same will be true of the study of human behavior. Actually this is putting it too mildly. Most believe that the scientific study of behavior has *already* enriched our understanding in just the way Frankel stated. There is, however, a cost—a cost that accounts for much of the resistance to psychology. We must give up the idea that personal recipe knowledge of human behavior is adequate, that this is the only psychology that we need. The cost is "specialized study . . . not easily available to the man on the run." Not everyone is a physicist, even though we all hold intuitive physical theories. But in giving up the claim that our personal physical theories must usurp scientific physics, we make way for a true science of the physical universe whose theories, because science is public, will be available to us all. Likewise, everyone is not a psychologist. But the facts and theories uncovered by the science of psychology are available to be put to practical ends and to enrich the understanding of all of us.

The Final Word

We are thus at the end of our sketch of how to think straight about psychology. It is a rough sketch, but it can be of considerable help in comprehending how the discipline of psychology works and in evaluating new psychological claims. Our sketch has revealed that:

1. Psychology progresses by investigating solvable empirical problems. This progress is uneven because psychology is composed of many

different subareas, and the problems in some areas are more difficult than in others.

2. Psychologists propose falsifiable theories to explain the findings that they uncover.
3. The concepts in the theories are operationally defined, and these definitions evolve as evidence accumulates.
4. These theories are tested by means of systematic empiricism, and the data obtained are in the public domain, in the sense that they are presented in a manner that allows replication and criticism by other scientists.
5. What makes the empiricism systematic is that it strives for the logic of control and manipulation that characterizes a true experiment.
6. Psychologists use many different methods to arrive at their conclusions, and the strengths and weaknesses of these methods vary.
7. Most often, conclusions are drawn only after a slow accumulation of data from many experiments.
8. The behavioral principles that are eventually uncovered are almost always probabilistic relationships.
9. The data and theories of psychologists are accepted only after publication in peer-reviewed scientific journals.

In 1961 British psychologist Donald Broadbent made a statement that is just as relevant today as it was then. For us it could serve as a condensed summary of how to think straight about psychology:

> We end then upon a note of doubt, with no certainty about the beliefs which future psychologists will hold. This is as it should be. Nobody can grasp the nature of things from an armchair, and until fresh experiments have been performed we do not know what their results will be. The confident dogmatisms about human nature which fall so readily from pulpits, newspaper editorials, and school prize-givings are not for us. Rather, we must be prepared to live with an incomplete knowledge of behavior but with confidence in the power of objective methods to give us that knowledge some day. (pp. 200–201)

References

Aaron, P. G., & Joshi, R. M. (1992). *Reading problems: Consultation and remediation.* New York: Guilford Press.

Abrahamsen, D. (1977). *Nixon vs. Nixon: An emotional tragedy.* New York: Farrar, Straus & Giroux.

Adams, M. J. (1990). *Beginning to read: Thinking about learning about print.* Cambridge: MIT Press.

Adams, M. J., & Bruck, M. (1993). Word recognition: The interface of educational policies and scientific research. *Reading and Writing: An Interdisciplinary Journal, 5,* 113–139.

Adelman, K. A., & Adelman, H. S. (1987). Rodin, Patton, Edison, Wilson, Einstein: Were they really learning disabled? *Journal of Learning Disabilities, 20,* 270–279.

Alcock, J. E. (1981). *Parapsychology: Science or magic?* Oxford: Pergamon Press.

Alcock, J. E. (1984). Parapsychology's past eight years: A lack-of-progress report. *Skeptical Inquirer, 8,* 312–320.

Alcock, J. E. (1990). *Science and supernature: A critical appraisal of parapsychology.* Buffalo, NY: Prometheus Books.

American Psychiatric Association. (1980). *Diagnostic and Statistical Manual of Mental Disorders* (3rd ed.—DSM-III). Washington, DC: Author.

Anderson, C. A., & Gunderson, K. (1991). *Paul E. Meehl: Selected philosophical and methodological papers.* Minneapolis: University of Minnesota Press.

Anderson, J. R. (1991). Is human cognition adaptive? *Behavioral and Brain Sciences, 14,* 471–517.

Andreassen, P. (1987). On the social psychology of the stock market: Aggregate attributional effects and the regressiveness of prediction. *Journal of Personality and Social Psychology, 53,* 490–496.

Arkes, H., Faust, D., Guilmette, T., & Hart, K. (1988). Eliminating the hindsight bias. *Journal of Applied Psychology, 73,* 305–307.

Arkes, H., & Hammond, K. (Eds.). (1986). *Judgment and decision making.* Cambridge, England: Cambridge University Press.

Arkes, H., Wortmann, R., Saville, R., & Harkness, A. (1981). Hindsight bias among physicians weighing the likelihood of diagnosis. *Journal of Applied Psychology, 66,* 252–254.

Asher, W. (1990). Educational psychology, research methodology, and meta-analysis. *Educational Psychologist, 25,* 143–158.

Asimov, I. (1989). The relativity of wrong. *Skeptical Inquirer, 14,* 35–44.

Auletta, K. (1992). *Three blind mice: How the TV networks lost their way.* New York: Vintage Books.

Bachman, J. G., & Schulenberg, J. (1993). How part-time work intensity relates to drug use, problem behavior, time use, and satisfaction among high school seniors: Are these consequences or merely correlates? *Developmental Psychology, 29,* 220–235.

Backman, L., & Dixon, R. A. (1992). Psychological compensation: A theoretical framework. *Psychological Bulletin, 112,* 259–283.

Bainbridge, W. S., & Stark, R. (1980). Superstitions: Old and new. *Skeptical Inquirer, 4,* 18–21.

Banaji, M. R., & Crowder, R. G. (1989). The bankruptcy of everyday memory. *American Psychologist, 44,* 1185–1193.

Bandura, A. (1982). The psychology of chance encounters and life paths. *American Psychologist, 37*, 747–755.

Baron, J. (1994). *Thinking and deciding* (2nd ed.). Cambridge, England: Cambridge University Press.

Bastedo, R. W. (1981). An empirical test of popular astrology. In K. Frazier (Ed.), *Paranormal borderlands of science*. Buffalo, NY: Prometheus Books.

Baumeister, R. (1987). New insights into self-deception. *Contemporary Psychology, 32*, 698–699.

Ben-Shakhar, G., Bar-Hillel, M., Blui, Y., Ben-Abba, E., & Flug, A. (1989). Can graphological analysis predict occupational success? *Journal of Applied Psychology, 71*, 645–653.

Benton, A., & Pearl, D. (1978). *Dyslexia: An appraisal of current knowledge*. New York: Oxford University Press.

Berkowitz, L. (1984). Some effects of thought on anti- and prosocial influences of media events: A cognitive-neoassociation analysis. *Psychological Bulletin, 95*, 410–427.

Berkowitz, L., & Donnerstein, E. (1982). External validity is more than skin deep. *American Psychologist, 37*, 245–257.

Berman, J., & Norton, N. (1985). Does professional training make a therapist more effective? *Psychological Bulletin, 98*, 401–407.

Berra, T. M. (1990). *Evolution and the myth of creation*. Stanford, CA: Stanford University Press.

Bersoff, D. (1981). Testing and the law. *American Psychologist, 36*, 1047–1056.

Bersoff, D. (1982). Larry P. and PASE: Judicial report cards on the validity of intelligence tests. In T. R. Kratochwill (Ed.), *Advances in school psychology*. Hillsdale, NJ: Erlbaum.

Best, J. (1982). Misconceptions about psychology among students who perform highly. *Psychological Reports, 51*, 239–244.

Bevan, W. (1982). A sermon of sorts in three plus parts. *American Psychologist, 37*, 1303–1322.

Bevan, W. (1986). The journey is everything: General-experimental psychology in the United States after a hundred years. In S. Hulse & B. Green (Eds.), *One hundred years of psychological research in America*. Baltimore: Johns Hopkins University Press.

Blum, J. (1978). *Pseudoscience and mental ability*. New York: Monthly Review Press.

Boden, M. A. (1987). *Artificial intelligence and natural man* (2nd ed.). New York: Basic Books.

Bok, S. (1974). The ethics of giving placebos. *Scientific American, 23*, 17–23.

Boneau, C. A. (1990). Psychological literacy: A first approximation. *American Psychologist, 45*, 891–900.

Borgida, E., & Nisbett, R. E. (1977). The differential impact of abstract vs. concrete information on decisions. *Journal of Applied Social Psychology, 7*, 258–271.

Bornstein, R. F. (1989). Exposure and affect. *Psychological Bulletin, 106*, 265–289.

Bower, B. (1990, July 21). The ticing link. *Science News, 138*, 42–44.

Brandt, A. M. (1990). The cigarette, risk, and American culture. *Daedalus, 119*, 155–176.

Braun, P. A., & Yaniv, I. (1992). A case study of expert judgment: Economists' probabilities versus base-rate model forecasts. *Journal of Behavioral Decision Making, 5*, 217–231.

Breitmeyer, B. J., & Ramey, C. T. (1986). Biological nonoptimality and quality of postnatal environment as codeterminants of intellectual development. *Child Development, 57,* 1151–1165.

Brenneman, R. (1990). *Deadly blessings: Faith healing on trial.* Buffalo, NY: Prometheus Books.

Broadbent, D. (1961). *Behaviour.* New York: Basic Books.

Broadbent, D. (1973). *In defense of empirical psychology.* London: Methuen.

Bronfenbrenner, U., & Mahoney, M. (1975). The structure and verification of hypotheses. In U. Bronfenbrenner & M. Mahoney (Eds.), *Influence on human development.* Hinsdale, IL: Dryden.

Broniarczyk, S., & Alba, J. W. (1994). Theory versus data in prediction and correlation tasks. *Organizational Behavior and Human Decision Processes, 57,* 117–139.

Bronowski, J. (1956). *Science and human values.* New York: Harper & Row.

Bronowski, J. (1973). *The ascent of man.* Boston: Little, Brown.

Bronowski, J. (1974). Science, poetry, and human specificity. *American Scholar, 43,* 386–404.

Bronowski, J. (1977). *A sense of the future.* Cambridge: MIT Press.

Bronowski, J. (1978a). *The common sense of science.* Cambridge: Harvard University Press.

Bronowski, J. (1978b). *Magic, science, and civilization.* New York: Columbia University Press.

Brown, J. (1987). Hunger in the U.S. *Scientific American, 256,* 37–47.

Bruck, M. (1992). Persistence of dyslexics' phonological awareness deficits. *Developmental Psychology, 28,* 874–886.

Budiansky, S. (1984, April 22). The meat of the matter. *Washington Post Book World,* p. 7.

Bulgatz, J. (1992). *Ponzi schemes, invaders from Mars, and more extraordinary popular delu-sions and the madness of crowds.* New York: Harmony Books.

Bunge, M. (1983). Speculation: Wild and sound. *New Ideas in Psychology, 1,* 3–6.

Burnham, J. C. (1987). *How superstition won and science lost.* New Brunswick, NJ: Rutgers University Press.

Buss, D. M. (1985). Human mate selection. *American Scientist, 73,* 47–51.

Buss, D. M. (1992). Is there a universal human nature? *Contemporary Psychology, 37,* 1262–1263.

Buss, D. M., & Barnes, M. (1986). Preferences in human mate selection. *Journal of Personality and Social Psychology, 50,* 559–570.

Byrnes, G., & Kelly, I. (1992). Crisis calls and lunar cycles: A twenty-year review. *Psychological Reports, 71,* 779–795.

Caramazza, A., McCloskey, M., & Green, B. (1981). Naive beliefs in "sophisticated" subjects: Misconceptions about trajectories of objects. *Cognition, 9,* 117–123.

Carroll, M., & Nelson, T. O. (1993). Failure to obtain a generation effect during naturalistic learning. *Memory and Cognition, 21,* 361–366.

Casscells, W., Schoenberger, A., & Graboys, T. (1978). Interpretation by physicians of clinical laboratory results. *New England Journal of Medicine, 299,* 999–1001.

Caudill, M., & Butler, C. (1990). *Naturally intelligent systems.* Cambridge: MIT Press.

Ceci, S. J., & Bruck, M. (1993a). Child witnesses: Translating research into policy. *Social Policy Report: Society for Research in Child Development, 7*(3), 1–30.

Ceci, S. J., & Bruck, M. (1993b). Suggestibility of the child witness: A historical review and synthesis. *Psychological Bulletin, 113,* 403–439.

Chall, J. S. (1983). *Learning to read: The great debate* (2nd ed.). New York: McGraw-Hill.

Chall, J. S. (1989). Learning to read: The great debate 20 years later. *Phi Delta Kappan, 70*(7), 521–538.

Chapman, L., & Chapman, J. (1967). Genesis of popular but erroneous psychodiagnostic observations. *Journal of Abnormal Psychology, 72*, 193–204.

Chapman, L., & Chapman, J. (1969). Illusory correlation as an obstacle to the use of valid psychodiagnostic signs. *Journal of Abnormal Psychology, 74*, 271–280.

Chase, A. (1977). *The legacy of Malthus*. New York: Knopf.

Christensen, A., & Jacobson, N. S. (1994). Who (or what) can do psychotherapy: The status and challenge of nonprofessional therapies. *Psychological Science, 5*, 8–14.

Churchland, P. M. (1984). *Matter and consciousness*. Cambridge: MIT Press.

Cicchetti, D., & Grove, W. (Eds.). (1991). *Thinking clearly about psychology: Essays in honor of Paul E. Meehl*. Minneapolis: University of Minnesota Press.

Clotfelter, C., & Cook, P. (1989). *Selling hope: State lotteries in America*. Cambridge: Harvard University Press.

Coates, W., Jehle, D., & Cottington, E. (1989). Trauma and the full moon: A waning theory. *Annals of Emergency Medicine, 18*, 763–765.

Cohen, R. (1985, December 17). Despair: America's double standard. *Detroit Free Press*, p. 11.

Coles, G. (1987). *The learning mystique*. New York: Pantheon Books.

Comstock, G., & Paik, H. (1991). *Television and the American child*. San Diego: Academic Press.

Cournaud, A. (1977). The code of the scientist and its relationship to ethics. *Science, 198*, 699–705.

Cowley, G., & Biddle, N. A. (1994, June 20). Waving away the pain. *Newsweek*, pp. 70–71.

Crease, R. P., & Samios, N. P. (1991, January). Managing the unmanageable. *The Atlantic*, p. 80–88.

Crews, F. (1993, November 18). The unknown Freud. *The New York Review of Books*, pp. 55–66.

Culver, R., Rotton, J., & Kelly, I. W. (1988). Moon mechanisms and myths. *Psychological Reports, 62*, 683–710.

Cummins, R. A., & Prior, M. P. (1992). Autism and assisted communication: A response to Bilken. *Harvard Educational Review, 62*, 228–241.

Davis, D., & Holt, C. (1993). *Experimental economics*. Princeton: Princeton University Press.

Davis, S., Thomas, R., & Weaver, M. (1982). Psychology's contemporary and all-time notables: Student, faculty, and chairperson viewpoints. *Bulletin of the Psychonomic Society, 20*, 3–6.

Dawes, R. M. (1988). *Rational choice in an uncertain world*. San Diego: Harcourt Brace & Jovanovich.

Dawes, R. M. (1991). Probabilistic versus causal thinking. In D. Cicchetti & W. Grove (Eds.), *Thinking clearly about psychology: Essays in honor of Paul E. Meehl* (Vol. 1, pp. 235–264). Minneapolis: University of Minnesota Press.

Dawes, R. M. (1994). *House of cards: Psychology and psychotherapy built on myth*. New York: Free Press.

Dawes, R. M., Faust, D., & Meehl, P. E. (1989). Clinical versus actuarial judgment. *Science, 243*, 1668–1673.

Dawes, R. M., Mirels, H., Gold, E., & Donahue, E. (1993). Equating inverse probabilities in implicit personality judgments. *Psychological Science, 4,* 396–400.

DeBondt, W., & Thaler, R. H. (1985). Does the stock market overreact? *Journal of Finance, 40,* 793–805.

Dembroski, T., & Costa, P. (1988). Assessment of coronary-prone behavior: A review. *Annals of Behavioral Medicine, 10,* 60–63.

Dembroski, T. M., & Costa, P. T. (1987). Coronary prone behavior: Components of the Type A pattern and hostility. *Journal of Personality, 55,* 211–235.

Dennett, D. (1985). Can machines think? In M. Shafto (Ed.), *How we know* (pp. 121–145). New York: Harper & Row.

Diamond, S. S. (1993). Instructing on death: Psychologists, juries, and judges. *American Psychologist, 48,* 423–434.

Dickson, D. H., & Kelly, I. W. (1985). The "Barnum effect" in personality assessment: A review of the literature. *Psychological Reports, 57,* 367–382.

Dillon, K. (1993, Spring). Facilitated communication, autism, and ouija. *Skeptical Inquirer, 17,* 281–287.

Dos Passos, J. (1964). *Occasions and protests.* New York: Henry Regnery.

Dowie, J., & Elstein, A. (Eds.). (1988). *Professional judgment: A reader in clinical decision making.* New York: Cambridge University Press.

Druckman, D., & Swets, J. A. (1988). *Enhancing human performance: Issues, theories and techniques.* Washington, DC: National Academy Press.

Dunn, K. (1993, July 10). Fibbing: The lies the good guys tell. *Toronto Globe and Mail.*

Eddy, D. (1982). Probabilistic reasoning in clinical medicine: Problems and opportunities. In D. Kahneman, P. Slovic, & A. Tversky (Eds.), *Judgment*

under uncertainty: Heuristics and biases (pp. 249–267). Cambridge, England: Cambridge University Press.

Ehri, L. C. (1989). The development of spelling knowledge and its role in reading acquisition and reading disability. *Journal of Learning Disabilities, 22,* 356–365.

Einhorn, H. J. (1986). Accepting error to make less error. *Journal of Personality Assessment, 50,* 387–395.

Eisenberg, L. (1977). The social imperatives of medical research. *Science, 198,* 1105–1110.

Elkind, D. (1987). Child rearing without guilt. *Psychology Today, 21,* 66–67.

Ellis, A. (1985). The cognitive neuropsychology of developmental (and acquired) dyslexia: A critical survey. *Cognitive Neuropsychology, 2,* 169–205.

Eron, L. D. (1982). Parent-child interaction, television violence, and aggression of children. *American Psychologist, 37,* 197–211.

Estes, W. (1979). Experimental psychology: An overview. In E. Hearst (Eds.), *The first century of experimental psychology.* Hillsdale, NJ: Erlbaum.

Estes, W. K. (1993). Concepts, categories, and psychological science. *Psychological Science, 4,* 143–153.

Etzioni, A. (1988). Normative-affective factors: Toward a new decision-making model. *Journal of Economic Psychology, 9,* 125–150.

Evans, C. (1980). *The micro millennium.* New York: Viking Press.

Falk, R. (1989). Judgment of coincidences: Mine versus yours. *American Journal of Psychology, 102,* 477–493.

Falk, R., & MacGregor, D. (1983). The surprisingness of coincidences. In P. Humphreys, O. Svenson, & A. Vari (Eds.), *Analysis and aiding decision processes* (pp. 489–502). Budapest: Akademiai Kiado.

Fama, E. (1965). Random walks in stock market prices. *Financial Analysts Journal, 21,* 55–59.

Fancher, R. (1985). *The intelligence men.* New York: W. W. Norton.

Farber, S. (1981). *Identical twins reared apart.* New York: Basic Books.

Farley, F., & Null, C. H. (1987). *Using psychological science: Making the public case.* Washington, DC: Federation of Behavioral, Psychological and Cognitive Sciences.

Faust, D., Hart, T., Guilmette, T., & Arkes, H. (1988). Neuropsychologists' capacity to detect adolescent malingerers. *Professional Psychology: Research and Practice, 19,* 578–582.

Feeney, D. (1987). Human rights and animal welfare. *American Psychologist, 42,* 593–599.

Fernald, D. (1984). *The Hans legacy.* Hillsdale, NJ: Erlbaum.

Fischer, F. W., Liberman, I. Y., & Shankweiler, D. (1978). Reading reversals and developmental dyslexia: A further study. *Cortex, 14,* 496–510.

Fischhoff, B. (1975). Hindsight ≠ foresight: The effect of outcome knowledge on judgment under certainty. *Journal of Experimental Psychology: Human Perception and Performance, 1,* 288–299.

Fischhoff, B. (1977). Perceived informativeness of facts. *Journal of Experimental Psychology: Human Perception and Performance, 3,* 349–358.

Fischhoff, B. (1988). Judgment and decision making. In R. J. Sternberg & E. E. Smith (Eds.), *The psychology of human thought* (pp. 153–187). Cambridge, England: Cambridge University Press.

Fletcher, J. M., Shaywitz, S. E., Shankweiler, D., Katz, L., Liberman, I., Stuebing, K.,

Francis, D. J., Fowler, A., & Shaywitz, B. A. (1994). Cognitive profiles of reading disability: Comparisons of discrepancy and low achievement definitions. *Journal of Educational Psychology, 86,* 6–23.

Fong, G. T., Lurigio, A. J., & Stalans, L. J. (1990). Improving probation decisions through statistical training. *Criminal Justice and Behavior, 17,* 370–388.

Forsyth, B. (1976). Crucial experiments and social psychological inquiry. *Personality and Social Psychology Bulletin, 2,* 454–459.

Frankel, C. (1973). The nature and sources of irrationalism. *Science, 180,* 927–931.

Frazier, K. (1981). *Paranormal borderlands of science.* Buffalo, NY: Prometheus Books.

Fridson, M. S. (1993). *Investment illusions.* New York: Wiley.

Friedman, M., & Booth-Kewley, S. (1987). The "disease-prone personality." *American Psychologist, 41,* 539–555.

Friedman, M., & Ulmer, D. (1984). *Treating Type A behavior and your heart.* New York: Knopf.

Friedrich-Cofer, L., & Huston, A. (1986). Television violence and aggression: The debate continues. *Psychological Bulletin, 100,* 364–371.

Frith, U. (1989). *Autism: Explaining the enigma.* Oxford, England: Basil Blackwell.

Frith, U. (1993, June). Autism. *Scientific American, 268*(6), 108–114.

Gage, N., & Berliner, D. (1984). *Educational psychology* (3rd ed.). San Francisco: Freeman.

Galaburda, A. (1994). Developmental dyslexia and animal studies: At the interface between cognition and neurology. *Cognition, 50,* 133–149.

Gardner, H. (1985). *The mind's new science.* New York: Basic Books.

Gardner, M. (1972). Mathematical games: Why the long arm of coincidence is usually not as long as it seems. *Scientific American, 227,* 110–112.

Gardner, M. (1981). *Science: Good, bad, and bogus.* Buffalo, NY: Prometheus Books.

Gardner, M. (1983). *The whys of a philosophical scrivener.* New York: Quill.

Gelman, S., Epp, D., Downing, R., Twatrk, R., & Eyerly, R. (1989). Impact of group homes on the values of adjacent residential properties. *Mental Retardation, 27,* 127–134.

Geschwind, N. (1985). The biology of dyslexia. In D. Gray & J. Kavanagh (Eds.), *Behavioral measures of dyslexia.* Parkton, MD: York Press.

Ghiselin, M. T. (1989). *Intellectual compromise.* New York: Paragon House.

Gibson, E. J. (1994). Has psychology a future? *Psychological Science, 5,* 69–76.

Gigerenzer, G. (1984). External validity of laboratory experiments: The frequency-validity relationship. *American Journal of Psychology, 97,* 185–195.

Gilovich, T. (1991). *How we know what isn't so: The fallibility of human reason in everyday life.* New York: Free Press.

Gilovich, T., Vallone, R., & Tversky, A. (1985). The hot hand in basketball: On the misperception of random sequences. *Cognitive Psychology, 17,* 295–314.

Glass, D. C. (1977). Stress, behavior patterns, and coronary disease. *American Scientist, 65,* 177–187.

Gleick, J. (1988). *Chaos: Making a new science.* New York: Penguin Books.

Gleick, J. (1990, March 4). Uh-oh, Here comes the mailman. *New York Times Book Review,* p. 32.

Gleitman, H. (1981). *Psychology.* New York: W. W. Norton.

Goldberg, L. R. (1959). The effectiveness of clinicians' judgments: The diagnosis of organic brain damage from the Bender Gestalt Test. *Journal of Consulting Psychology, 23,* 25–33.

Goldberg, L. R. (1968). Simple models or simple processes? Some research on clinical judgments. *American Psychologist, 23,* 483–496.

Goldberg, L. R. (1991). Human mind versus regression equation: Five contrasts. In D. Cicchetti & W. Grove (Eds.), *Thinking clearly about psychology: Essays in honor of Paul E. Meehl* (Vol. 1, pp. 173–184). Minneapolis: University of Minnesota Press.

Goldstein, M., & Goldstein, I. (1978). *How we know: An exploration of the scientific process.* New York: Plenum Press.

Goodfield, J. (1981). *An imagined world.* New York: Harper & Row.

Gough, P., Ehri, L., & Treiman, R. (Eds.). (1992). *Reading acquisition.* Hillsdale, NJ: Erlbaum.

Gould, S. J. (1987). Justice Scalia's misunderstanding. *Natural History, 96,* 14–21.

Green, M., & MacColl, G. (1983). *There he goes again: Ronald Reagan's reign of error.* New York: Pantheon Books.

Greenberger, D., & Steinberg, L. (1986). *When teenagers work.* New York: Basic Books.

Greenwald, A. G., Spangenberg, E., Pratkanis, A., & Eskenazi, J. (1991). Double-blind tests of subliminal self-help audiotapes. *Psychological Science, 2,* 119–122.

Greider, W. (1992). *Who will tell the people?* New York: Simon & Schuster.

Griffin, D., & Tversky, A. (1992). The weighing of evidence and the determinants of confidence. *Cognitive Psychology, 24,* 411–435.

Griffith, T. (1982, April 5). Reagan's TV troubles. *Time,* p. 570.

Grimmer, M. R. (1992). Searching for security in the mystical: The function of paranormal beliefs. *Skeptical Inquirer, 16,* 173–176.

Hamill, R., Wilson, T. D., & Nisbett, R. E. (1980). Insensitivity to sample bias: Generalizing from atypical cases. *Journal of Personality and Social Psychology, 39,* 578–589.

Hammond, K. R., Harvey, L. O., & Hastie, R. (1992). Making better use of scientific knowledge: Separating truth from justice. *Psychological Science, 3,* 80–87.

Hansel, C. E. M. (1980). *ESP and parapsychology: A critical re-evaluation.* Buffalo, NY: Prometheus Books.

Haugeland, J. (1985). *Artificial intelligence: The very idea.* Cambridge: MIT Press.

Hearst, E. (1979). *The first century of experimental psychology.* Hillsdale, NJ: Erlbaum.

Hedges, L. (1987). How hard is hard science, how soft is soft science? *American Psychologist, 41,* 443–455.

Henshel, R. (1980). The purposes of laboratory experimentation and the virtues of deliberate artificiality. *Journal of Experimental Social Psychology, 16,* 466–478.

Hines, T. (1988). *Pseudoscience and the paranormal.* Buffalo, NY: Prometheus Books.

Holmes, D. L., & Peper, R. J. (1977). An evaluation of the use of spelling error analysis in the diagnosis of reading disabilities. *Child Development, 48,* 1708–1711.

Holton, G., & Roller, D. (1958). *Foundations of modern physical science.* Reading, MA: Addison-Wesley.

Huber, P. W. (1990). Pathological science in court. *Daedalus, 119,* 97–118.

Hudson, A., Melita, B., & Arnold, N. (1993). A case study assessing the validity of facilitated communication. *Journal of Autism and Developmental Disorders, 23,* 165–173.

Huesmann, L. R., & Eron, L. D. (1986). *Television and the aggressive child: A cross-national comparison.* Hillsdale, NJ: Erlbaum.

Huesmann, L. R., Lagerspetz, K., & Eron, L. D. (1984). Intervening variables in the TV violence-aggression relation: Evidence from two countries. *Developmental Psychology, 20,* 746–775.

Hurley, J. (1990, June). Confessions of a RD. *Nutrition Action Healthletter,* p. 8.

Hyman, R. (1964). *The nature of psychological inquiry.* Englewood Cliffs, NJ: Prentice-Hall.

Hyman, R. (1981). Cold reading: How to convince strangers that you know all about them. In K. Frazier (Eds.), *Paranormal borderlands of science.* Buffalo, NY: Prometheus Books.

Hyman, R. (1984–1985). Outracing the evidence: The muddled "mind race." *Skeptical Inquirer, 9,* 125–145.

Hyman, R. (1992). What does Goodfellow's classic analysis tell researchers today? *Journal of Experimental Psychology: General, 121,* 128–129.

Hynd, G. S., Marshall, R., & Gonzalez, J. (1991). Learning disabilities and presumed central nervous system dysfunction. *Learning Disability Quarterly, 14,* 283–296.

If it sounds just ducky, it probably quacks. (1990, March 23). *Detroit Free Press.*

Jeffrey, R., & Pasewark, R. (1983). Altering opinions about the insanity plea. *Journal of Psychiatry and Law, 11,* 29–44.

Jeffrey, R. W. (1989). Risk behaviors and health. *American Psychologist, 44,* 1194–1202.

Jencks, C. (1985). How much do high school students learn? *Sociology of Education, 58,* 128–135.

Jencks, C., & Riesman, D. (1968). *The academic revolution*. Garden City, NY: Doubleday.

Jenkins, C. D., Zyzanski, S. J., & Rosenman, R. H. (1976). Risk of new myocardial infarction in middle-aged men with manifest coronary heart disease. *Circulation, 53,* 342–347.

Johnson, G. (1986). *Machinery of the mind.* Redmond, WA: Microsoft Press.

Johnson, H. (1991). *Sleepwalking through history: America in the Reagan years.* New York: Anchor Books.

Josephson, W. (1987). Television violence and children's aggression: Testing the priming, social script, and disinhibition predictions. *Journal of Personality and Social Psychology, 53,* 882–890.

Joshi, R. M., & Leong, C. K. (Eds.). (1993). *Reading disabilities: Diagnosis and component processes.* Dordrecht, The Netherlands: Kluwer Academic.

Judson, H. F. (1979). *The eighth day of creation.* New York: Simon & Schuster.

Kahneman, D., Slovic, P., & Tversky, A. (1982). *Judgment under uncertainty: Heuristics and biases.* Cambridge, England: Cambridge University Press.

Kahneman, D., & Tversky, A. (1973). On the psychology of prediction. *Psychological Review, 80,* 237–251.

Kavale, K. A., & Mattson, P. (1983). "One jumped off the balance beam": Meta-analysis of perceptual-motor training. *Journal of Learning Disabilities, 16,* 165–173.

Kelly, I., Rotton, J., & Culver, R. (1985). The moon was full and nothing happened: A review of studies on the moon and human behavior and lunar beliefs. *Skeptical Inquirer, 10,* 129–143.

Kershaw, A. (1991, July 21). The psychic guide to hiring and firing. *London Independent.*

Kety, S. (1974). Preface. In J. Swazey, *Chlorpromazine in psychiatry: A study of therapeutic intervention.* Cambridge: MIT Press.

Kim, J. (1994, September). Watch out for investing newsletters luring you with outdated returns. *Money Magazine,* pp. 12–13.

Kimble, G. A. (1990). Mother Nature's bag of tricks is small. *Psychological Science, 1,* 36–41.

Kimble, G. A. (1994). A frame of reference for psychology. *American Psychologist, 49,* 510–519.

King, F. (1993, March). Science literacy and public support of science. *American Psychological Society Observer, 6*(2), 2–11.

Knight, G. P., Johnson, L., Carlo, G., & Eisenberg, N. (1994). A multiplicative model of the dispositional antecedents of a prosocial behavior: Predicting more of the people more of the time. *Journal of Personality and Social Psychology, 66,* 178–183.

Kohn, A. (1990). *You know what they say . . . : The truth about popular beliefs.* New York: HarperCollins.

Kolb, B., & Whishaw, I. (1990). *Fundamentals of human neuropsychology* (3rd ed.). New York: Freeman.

Kramer, S. P. (1987). *How to think like a scientist: Answering questions by the scientific method.* New York: Thomas Y. Crowell Junior Books.

Krauthammer, C. (1985, December 29). The twilight of psychotherapy? *Detroit News.*

Krippner, S. (1977). *Advances in parapsychological research: 1. Psychokinesis.* New York: Plenum Press.

Kruglanski, A. W. (1975). The human subject in the psychology experiment: Fact and artifact. In L. Berkowitz (Ed.), *Advances in experimental social psychology.* New York: Academic Press.

Kruglanski, A. W. (1976). On the paradigmatic objections to experimental psychology. *American Psychologist, 31,* 655–663.

Kurtz, P. (1987). *A skeptic's handbook of parapsychology.* Buffalo, NY: Prometheus Books.

Lakatos, I. (1970). Falsification and the methodology of scientific research programmes. In I. Lakatos & A. Musgrave (Eds.), *Criticism and the growth of knowledge.* Cambridge, England: Cambridge University Press.

Landman, J. T., & Dawes, R. M. (1982). Psychotherapy outcome. *American Psychologist, 37,* 504–516.

Langer, E. J. (1975). The illusion of control. *Journal of Personality and Social Psychology, 32,* 311–328.

Langewiesche, W. (1993, December). The turn. *The Atlantic Monthly, 272*(6), 115–122.

Latané, B., & Darley, J. (1970). *The unresponsive bystander: Why doesn't he help?* New York: Appleton-Century-Crofts.

Laudan, R. (1980). The recent revolution in geology and Kuhn's theory of scientific change. In G. Gutting (Ed.), *Paradigms and revolutions.* Notre Dame, IN: University of Notre Dame Press.

Lazar, I., Darlington, R., Murray, H., Royce, J., & Sniper, A. (1982). Lasting effects of early education: A report from the Consortium of Longitudinal Studies. *Monographs of the Society for Research in Child Development, 47* (Serial No. 195).

Leary, M. R. (1979). Levels of disconfirmability and social psychological theory: A response of Greenwald. *Personality and Social Psychology Bulletin, 5,* 149–153.

Leavy, J. (1992). Our spooky presidential coincidences contest. *Skeptical Inquirer, 16,* 316–319.

Lee, V., Brooks-Gunn, J., Schnur, E., & Liaw, F. (1990). Are Head Start's effects sustained? A longitudinal follow-up comparison of disadvantaged children attending Head Start, no preschool, and other preschool programs. *Child Development, 61,* 495–507.

Leli, D., & Filskov, S. (1981). Clinical-actuarial detection and description of brain impairment with the W-B Form 1. *Journal of Clinical Psychology, 37,* 623–629.

Lerner, M. J., & Miller, D. T. (1978). Just world research and the attribution process: Looking back and ahead. *Psychological Bulletin, 85,* 1030–1051.

Levine, K., Shane, H., & Wharton, R. (1994). What if . . . : A plea to professionals to consider the risk-benefit ratio of facilitated communication. *Mental Retardation, 32,* 300–304.

Li, C. (1975). *Path analysis: A primer.* Pacific Grove, CA: Boxwood Press.

Lichtenstein, S., Slovic, P., Fischhoff, B., Layman, M., & Combs, B. (1978). Judged frequency of lethal events. *Journal of Experimental Psychology: Human Learning and Memory, 4,* 551–578.

Liebert, R. M., & Sprafkin, J. (1988). *The early window: Effects of television on children and youth* (3rd ed.). Oxford, England: Pergamon Press.

Liebert, R. S. (1977). Nixon and the enemy within. *Psychology Today, 10,* 68–69.

Lipsey, M. W., & Wilson, D. B. (1993). The efficacy of psychological, educational, and behavioral treatment: Confirmation from meta-analysis. *American Psychologist, 48,* 1181–1209.

Loftus, E. F. (1993). Psychologists in the eyewitness world. *American Psychologist, 48,* 550–552.

Loftus, E. F. (1994). The repressed memory controversy. *American Psychologist, 49,* 443–445.

Loftus, E. F., & Ketcham, K. (1991). *Witness for the defense.* New York: St. Martin's Press.

Lopes, L., & Oden, G. (1987). Distinguishing between random and nonrandom events. *Journal of Experimental Psychology: Learning, Memory, and Cognition, 13,* 392–400.

Lundeberg, M. A., Fox, P. W., & Puncochar, J. (1994). Highly confident but wrong: Gender differences and similarities in confidence judgments. *Journal of Educational Psychology, 86,* 114–121.

Lyon, D., & Slovic, P. (1976). Dominance of accuracy information and neglect of base rates in probability estimation. *Acta Psychologica, 40,* 287–298.

Lyon, G. R. (Ed.). (1994). *Frames of reference for the assessment of learning disabilities.* Baltimore: Paul Brookes.

MacDonald, A. (1990, October 3). Parents fear wrong things, survey suggests. *Ann Arbor News* (taken from New York Times wire service).

MacDougall, C. D. (1983). *Superstition and the press.* Buffalo, NY: Prometheus Books.

Magee, B. (1985). *Philosophy and the real world: An introduction to Karl Popper.* LaSalle, IL: Open Court.

Malkiel, B. G. (1990). *A random walk down Wall Street.* New York: W. W. Norton.

Mandler, G. (1984). *Mind and body.* New York: W. W. Norton.

Marcus, G. B. (1986). Stability and change in political attitudes: Observe, recall, and "explain." *Political Behavior, 8,* 21–44.

Market Facts, I. (1984). *1983 Consumer research study on reading and book purchasing.* New York: Book Industry Study Group.

Markovits, H., & Nantel, G.(1989). The belief-bias effect in the production and evaluation of logical criticisms. *Memory and Cognition, 17,* 11–17.

Marks, D., & Kammann, R. (1980). *The psychology of the psychic.* Buffalo, NY: Prometheus Books.

Marshall, E. (1980). Police science and psychics. *Science, 210,* 994–995.

Matthews, K. A. (1982). Psychological perspectives on the Type A behavior pattern. *Psychological Bulletin, 91,* 293–323.

Maughan, B., Hagell, A., Rutter, M., & Yule, W. (1994). Poor readers in secondary school. *Reading and Writing: An Interdisciplinary Journal, 6,* 125–150.

McBurney, D. (1983). *Experimental psychology.* Belmont, CA: Wadsworth.

McCall, R. (1988). Science and the press. *American Psychologist, 43,* 87–94.

McCarthy, J. (1983). The little thoughts of thinking machines. *Psychology Today, 17,* 46–49.

McCloskey, M. (1983). Intuitive physics. *Scientific American, 248,* 122–130.

McCorduck, P. (1979). *Machines who think.* San Francisco: Freeman.

McKeachie, W. J. (1960). Changes in scores on the Northwestern Misconceptions Test in six elementary psychology courses. *Journal of Educational Psychology, 51,* 240–244.

McKinney, J. D. (1987). Research on the identification of learning disabled children: Perspectives on changes in educational policy. In S. Vaughn & C. Bos (Eds.), *Research in learning disabilities* (pp. 215–233). Boston: College-Hill.

McNeil, B., Pauker, S., Sox, H., & Tversky, A. (1982). On the elicitation of preferences for alternative therapies. *New England Journal of Medicine, 306,* 1259–1262.

Medawar, P. B. (1967). *The art of the soluble.* London: Methuen.

Medawar, P. B. (1979). *Advice to a young scientist.* New York: Harper & Row.

Medawar, P. B. (1982). *Pluto's republic.* Oxford: Oxford University Press.

Medawar, P. B. (1984). *The limits of science.* New York: Harper & Row.

Medawar, P. B. (1990). *The threat and the glory.* New York: HarperCollins.

Medawar, P. B., & Medawar, J. S. (1983). *Aristotle to zoos: A philosophical dictionary of biology.* Cambridge: Harvard University Press.

Meehl, P. E. (1954). *Clinical versus statistical prediction: A theoretical analysis and review of the literature.* Minneapolis: University of Minnesota Press.

Meehl, P. E. (1986). Causes and effects of my disturbing little book. *Journal of Personality Assessment, 50,* 370–375.

Miller, N. E. (1985a). Rx: Biofeedback. *Psychology Today, 19,* 54–59.

Miller, N. E. (1985b). The value of behavioral research on animals. *American Psychologist, 40,* 423–440.

Miller, T. Q., Turner, C., Tindale, R., Posavac, E., & Dugoni, B. (1991). Reasons for the trend toward null findings in research on Type A behavior. *Psychological Bulletin, 110,* 469–485.

Mook, D. G. (1982). *Psychological research: Strategies and tactics.* New York: Harper & Row.

Mook, D. G. (1983). In defense of external invalidity. *American Psychologist, 38,* 379–387.

Mook, D. G. (1989). The myth of external validity. In L. W. Poon, D. C. Rubin, & B. A. Wilson (Eds.), *Everyday cognition in adulthood and late life* (pp. 25–43). Cambridge, England: Cambridge University Press.

Moore, R. L. (1977). *In search of white crows.* New York: Oxford University Press.

Morrison, P. (1983). Science and lost opportunity. *Skeptical Inquirer, 7,* 56.

Mulick, J., Jacobson, J., & Kobe, F. (1993, Spring). Anguished silence and helping hands: Autism and facilitated communication. *Skeptical Inquirer, 17,* 270–280.

Murchison, C. (1934). *Handbook of general experimental psychology.* Worcester, MA: Clark University Press.

Murstein, B. (1980). Mate selection in the 1970s. *Journal of Marriage and Family, 42,* 51–66.

National Safety Council. (1990). *Accident facts* (1990 edition). Chicago: Author.

Neisser, U. (1982). *Memory observed: Remembering in natural contexts.* New York: Freeman.

Neter, E., & Ben-Shakhar, G. (1989). Predictive validity of graphological inferences: A meta-analysis. *Personality and Individual Differences, 10,* 737–745.

Neuman, S. B. (1988). The displacement effect: Assessing the relation between television viewing and reading performance. *Reading Research Quarterly, 23,* 414–440.

Newell, A. (1990). *Unified theories of cognition.* Cambridge: Harvard University Press.

Nickerson, R. (1992). *Looking ahead: Human factors challenges in a changing world.* Hillsdale, NJ: Erlbaum.

Niemeyer, W., & Starlinger, I. (1981). Do the blind hear better? *Audiology, 20,* 503–515.

Nisbett, R. E., & Ross, L. (1980). *Human inference: Strategies and shortcomings of social judgment.* Englewood Cliffs, NJ: Prentice-Hall.

Olson, R., Kliegl, R. & Davidson, B. (1983). Dyslexia and normal readers' eye movements. *Journal of Experimental Psychology: Human Perception and Performance, 9,* 816–825.

Olson, R., Wise, B., Conners, F., Rack, J., & Fulker, D. (1989). Specific deficits in component reading and language skills: Genetic and environmental influences. *Journal of Learning Disabilities, 22,* 339–348.

Olson, R. K., Rack, J., Conners, F., DeFries, J., & Fulker, D. (1991). Genetic etiology of individual differences in reading disability. In L. Feagans, E. Short, & L. Meltzer (Eds.), *Subtypes of learning disabilities* (pp. 113–135). Hillsdale, NJ: Erlbaum.

Page, E., & Keith, T. (1981). Effects of U.S. private schools: A technical analysis of two recent claims. *Educational Researcher, 10,* 7–17.

Pallak, M., & Kilburg, M. (1986). Psychology, public affairs, and public policy. *American Psychologist, 41,* 933–940.

Paloutzian, R. F. (1983). *Invitation to the psychology of religion.* Glenview, IL: Scott, Foresman.

Paul, G. L. (1966). *Insight vs. desensitization in psychotherapy.* Stanford, CA: Stanford University Press.

Paul, G. L. (1967). Insight vs. desensitization in psychotherapy two years after termination. *Journal of Consulting Psychology, 31,* 333–348.

Paulos, J. A. (1988). *Innumeracy: Mathematical illiteracy and its consequences.* New York: Vintage Books.

Pearl, D., Bouthilet, L., & Lazar, J. (Eds.). (1982). *Television and behavior: Ten years of scientific progress and implications for the eighties.* Rockville, MD: National Institute of Mental Health.

Pennington, B. F. (1990). The genetics of dyslexia. *Journal of Child Psychology and Psychiatry, 31,* 193–201.

Phillips, M. R., Wolf, A. S., & Coons, D. J. (1988). Psychiatry and the criminal justice system. *American Journal of Psychiatry, 145,* 605–610.

Phillips, P., & Shafer, M. (1982). Exploratory research with two new psychic metal benders. In W. Roll, R. Morris, & R. White (Eds.), *Research in parapsychology, 1981.* Metuchen, NJ: Scarecrow Press.

Pillemer, R. (1991). One- versus two-tailed hypothesis tests in contemporary educational research. *Educational Researcher, 20*(9), 13–17.

Poon, L. W., Rubin, D. C., & Wilson, B. A. (Eds.). (1989). *Everyday cognition in adulthood and late life.* Cambridge, England: Cambridge University Press.

Popper, K. R. (1959). *The logic of scientific discovery.* New York: Harper & Row.

Popper, K. R. (1963). *Conjectures and refutations.* New York: Harper & Row.

Popper, K. R. (1972). *Objective knowledge.* Oxford, England: Oxford University Press.

Popper, K. R. (1976). *Unended quest: An intellectual biography.* La Salle, IL: Open Court.

Posner, M. I. (Ed.). (1989). *Foundations of cognitive science.* Cambridge: MIT Press.

Postman, N. (1985). *Amusing ourselves to death.* New York: Viking Penguin.

Postman, N. (1988). *Conscientious objections.* New York: Vintage Books.

Powell, B. (1993, December). Sloppy reasoning, misused data. *Phi Delta Kappan, 75*(4), 283, 352.

Prioleau, L., Murdock, M., & Brody, N. (1983). An analysis of psychotherapy versus placebo studies. *Behavioral and Brain Sciences, 6,* 275–310.

Prior, M. P., & Cummins, R. A. (1992). Questions about facilitated communication and autism. *Journal of Autism and Developmental Disorders, 22,* 331–338.

Quinlan, P. (1991). *Connectionism and psychology.* New York: Harvester Wheatsheaf.

Rabbitt, P. (1993). Does it all go together when it goes? *Quarterly Journal of Experimental Psychology, 46A,* 385–434.

Randi, J. (1980). *Flim-flam.* Buffalo, NY: Prometheus Books.

Randi, J. (1983). The project alpha experiment: 1. The first two years. *Skeptical Inquirer, 7,* 24–33.

Randi, J. (1987). *The faith healers.* Buffalo, NY: Prometheus Books.

Rayner, K. (1985). Do faulty eye movements cause dyslexia? *Developmental Neuropsychology, 1,* 3–15.

Reeves, R. (1986, March 3). The new Democrats take on the GOP. *Detroit News,* p. 7.

Reiser, M., Ludwig, A., Saxe, M., & Wagner, B. (1979). An evaluation of the use of psychics in the investigation of major crimes. *Journal of Police Science and Administration, 7,* 18–25.

Reynolds, C. R. (1985). Measuring the aptitude-achievement discrepancy in learning disability diagnosis. *Remedial and Special Education, 6,* 37–55.

Rodin, J. (1981). Current status of the internal-external hypothesis for obesity. *American Psychologist, 36,* 361–372.

Rosen, G. (1987). Self-help treatment books and the commercialization of psychotherapy. *American Psychologist, 42,* 46–51.

Rosenthal, R. (1990). How are we doing in soft psychology? *American Psychologist, 46,* 775–776.

Rotton, J., & Kelly, I. W. (1985). Much ado about the full moon. *Psychological Bulletin, 97,* 286–306.

Rowe, D. C., Vazsonyi, A. T., & Flannery, D. J. (1994). No more than skin deep: Ethnic and racial similarity in developmental process. *Psychological Review, 101,* 396–413.

Rowe, W. (1993). Psychic detectives: A critical examination. *Skeptical Inquirer, 17,* 159–165.

Rubenstein, E. A. (1983). Television and behavior: Research conclusions of the 1982 NIMH Report and their policy implications. *American Psychologist, 38,* 820–825.

Rutter, M. (1979). Maternal deprivation, 1972–1978: New findings, new concepts, and new approaches. *Child Development, 50,* 283–305.

Ryan, C. S., & Coyne, A. (1985). Effects of group homes on neighborhood property values. *Mental Retardation, 23,* 241–245.

Rynders, J. E., & Horrobin, J. M. (1990). Always trainable? Never educable? Updating educational expectations concerning children with Down Syndrome. *American Journal of Mental Retardation, 95,* 77–83.

Rzewnicki, R., & Forgays, D. G. (1987). Recidivism and self-cure of smoking and obesity: An attempt to replicate. *American Psychologist, 42,* 97–100.

Saks, M., & Kidd, R. (1980–1981). Human information processing and adjudication: Trial by heuristics. *Law and Society Review, 15,* 123–160.

Salthouse, T. A. (1991). *Theoretical perspectives on cognitive aging.* Hillsdale, NJ: Erlbaum.

Salthouse, T. A. (1993). Speed mediation of adult age differences in cognition. *Developmental Psychology, 29,* 722–738.

Salthouse, T. A. (1994). The nature of the influence of speed on adult age differences in cognition. *Developmental Psychology, 30,* 240–259.

Sandoval, J., & Miille, M. (1980). Accuracy of judgments of WISC-R item difficulty for minority groups. *Journal of Consulting and Clinical Psychology, 48,* 249–253.

Sapolsky, R. (1994, March–April). Measures of life. *The Sciences, 34*(2), 10–13.

Sassenrath, J., Croce, M., & Penaloza, M. (1984). Private and public schools students: Longitudinal achievement differences? *American Educational Research Journal, 21,* 557–563.

Sawyer, J. (1966). Measurement and prediction, clinical and statistical. *Psychological Bulletin, 66,* 178–200.

Schachter, S. (1982). Recidivism and self-cure of smoking and obesity. *American Psychologist, 37,* 436–444.

Schmidt, F. (1992). What do data really mean? Research findings, meta-analysis, and cumulative knowledge in psychology. *American Psychologist, 47,* 1173–1181.

Schneider, S. F. (1990). Psychology at a crossroads. *American Psychologist, 45,* 521–529.

Schwartz, S., & Griffin, T. (Eds.). (1986). *Medical thinking: The psychology of medical judgment and decision making.* New York: Springer-Verlag.

Scott, T. (1991). A personal view of the future of psychology departments. *American Psychologist, 46,* 975–976.

Seligmann, J., & Chideya, F. (1992, September 21). Horror story or big hoax? *Newsweek,* p. 75.

Shaffer, L. (1977). The golden fleece: Anti-intellectualism and social science. *American Psychologist, 32,* 814–823.

Shaffer, L. (1981). The growth and limits of recipe knowledge. *The Journal of Mind and Behavior, 2,* 71–83.

Shane, H. (1993, June). FC: Facilitated or "factitious" communication. *Communicating Together, 11*(2), 11–13.

Shapiro, A. (1960). A contribution to a history of the placebo effect. *Behavioral Science, 5,* 109–135.

Shapiro, A., Shapiro, E., Bruun, R., & Sweet, R. (1978). *Gilles de la Tourette syndrome.* New York: Raven Press.

Shefrin, H., & Statman, M. (1986). How not to make money in the stock market. *Psychology Today, 20,* 53–57.

Shepard, L. (1980). An evaluation of the regression discrepancy method for identifying children with learning disabilities. *Journal of Special Education, 14,* 79–91.

Shepard, R. (1983). "Idealized" figures in textbooks versus psychology as an empirical science. *American Psychologist, 38,* 855.

Shiller, R. (1987). The volatility of stock market prices. *Science, 235,* 33–37.

Shontz, F., & Green, P. (1992). Trends in research on the Rorschach: Review and recommendations. *Applied and Preventive Psychology, 1,* 149–156.

Siegel, L. S. (1988). Evidence that IQ scores are irrelevant to the definition and analysis of reading disability. *Canadian Journal of Psychology, 42,* 201–215.

Siegel, L. S. (1989). IQ is irrelevant to the definition of learning disabilities. *Journal of Learning Disabilities, 22,* 469–479.

Simmons, R., Burgeson, R., Carlton-Ford, S., & Blyth, D. (1987). The impact of cumulative change in early adolescence. *Child Development, 58,* 1220–1234.

Simon, H. A. (1992). What is an "explanation" of behavior? *Psychological Science, 3,* 150–161.

Singer, M. (1982). Comparing memory for natural and laboratory reading. *Journal of Experimental Psychology: General, 111,* 331–347.

Slovic, P., & Fischhoff, B. (1977). On the psychology of experimental surprises. *Journal of Experimental Psychology: Human Perception and Performance, 3,* 544–551.

Smith, M., & Belcher, R. (1993). Facilitated communication with adults with autism. *Journal of Autism and Developmental Disorders, 23,* 175–183.

Smith, M. L., Glass, G. V., & Miller, T. I. (1980). *The benefits of psychotherapy*. Baltimore: Johns Hopkins University Press.

Smith, R. E., Wheeler, G., & Diener, E. (1975). Faith without works. *Journal of Applied Social Psychology, 5,* 320–330.

Snowling, M. (1991). Developmental reading disorders. *Journal of Child Psychology and Psychiatry, 32,* 49–77.

Snyder, C., Shenkel, R., & Lowery, C. (1977). Acceptance of personality interpretations: The "Barnum effect" and beyond. *Journal of Consulting and Clinical Psychology, 45,* 104–114.

Spearman, C. (1904). "General intelligence" objectively determined and measured. *American Journal of Psychology, 15,* 201–293.

Spence, J. T. (1987). Centrifugal versus centripetal tendencies in psychology: Will the center hold? *American Psychologist, 42,* 1052–1054.

Spreen, O. (1988). Prognosis of learning disability. *Journal of Consulting and Clinical Psychology, 56,* 836–842.

Stankov, L., & Spilsbury, G. (1978). The measurement of auditory abilities of blind, partially sighted, and sighted children. *Applied Psychological Measurement, 2,* 491–503.

Stanovich, K. E. (1986a). Cognitive processes and the reading problems of learning disabled children: Evaluating the assumption of specificity. In J. Torgesen & B. Wong (Eds.), *Psychological and educational perspectives on learning disabilities* (pp. 87–131). New York: Academic Press.

Stanovich, K. E. (1986b). Matthew effects in reading: Some consequences of individual differences in the acquisition of literacy. *Reading Research Quarterly, 21,* 360–407.

Stanovich, K. E. (1989). Implicit philosophies of mind: The dualism scale and its relationships with religiosity and belief in extrasensory perception. *Journal of Psychology, 123,* 5–23.

Stanovich, K. E. (1991). Cognitive science meets beginning reading. *Psychological Science, 2,* 70–81.

Stanovich, K. E. (1993). Romance and reality. *The Reading Teacher, 47*(4), 280–291.

Stanovich, K. E. (1994). Does dyslexia exist? *Journal of Child Psychology and Psychiatry, 35,* 579–595.

Stanovich, K. E., & Siegel, L. S. (1994). The phenotypic performance profile of reading-disabled children: A regression-based test of the phonological-core variable-difference model. *Journal of Educational Psychology, 86,* 24–53.

Steadman, H., & Cocozza, J. (1978). Selective reporting and the public's misconceptions of the criminally insane. *Public Opinion Quarterly, 41,* 523–533.

Steen, L. A. (1990). Numeracy. *Daedalus, 119,* 211–231.

Steinberg, L., Fegley, S., & Dornbusch, S. M. (1993). Negative impact of part-time work on adolescent adjustment: Evidence from a longitudinal study. *Developmental Psychology, 29,* 171–180.

Sternberg, R. J. (1982). *Handbook of human intelligence*. Cambridge, England: Cambridge University Press.

Sternberg, R. J. (1990). *Metaphors of mind: Conceptions of the nature of intelligence*. Cambridge, England: Cambridge University Press.

Stevenson, H., Stigler, J., Lee, S., Lucker, G., Kitamura, S., & Hsu, C. (1985). Cognitive performance and academic achievement of Japanese, Chinese, and American children. *Child Development, 56,* 718–734.

Stevenson, J. (1992). Genetics. In N. Singh & I. Beale (Eds.), *Learning disabilities: Nature, theory, and treatment* (pp. 327–351). New York: Springer-Verlag.

Stevenson, J., Graham, P., Fredman, G., & McLoughlin, V. (1987). A twin study of genetic influences on reading and spelling ability and disability. *Journal of Child Psychology and Psychiatry, 28,* 229–247.

Stone, G. (1984). Reaction: In defense of the "artificial." *Journal of Counseling Psychology, 31,* 108–110.

Strupp, H. H. (1989). Psychotherapy: Can the practitioner learn from the researcher? *American Psychologist, 44,* 717–724.

Sutherland, S. (1992). *Irrationality: The enemy within.* London: Constable.

Sutton, R. (1987, June 22). That old-time nutrition. *Washington Post.*

Svenson, O. (1981). Are we all less risky and more skillful than our fellow drivers? *Acta Psychologica, 47,* 143–148.

Swanson, H. L. (Ed.). (1991). *Handbook on the assessment of learning disabilities.* Austin, TX: Pro-Ed.

Taube, K. T., & Linden, K. W. (1989). State mean SAT score as a function of participation rate and other educational and demographic variables. *Applied Measurement in Education, 2,* 143–159.

Taylor, H. G., Satz, P., & Friel, J. (1979). Developmental dyslexia in relation to other childhood reading disorders: Significance and clinical utility. *Reading Research Quarterly, 15,* 84–101.

Thaler, R. H. (1992). *The winner's curse: Paradoxes and anomalies of economic life.* New York: Free Press.

Thomas, G., Alexander, K., & Eckland, B. (1979). Access to higher education: The importance of race, sex, social class, and academic credentials. *School Review, 87,* 133–156.

Thornton, E. (1986). *The Freudian fallacy.* London: Paladin Books.

Thurow, L. C. (1987). A weakness in process technology. *Science, 238,* 1659–1663.

Torgesen, J. K., Wagner, R. K., & Rashotte, C. A. (1994). Longitudinal studies of phonological processing and reading. *Journal of Learning Disabilities, 27,* 276–286.

Townsend, J., & Kadlec, H. (1990). Psychology and mathematics. In R. Mickens (Ed.), *Mathematics and science.* Teaneck, NJ: World Scientific Press.

Turing, A. (1950). Computing machinery and intelligence. *Mind, 59,* 433–460.

Turner, C., Simons, L., Berkowitz, L., & Frodi, A. (1977). The stimulating and inhibiting effects of weapons on aggressive behavior. *Aggressive Behavior, 3,* 355–378.

Tversky, A., & Edwards, W. (1966). Information versus reward in binary choice. *Journal of Experimental Psychology, 71,* 680–683.

Tversky, A., & Kahneman, D. (1974). Judgment under uncertainty: Heuristics and biases. *Sciences, 185,* 1124–1131.

Tversky, A., & Kahneman, D. (1982). Evidential impact of base rates. In D. Kahneman, P. Slovic, & A. Tversky (Eds.), *Judgment under uncertainty: Heuristics and biases.* Cambridge, England: Cambridge University Press.

Tversky, A., & Kahneman, D. (1983). Extensional versus intuitive reasoning: The conjunction fallacy in probability judgment. *Psychological Review, 90,* 93–315.

U.S. Congress House Select Committee on Aging. (1984, May 31). *Quackery: A*

$10 billion scandal. 0Washington, DC: U.S. Government Printing Office.

University of California, Berkeley. (1991, January). The 18-year gap. *Berkeley Wellness Letter,* p. 2.

Vallone, R., Griffin, D. W., Lin, S., & Ross, L. (1990). Overconfident prediction of future actions and outcomes by self and others. *Journal of Personality and Social Psychology, 58,* 582–592.

Varela, J. A. (1977). Social technology. *American Psychologist, 32,* 914–923.

Vaughan, E. D. (1977). Misconceptions about psychology among introductory psychology students. *Teaching of Psychology, 4,* 138–141.

Vellutino, F. (1979). *Dyslexia: Theory and research.* Cambridge: MIT Press.

Violato, C. (1984). Effects of Canadianization of American-biased items on the WAIS and WAIS-R information subtests. *Canadian Journal of Behavioral Science, 16,* 36–41.

Violato, C. (1986). Canadian versions of the information subtests of the Wechsler tests of intelligence. *Canadian Psychology, 27,* 69–74.

Wagenaar, W. A. (1988). *Paradoxes of gambling behavior.* Hove, England: Erlbaum.

Wagenaar, W. A., & Keren, G. (1986). The seat belt paradox: Effect of adopted roles on information seeking. *Organizational Behavior and Human Decision Processes, 38,* 1–6.

Wainer, H. (1989). Eelworms, bullet holes, and Geraldine Ferraro: Some problems with statistical adjustment and some solutions. *Journal of Educational Statistics, 14,* 121–140.

Wainer, H. (1993). Does spending money on education help? A reaction to the Heritage Foundation and the *Wall Street Journal. Educational Researcher, 22*(9), 22–24.

Walberg, H., & Shanahan, T. (1983). High school effects on individual students. *Educational Researcher, 12,* 4–9.

A wealth of financial-aid misconceptions. (1988, October 26). *Education Week,* p. 3.

Wheeler, D. L., Jacobson, J. W., Paglieri, R. A., & Schwartz, A. A. (1993). An experimental assessment of facilitated communication. *Mental Retardation, 31,* 49–60.

Wickens, C. D. (1992). *Engineering psychology and human performance* (2nd ed.). New York: HarperCollins.

Widiger, T., & Schilling, M. (1980). Towards a construct validation of the Rorschach. *Journal of Personality Assessment, 44,* 450–459.

Williams, P., Haertel, E., Haertel, G., & Walberg, H. (1982). The impact of leisure-time television on school learning: A research synthesis. *American Educational Research Journal, 19,* 19–50.

Williams, T. (1986). *The impact of television: A natural experiment in three communities.* New York: Academic Press.

Willis, C. (1990, June). The ten mistakes to avoid with your money. *Money Magazine,* pp. 84–94.

Wilson, T. D., & Brekke, N. (1994). Mental contamination and mental correction: Unwanted influences on judgments and evaluations. *Psychological Bulletin, 116,* 117–142.

Wolfle, L. M. (1987). Enduring cognitive effects of public and private schools. *Educational Researcher, 16,* 5–11.

Wood, W., Young, F. Y., & Chachere, J. G. (1991). Effects of media violence on viewers' aggression in unconstrained social interaction. *Psychological Bulletin, 109,* 371–383.

Woodcock, R. W. (1987). *Woodcock Reading Mastery Tests—Revised.* Circle Pines, MN: American Guidance Service.

Wright, L. (1988). The Type A behavior pattern and coronary artery disease. *American Psychologist, 43,* 2–14.

Wright, R. (1988). *Three scientists and their gods.* New York: Harper & Row.

Wrightsman, L. (1969). Wallace supporters and adherence to "law and order." *Journal of Personality and Social Psychology, 13,* 17–22.

Wyatt, W., Posey, A., Welker, W., & Seamonds, C. (1984). Natural levels of similarities between identical twins and between unrelated people. *Skeptical Inquirer, 9,* 62–66.

Yates, J. F. (Ed.). (1992). *Risk-taking behavior.* Chichester, England: John Wiley.

Zill, N., & Winglee, M. (1990). *Who reads literature?* Cabin John, MD: Seven Locks Press.

Index